CALL TO CAMBRIA

A Novel

by

Bartie Jones

For a favorite Library

Bartie Jones

8/30/2002

ISBN: 0-7596-8607-6

This book is printed on acid free paper.

1stBooks - rev. 3/27/02

I'm proud to dedicate this,
my first novel,
to my three children:
Judy Bebb Jones Muhn
Lynn Ann Jones
John Bart Jones
who grew up in the Welsh community of focus
and are descendants of one
of the original settlers.

"Call to Cambria" is the delightful story of a pastor and congregation discovering one another and falling in love. It reflects well the uncertainties and fears that lead to misunderstandings and conflict within local congregations. It also demonstrates how love and hope triumph over the human frailties and the challenges we face. Get lost in Cambria for a weekend and you will find your spirit renewed and your outlook brightened."

Reverend Wendy S. Pratt
Pastor, Salem Presbyterian Church

(Reverend Pratt is the first woman pastor of the church of focus in the novel but is not the character written by the author.)

TABLE OF CONTENTS

Acknowledgments

In 1978 the beginning of this novel found its way onto paper as I sat alone house-bound through the great blizzard. Through the years only pieces of it came together until 1995 when I seriously set about completing what had haunted me for years. Writing, completing and publishing a first novel can only be done with a great deal of help.

Let me begin with Jane Jordan Browne of Multimedia Product Development whose straightforwardness gave me courage too proceed; to Sybil Downing who recommended Jane, and Betsy O'Herin who introduced me to Sybil. Next, to the good people of 1st Books, the new wave of publishing, about whom I can't say enough. They led me step by step through the process.

As to teachers, book reviewers, ministers and writers, Lila McGinnis shines, Clare Sanford was stringent, Reverend Mary Albert thoughtful, Doctor Gail Ahumada exacting, and Reverend-Doctor Marilyn Stavenger faithful. My deepest gratitude too, to Jory Blakemore Johnson and Frances Hurd Stadler (now deceased) for a thorough read, to Russ Roberts for mechanical advice; to Doris Price for authenticity; to Latimer Breese, Becky Zirkle, Maxine Morgan and Minnie Jones for historical data, and Chris Reinhard for technological aid. My Sunday night Spirit Group encouraged me at every point in its process and countless others along the way added encouragement and interest. My thanks to all of you and I hope it is everything you'd hoped for.

Finally, and above all, I am indebted to Helen Kuester Davis who provided the perfect surroundings in which to work, proof-read my manuscripts and did countless things to support me throughout from meal-making, net-working, problem-solving and encouragement to enduring love and patience.

Author's Note

Although this novel is based on historical events, it is a work of imagination.

While I used the village of Venedocia, Ohio and surrounding area between Van Wert and Lima as a setting, my characters were created to fit the story.

Descriptions of characters may seem familiar because I used general Welsh features and traits of various people I knew there to compile into my own characters as I imagined them and wanted them to be. The characters in this book act in their own way to create the story I wanted to tell. While it is based on some of the events that happened while I lived there, it by no means was the true story of what did happen. It was never my intention to reflect negatively on any of the people or the church but rather, give the community an attractive image.

I wanted to tell a story of the Welsh immigrants love for music and particularly of a time when their language was giving away to English and their identities as "pure-blooded Welsh" were waning; and I wanted to tell of the struggles that young women pastors have in establishing themselves in what has generally been accepted as a male profession. Megan is a strong woman but she has to work hard at being who she wants to be which shows the strength of character the Welsh people have. In this story, Megan is all the time becoming a better pastor.

PART ONE

Chapter One

CHAPTER ONE - MEGAN ARRIVES

At ten years of age, Megan Brown was a natural mimic. She imitated Reverend Bell so perfectly that her mother's friends fell into hysterics.

"Good Morning. I said, 'Good Morning.' My goodness, have you fallen asleep before I've even begun my sermon this morning? Let's try again. Good Morning! Well, now, that's more like it. Bless you, you are good people and I love every one of you."

Megan knew most of the Bible stories: "Now when Jonah was sitting in the dark belly of that whale, Jonah had one big problem…"

At twelve she joined the church and was told by Reverend Bell that she could grow up to be anything she wanted to be.

"Even a preacher?" she asked.

"Even a preacher," he answered and so the seed was planted.

On September 15, 1971, the Reverend Megan Brown, now twenty-eight, with a Masters of Divinity from Princeton University and two years of Peace Corps experience behind her, drove across Ohio on Route 30 in her brand new red convertible. She was on the way to her first call as minister of the Welsh Presbyterian Church of Cambria, Ohio, and she was anxious.

It wasn't that she was afraid of small towns. She grew up in Medina, Ohio where she worked in her father's hardware store and knew all his friendly customers. In her first years at Ohio University and even in Princeton she had experienced little towns. In Africa with the Peace Corps she'd experienced a different culture, so surely she had no reason to worry about people who were Welsh or their small community. Perhaps it was because they were farmers. She didn't know much about farming.

She did know she was the first woman pastor, as well as the first non-Welsh for the church. For those reasons she wondered how she would be accepted.

Megan had waited all summer since her graduation for a call. Only three weeks ago, Professor Jarvis summoned her into his book-lined office at Princeton to tell her about this "small, unique, Welsh-American community," as he put it. He, himself, had ministered there right out of seminary, he said, and it was one of the most rewarding experiences of his life.

So she went for an interview and knew immediately what they needed. Furthermore, she believed she could make it happen for them. She sold herself quickly.

While waiting for their decision, she noticed an impressive stained-glass window at the rear of the sanctuary. It was the Good Shepherd, holding a lamb in his arms. As she'd gazed up at it, it seemed He looked directly at her saying, "Come, be a shepherd." Her whole being seemed to freeze in time. She was sure it was God's voice. But, whatever she had heard she knew for certain that God was calling her to this place and a strange tingling shivered through her all the way to her toes. *This is my calling*, she whispered to herself. So when they issued the invitation officially, she accepted immediately and joyfully. Only for a fleeting second did it cross her mind that she might be the only candidate they had who was willing to come. Her stronger feeling was that this is where she must be. So, here she was on her way driving her brand new red convertible.

She had thought the convertible a wonderful idea when her parents let her choose her own car as a graduation gift. It was a peace offering from her father, she knew. He had refused to pay for her seminary schooling, and she had worked her own way through. So she decided she deserved whatever she wanted. Now, however, she wondered what these people would think, and even more, how would they react to their new, single, 28-year-old woman pastor who drove a red convertible.

Fear gripped her throat. Tears came to her eyes. She groped for a handkerchief and pulled to the side of the road. Blowing her nose, she acknowledged to herself that she really was afraid. "God, I don't know why I'm afraid, but I am," she spoke aloud. "I sure could use a little more courage right now if you have any extra." Drawing in a deep breath and trying to relax, she made herself drive on.

She seemed to be alone on this narrow back road driving by neatly groomed yards, freshly painted buildings, and lush vegetable gardens. One of the Session members had earlier told her, "If the barn is better kept, the farmer is in charge. If the house looks better, it's the wife who's in charge. If both look good it's a happy marriage." Here, all the buildings and gardens looked well cared-for. They must all be getting along well, perhaps even well-to-do. Maybe even enough to tithe to the church.

The land lay flat and open with only small clusters of woods scattered about leaving wide expanses of space where winter winds could blow through with force. She imagined snow piled into drifts making the roads impassable and she was glad to be getting settled in now so she could watch the harvest and have time to prepare for their harsh winter.

Megan turned the rear-view mirror toward her face to check her lipstick. Her hair shone auburn in the sun. Strands whipped across her face and she tipped her head, catching the breeze to blow them back. Her slender hands played loosely on the steering wheel. She wore navy slacks and pale blue shirt which were comfortable for driving. She had thought about wearing a tailored suit, but, knowing no one would be there to meet her, opted for comfort.

Restless, she clicked on the radio. Only two stations could be found. One was a raspy voice churning out hog prices; the other, was the same weather being repeated over and over. She snapped it off.

Another wave of anxiety swept over her reminding her she was totally on her own. It wasn't like going to Africa for the Peace Corps. There, Charles had helped her, teaching her so much about the African culture. Here, there was no

4

one. She hoped she could find a friend she could trust. Maybe her father was right, after all. Maybe she wasn't cut out to minister a whole church. No, she wasn't giving in to that thought. This was her chance to prove him wrong, to stand up for what she truly believed in, to prove that women could minister as well as men. But more important, to prove she had really been called.

David Jones Thomas, Chair of the Search Committee, had written her to drive straight to the manse and get settled. He and others would be working in the fields and would see her in the evening at the Session meeting. They would know she had arrived. No need to call anyone.

Just then she approached a single railroad track that lay on a raised bed preventing her from seeing beyond it until she was on the top, at which point she stopped dead on the tracks and honked her horn. Directly in front of her was a tractor, sitting crossways on the road. The driver turned and stared straight at her. For an immeasurable moment their eyes met, sizing up one another.

Then the farmer slowly climbed down and limped toward her. *What's the matter with him? Why isn't he moving that machine out of my way?* He continued to walk laboriously toward her, his stocky build emphasizing his shortness.

"No harm done," he said, a bit out of breath. He slipped off his green John Deere cap at an attempt to straighten his disheveled hair. It was pure white against his sun-burned Santa Claus cheeks and his glasses were so dusty she wondered whether he could see anything at all. He flipped the cap back on his head and pulled the visor to set it straight. With a knowing smile he moved in closer. "I'd guess you to be the new preacher lady we've been expectin'."

"That's right. Have we met?"

"We have now," he said slipping his work glove off and offering his hand. His skin was callused and rough, but warm.

"I really don't feel too safe on this track," she said.

"Oh, don'tcha worry about that none. Train only comes onc't a week anymore. Since the elevator moved, we don't have no need of it much. My name's Willie Williams. Folks here-about call me Tadcu. You can have your choice."

"Is that — Tah-ky a Welsh name?" she asked smiling at his accent.

"Yep. Tahd-key." He emphasized the d sound. "It's Welsh for grandfather."

"Oh, well in that case, I'd just better call you Mr. Williams."

He nodded. "Welcome to Cambria. I hope you'll like it here."

"Thank you."

"Do you know your way to the manse?"

"I do. I saw it from the outside when I came for the interview."

"Well, everything's ready. Key's hangin' in the garage on a hook to the left of the door. Make yerself to home."

She thanked him, noticing a gleam in his mahogany eyes. He slowly limped back to his big green tractor and pulled himself up onto the seat. He revved up the engine and turned the old John Deere over to the side for her to pass.

"Thanks again," she called and waved as she pulled around. At the next turn the fields opened up and there across the broad expanse she saw the church of Cambria. It stood like a castle larger and higher than all the other buildings in the village. The golden afternoon sun shone down through the dust particles from the harvest, casting a haze like an old pastoral painting. Seeing it soothed her and a familiar hymn came to mind. "Guide Me, Oh, Thou Great Jehovah, pilgrim in this barren land." Like a prayer, she hummed it. "I am weak, but Thou art mighty. Hold me with Thy powerful hand." It calmed her anxieties and reminded her of her mission. She did not realize that the hymn was a Welsh one, or that she would hear it sung many times in the church she was about to pastor.

To her left as she approached the village was a small baseball field with a single set of bleachers. A row of small homes lined the street. Cambria was laid out on one north/south street called Main Street. Turning left onto Main, she saw that maple trees lined both sides. There was a small service garage to her right. Good, someone to take care of my car, she thought. Two men in overalls and caps stood by the door watching her. She nodded and drove on past. They tipped their caps.

Next, there was a small porch-front building on the left with a pole bearing the Stars and Stripes, and across from it, a general store. *Post Office and store, okay.* A small cluster of people stood watching. *Dog-gone it! If they had time to stand around waiting to see what their new pastor looks like, someone could have been at the manse to greet me. Looks as if common courtesy is one of the first things to teach them.* Suddenly, she felt quite vulnerable in her open convertible and wished it were more conservative. A man looked through the window of the small general store. It was open. Another man sat on a cast-off pew bench in front of it. Unnoticed by her, he watched her closely through town.

On the right she passed a larger building with "Cambrian Hall" painted above its door and next to it was the church. To her left, across from the church, was a parking lot for sixty to eighty cars. The gravel driveway between the church and the manse ended at a small white frame garage. Megan pulled up to the garage and looked for the key, then walked to the front of the house.

The yellow brick manse was impressive with its stone facings. It matched the church and was the only brick house in the village. It seemed, to her, symbolic of the respect the villagers gave their pastor and it gave her a brief boost of security. She walked up the sidewalk through a lean stand of grass and climbed the steep front steps. Rhododendron bushes graced both sides of the full front porch.

The two-story square house seemed huge for a single person. She knew most of its former occupants had had families, except for Professor Jarvis who was also single. Glancing at the house across the street her eyes caught the movement of a curtain in one of the windows. Megan's lips curled in amusement. Briskly, she turned and walked across the maroon tile porch. She opened the outside wooden-framed, leaded-glass door and then the inside etched-glass door. The oak floor gleamed with fresh varnish and the windows shone in the afternoon sun. It was an unusual entranceway and there was room between the two doors for boots and umbrellas. Closing both doors behind her, Megan leaned back against the inside door and took her first look at the place she would call home.

CHAPTER TWO – DAVID

David Jones Thomas was given his middle name, Jones, after his mother's family and his surname, Thomas, after his father's. At thirty years of age, David was the most sought after bachelor in the community. He was one of only a few young men to escape the Vietnam War. With flat feet, he didn't qualify for the service. As an only child, he expected to inherit the largest and wealthiest farm in the area. This morning he had two wagons loaded with soybeans, waiting to be taken to the elevator, and fifteen more acres to harvest. He was aware that the new young pastor would be driving in and that he would have to be at the church by 7:00 pm. David shaved, washed the upper part of his body and ran a brush through his soft wavy hair. His muscular arms were tan to an inch above his elbows.

He was five feet eleven inches tall, and had surpassed his father's height at age eighteen. He pulled on a fresh white cotton tee-shirt with short sleeves and the familiar gray work pants. After tying up his work shoes, he filled his pockets with his pocket knife, coins, mints, and stuffed a fresh bandanna handkerchief in his left hip pocket. Taking a last look in the mirror, he smiled at himself from under dark eyebrows and sun-tanned face through lucid blue eyes, common to the Welsh. The summer's toil had made him stronger and more muscular. Breathing in, he smacked his flat, hard belly. Surely the right woman is out there just waiting for me, he thought. All the possible candidates in the community had been swept up while he was away studying in college. The only possible prospect was his childhood sweetheart, Evie, whose farm he had been working. Somehow, there wasn't much excitement in that.

David liked challenge. *That gutsy new pastor might be an option.* The thought quickly passed and he tromped rapidly down the stairs into the kitchen. There was freshly brewed coffee sitting on the old coal stove. His mam already was out with her chickens. He slipped into his jacket and grabbed a blue enamel cup filling it with coffee and headed out the back door. Letting the screen door slam behind him he noticed the air was cool. The sweet scent of farm met his nostrils.

"Didja eat?" came a voice from the chicken house.

"No,' he answered and kept walking.

"Gotta eat," she called back.

"Later," he answered and kept walking.

"I'll bring somethin' out then," she shouted after him. He raised a hand in acknowledgment. Approaching the barn, he heard the cows mooing and knew his tad had already started milking. A quick whiff of the freshly baled hay gave him a feeling of satisfaction. Tad looked up from below the large Holstein as he attached the milking machine.

"Bit late, aren'tcha?"

David leaned on the railing and stroked Old Babe's neck. "Sorry. Can you do this alone this morning? I want to get those beans over to the elevator before the line gets too long."

"I can handle it."

David waited. His tad pulled a squirt of milk from Old Babe and added, "I'll get the combine ready."

"Good. I'd like to get in and out of there before everyone starts asking questions about beans again."

"Know whatcha mean."

"Okay, then." David left the milking parlor and walked across the barnyard to the big red International Harvester. He wasted no time driving out the lane and pulling onto the road with the two wagons trailing behind. A puff of smoke coughed out of the stack and disintegrated into the cool morning air. Across the fields the woods were showing signs of early frost and the ditches were still moist with dew. It was four miles to the elevator, a ride that always gave him time to think.

Most of the farmers grew corn, wheat, oats and hay. They had questioned him when he planted soy beans for the first time. Beans were a good crop. They brought six dollars a bushel compared to two dollars for corn, but were new to the community. David had learned about them in Agriculture school and convinced his tad to let him try growing them. Naturally, everybody had questions to ask. Same questions over and over. This was his first harvest of them and so far he was getting 60 bushels to the acre, already bringing in twice as much as corn. It made him wish he had put all their fields into beans. It would have made more money, but that wouldn't have been good farming.

Driving past a neighbor's farm he waved at him entering his barn. David was the first person in the community to go to college and he had graduated with honors. As long as he could remember, his tad had planned for him to go. For years he had saved all the extra money he could so when the time came he was able to pay cash for everything. John Thomas wanted his son to be well educated and to be on the forefront of new farming techniques.

"Farming is going to change," he had told David, "and I want you to make this farm a landmark."

David's parents had been childhood sweethearts. Their families' farms bordered each other and when they grew up and married, his tad worked both farms. Eventually, they inherited both, giving them over 600 acres, most of it tillable, except for 18 acres of woods and a creek.

David was an only child and the pride of both his parents, but particularly his tad. John Thomas had taken little David with him on the wagon to the barn and to the fields, and in his pick-up truck to town and to the elevator. He talked continuously to him, telling him about everything he did and why he did it.

9

At four, David learned to feed the chickens and gather the eggs. Later he filled buckets of grain and poured them into the mangers for the cows. He remembered how he learned what to do when a sow gave birth to one-too-many baby pigs.

"There's only so many dinner plates on an old sow's belly," his tad said, "so if she's got one too many for dinner what're you gonna do? You can't let the little booger starve, can you?"

David's puzzled look caused his tad to smile. He gently reached over into the pen and lifted out the little critter, carrying him, nestled in his arm over to the can of fresh cow's milk. Handing the squirming and squealing piglet to David, he said, "Here, hold onto her for a minute." He then took a baby's bottle from the shelf, dipped into the can of fresh milk, filling it. After screwing on a nipple lid, he handed it to David saying, "Here you go. See if she'll take this."

He remembered pressing it to the little pig's mouth and with a little probing getting her to take it. It was a joyful moment and David learned in a gratifying way that on the farm you can usually solve problems by yourself.

David's tad had been the first farmer in the community to retire his horses and buy a tractor. It had a loud rhythmic putt-putt sound that identified it before you saw it. When his tad started using that tractor, everyone driving by stopped to watch, waving him down to ask questions and looking it over from top to bottom. It was the most exciting thing to happen in a long while. That was back in 1954 when David was thirteen. A lot of changes had taken place in the last fifteen years. Some people lost their farms to others who were able to buy them out and farm with machinery. He remembered he could barely reach the pedals then but he hooked up the wagons and took them to the fields. In just a few years time, all the farmers had tractors and horses were kept only for pleasure.

David had ridden the wagons since he was four and done chores from age five. At eight he had harnessed the horses and by age ten lifted feed sacks and hay bales. He was shy and small but full of energy. When they got that John Deere, he suddenly had become very popular on the school bus. All the kids wanted to know what it was like and how fast it could go. Overnight he felt important. He would be first in many things through the years. That's the way John Thomas planned it.

David stretched up and became strong enough to hoist hay bales onto wagons and into the hayloft. He climbed and pulled and stacked in that stifling heat of summer. He also helped on other farms. The competition was keen among teenage farm boys as to who could move the most bales. One time his tad looked up at him in the top haymow. The heat was unbearable and David was complaining.

"Well, David," drawled his tad calmly, "you know you're workin' when the sweat runs down the crack of your ass."

"Well, I'm a workin' then," he'd replied and his tad let out a proud chortle.

They worked side by side. At the end of each day after a hearty meal of his mam's home-canned beef, mashed potatoes, green beans, biscuits and cherry pie, they would sit down to plan the next day's work.

"Most farmers plan the day's work at breakfast when they know what the weather's gonna be," John Thomas would say. "I say you have to have somethin' rollin' 'round in your mind to sleep on. That way you wake up ready to go. Then, if it's rainin', you plan somethin' else at breakfast. You always have things piled up for a rainy day, anyway."

David learned a lot from his tad growing up but after going to college he came home with new ideas his tad never heard of and it seemed he was ahead of his tad. Soon, he'll retire and leave it all to me, David thought. I'm ready. I'm really ready.

The line at the elevator was not long and he moved through quickly. He returned to the farm to find the combine greased, gassed and ready to go. Mam had placed a sandwich and an apple on the seat. He chomped down on both and was in the field by the time the crop had dried enough to run.

The crop was ready for harvesting and the day went fast as his monster machine gobbled up the rows and poured streams of beans into the wagons. By one o'clock mam arrived with their picnic lunch. The three of them ate while resting on the tailgate of the old yellow pick-up parked at the edge of the field.

David quietly ate his sandwiches while his mam and tad caught up with the news. He kept thinking about the new pastor. She would be driving in about now. He had arranged everything with her ahead of time because he knew he couldn't leave the field to meet her. He knew he had to get the beans off while the weather held.

He was apprehensive about working with a woman pastor. In particular, he couldn't imagine a woman who'd never lived in the country would know much of anything about the upkeep of a church building. Things needed fixing and he was sure he'd be the one stuck with the chore. Still, at the interview there weren't any fears on her part. In fact, she was downright cocky about saying just what the church needed. No doubt she'll be a handful, he thought, but he figured he could shepherd any ewe into the fold if he set his mind to it.

There was something more: that anonymous letter he had received addressed to him and the church session. Sworn to secrecy, he had to decide whether or not to mention it to the new pastor before the meeting. This letter could be controversial and he was wrestling with the best way to handle it.

"You're pretty quiet today," his mam remarked. "Anything special on your mind?"

"Just that meeting tonight." He camouflaged his answer.

"Everything's ready. That old manse cleaned up pretty good," said his tad, immediately assuming David's thoughts were on the new preacher's arrival at the manse.

"Real good," David agreed. "When Tadcu Willie puts his hand to something it generally turns out well. He'll be keeping an eye out for her arrival."

"What time is the meeting?" Tad asked.

"Seven," Then quickly, because he didn't want to get into a discussion, added, "Well, I'd better get moving."

As acting clerk of the Session and chairperson of the Search Committee, David had carried the leadership of the church during the interim, working with several different pastors who filled in until they found a new pastor. The church had confidence in his leadership. It was hard to find young leaders for the church since most of the youth were off to Vietnam. Church members called on David for many things.

He took pride in carrying out these tasks. He knew he was following the footsteps of four generations of leaders since the church's beginning. His father claimed he was a pure-blooded Welshman but Buck Jones said there was no such thing. However, most folks didn't put much weight on anything Buck said. Right now David was feeling anxious because there were some who had not wanted to hire a woman pastor, much less a young one and not Welsh. If he decided to read the letter it could be the torch that lit the fire that was already laid. He didn't want to risk his leadership position but he was sure Reverend Megan Brown wouldn't know what to do with that letter at this point.

The rest of the day passed quickly. At supper, Mam mentioned that Tadcu had called to tell them that Pastor Brown had arrived.

"Did he talk to her?" David asked.

"He saw her on the road and she stopped to talk a minute, he said."

"Good." Tadcu would see that she got in all right.

Keyed up, now, he quickly bathed and dressed, then paused a moment in front of his dresser. Then, making his decision, he took the letter from the drawer and tucked it into his shirt pocket. He made a short phone call and left for church.

CHAPTER THREE - THE LETTER

Tadcu Willie Williams was next to the oldest member of the church. His brother, Edwin, a retired history teacher, was two years younger. Edwin attended worship regularly, sitting at the right end of the third pew in the center section and promptly, when the sermon began, fell asleep.

Tadcu always sat alone on the left end of the sixth pew in the far right section where his family consistently sat. All his children were gone from the community. His wife had died just a year ago. He felt closer to her in that pew and saw no reason to sit with Edwin or bounce about trying other places. It was his pew and everyone knew it. When he wasn't there they knew that too.

Edwin, a bachelor, kept to himself. After their parents died, he lived on the home farm but rented out his land. He tutored students of history for awhile and then kept himself busy reading and trotting off to find historic markers. He knew how the land had been acquired from the Indians and had felt it not really right.

Tadcu claimed it was unused and undeveloped land and their parents had as much right as any other immigrants. They worked harder than the Indians had to make good profitable land of it, he argued.

Tadcu earned enough money shoeing horses to buy extra land on which he had raised his family. When his children left the farm he gradually sold off portions keeping only enough to enable him to live comfortably. In recent years he had taken on the job as custodian of the church and manse. It was he who had readied the manse for Megan. Also a Session member, he prepared the room for the Session to meet. He looked forward to seeing Pastor Brown again. Seeing her for the first time in a red convertible, young and vulnerable, he took pity on her and decided to champion her cause whatever it was. He finished making the coffee and walked to the vestibule to pull the heavy thick rope that rang the tower bell seven strokes as a reminder of the meeting.

When Megan entered the manse she took time to look carefully into each room. To the left of the front entrance was a study lined with empty bookshelves and a large walnut desk. Megan fell in love with the desk immediately. It felt like a reward for all the times she had worked on tables and small desks at school.

To the right was the living room with a large brick fireplace on the north wall and windows on either side from which she could see the church and beyond down the street of the village. Behind the living room was the kitchen and behind the study was the dining room. She imagined entertaining and holding meetings there.

The main stairway with a heavy oak railing led up to a landing. From the cushioned window seat one could see west across square flat fields to the wooded cemetery and beyond.

The second floor had four rooms. She chose the north-east corner room(above the living room), for her bedroom. From its windows she had a good view of the village. She would make the other three rooms into a guest room, a storage room and a reading room. Her sofa bed could be in the guest room as she hadn't yet acquired much furniture.

Next to the bathroom was a back stairway leading back down to the kitchen. Someone had already placed a quart of milk, three fresh eggs, a package of home-cured bacon, cheese, a jar of peanut butter and a loaf of bread in the refrigerator; and on the table a plate was stacked with home-made cookies. She helped herself to one right away. From the kitchen window she noticed a side entrance to the church, a way to enter and leave privately. Satisfied, she went about unpacking her car.

After organizing her things, she treated herself to a warm bath in the antique tub and dressed for the meeting. She made a sandwich and was just eating her cookies and milk when the phone rang. It took her a moment to locate it in the front hall. It was David welcoming her to Cambria and saying he would stop by for her. Pleased at his thoughtfulness, she hurriedly cleaned up the kitchen and sat down to wait.

Suddenly a loud clanging from the church belfry startled her. She ran to the living room window where she saw the large bell swinging in the belfry.

"That will take some getting used to," she said aloud. Fortunately it stopped after seven tolls. She decided to wait for David on the front porch.

The air was warm. A slight breeze ruffled her hair. She could hear farm machinery still running in the near-by fields. So far, there was only one car in the parking lot.

David drove his new green pick-up truck to the meeting thinking to impress the new pastor. He still planned to have "Golden Acres Farm" painted on the door in yellow but he had installed his CB and mounted his rifle in the back window.

This had been a good day. A farmer was, in his terms, a provider of life and a partner with God. All was fine when there was the right amount of sunshine and rain, but it seemed that farmers were never satisfied with their fields of plenty. It should always have been more or less of something: more corn, less rain, more sun, no hail; or it was the big snow that soaked the earth too long in the spring that kept them from the fields, or whatever else they could find to grumble about.

David liked the challenge of trying to beat the odds. He had grown up with the land and often could anticipate the weather. He paid attention to the sky.

It was the same way with the church. He could predict what might happen if a more creative member of the church wanted to try something new. One could always count on a "No" vote first. A "No" vote could buy time. Later, if it turned out to be a good idea, the vote could change. If not, it would eventually die away. David anticipated a "No" response to the letter tonight.

In the back of his mind he had decided to take things in his own hands reasoning it was too early to bother her with things of which she would have no understanding. It never occurred to him to ask her. Turning into her driveway, he was surprised to see her waiting on the porch.

"Mind if I park in your driveway tonight?" he called out the open truck window to her. She looked awfully young to be his new pastor. Still, it might turn out to his advantage.

"Help yourself." She, too, thought he was younger looking than she had remembered.

He pulled up behind her red convertible still parked with the top down. *Whooooeey, wouldja look at that. I don't believe that baby will get through a snow drift.* Amused, he walked to meet her and welcomed her with a broad smile and handshake. "How was the trip?" he asked politely.

"Beautiful! Your directions were perfect and the clouds were spectacular. You can really see the sky out here."

He grinned at the thought of her driving along in her convertible looking at the clouds. They walked over to the church. He made an effort at conversation.

"And the house, was everything all right there?"

"Immaculate. Whom do I thank for that?"

"Tadcu. Did he also put some food in to hold you over?"

"He did. Breakfast, even lunch. That was thoughtful."

"Tadcu is everyone's grandfather."

"What is that name again?"

"Tadcu. It's Welsh for grandfather."

"And does everyone call him that?"

"He wouldn't have it any other way."

"Did he tell you I met him on the road?"

"No. I haven't talked with him."

"He was parked on his tractor right in the middle of the road. I was stuck on the railroad track which scared me half to death, but he walked right up to the car and we got acquainted. How old is he?"

"Ninety, I think. I guess he told you that the railroad is almost defunct." They reached the door of the church. Wanting to put her at ease he said, "This won't be a long meeting. A couple of reports and that's it. Mostly, they just want to meet you before anyone else."

"Fine," she replied, immediately at ease.

As they entered the meeting room Tadcu called out "Dah-veed!"

"It's the way the older Welsh say my name," David whispered aside to her.

"Evening, Tadcu. Thanks for getting things ready."

Tadcu stood to greet them and took Megan's hand in one of his, patting it with the other. They chatted again about their meeting. She thanked him for the food and observed what a happy person he was. It would be very easy to call him Tadcu.

"Was it you who rang the bell? I about jumped out of my skin."

He bellowed out with a hearty laugh. "I'm afraid so. I guess it would seem pretty loud livin' right next door to it."

"Do you ring that for every meeting?" she asked, wondering how often she should be prepared for it.

"No, not every meetin', but for weddin's and funerals. I rang it tonight just as a reminder to anyone who might still be out farmin'. If there's a tornado or fire we sometimes ring it."

"A tornado?" She was surprised.

"Yessum. With these here wide open spaces we get a lot of wind."

As the other members arrived Megan watched for a female cohort but this group was all male. Next year, she vowed to herself, there will be a woman in this group. It's not right to have only men running a church.

Robert Jones arrived. He was acting clerk while David filled in as Moderator. He was short and slight of build with the ruddy complexion of a farmer. He acknowledged her quietly with a nod and quickly sat down to prepare his papers. He's a quiet one, she judged to herself, one to watch for his expressions because he probably won't tell you his thoughts.

Following Robert came Jim Morris. Jim announced to her that he was the treasurer of the church. He told her about his wife whose name was also Margaret. He then added that he had twin daughters named Cathy and Carol and a son, Kevin. Definitely an outgoing, friendly person, she thought and decided that he could be trusted.

Just then Squire Lloyd arrived. She remembered him at her interview asking if she liked to sing. She also remembered he was called Squire because it was rumored that he had descended from a member of King Arthur's court. His ruddy complexion and twinkling eyes brought to mind pictures in her childhood story books of knights and jesters.

"Welcome back. I'm glad you found your way. Now I remember you told me you like to sing so I want to be sure to invite you to sing with the church choir," he said right off.

"How can she do that, Squire?" asked Jim. "She's the pastor."

"Can be done," he snapped back. He chaired the Music Committee, a very important position in the Welsh church, she was told. Megan made a non-committal smile.

Paul Jenkins, a short, balding man banged the door shut accidentally and laughing about it, nervously pumped her hand. She later learned he was a banker who owned a turkey farm.

Tadcu was offering coffee when Thomas Evans arrived. Noting his expression and sidewise glance at Megan, Tadcu watched Thomas walk toward her. He had not wanted a woman pastor, nor a non-Welsh person, nor a youthful one. His was the only vote on the session against her,(having stated that men do best without women interfering) and he swore there were others who felt the same although they were never named.

Megan noticed his austere face and wide spread nostrils as he approached her. Their eyes met and locked.

"I'm Thomas Evans," he barked. "I'm the Director of Music. You're the first non-Welsh and first woman pastor for us. You may as well know, young lady, that I voted against you. I still think you are a bad choice for this church. However, since you are here, I've agreed to try to work with you."

"I'm sure we'll get along," replied Megan but by the time she spoke he had already turned away and chosen a seat where he wouldn't have to look at her directly.

Tadcu slammed a tray down and spit out "Catwceg!" Everyone turned in surprise to look at him. "Thomas Morrghan,(he rolled the r in anger) what's happened to your manners?" He growled with a tensely red face. "That was downright rude. A new pastor should be addressed as Reverend or Pastor, not by her first name unless SHE says it's all right to do so."

Thomas stood up prepared to yell back at Tadcu when David intervened. "Hold it right there! This is no way to act the first night we meet our new pastor." Tadcu turned back to the coffee pot and Thomas sat down with a tense smirk on his face. Megan spoke quickly.

"It's all right. I understand that there are some people in the church who don't want a woman pastor. Given time, I hope I can put them at ease. As for my name, I'd be content to be called Pastor Megan, if you like."

"Then Pastor Megan it is," said David quickly. Their eyes met in agreement and she felt a surge of support from him. "It's a good choice," he added, "because we already have three other Margarets." Megan looked surprised and David explained. "Jim's wife Margaret, Maggie Jones and Meg Richards. Yours is a very popular name." The group of men all chuckled and peace was temporarily restored.

Tadcu then took the opportunity to tell Megan a little history. "Nicknames are common to the Welsh because so many of us derive from the five families that come here from Wales back in the mid 19th century. We identify people with the same last names with somethin' about 'em, like David Jones Ditcher and David Jones Digger. Same names but one lays tile and the other digs graves."

"Exceptin' that Digger no longer digs graves 'cause he's in one," joked Squire and it brought a laugh.

Immediately they all began calling out examples.

"They was Biguil Williams - Biguil meanin' shepherd."

"Yeah, an' Tom Turkey."

"Don't ferget Jane Plum Orchard," Squire wiggled his body suggestively.

"Now don't start that, Squire." They all let out a guffaw.

"There's Billy Half-Way, who lived half way between Delphos and here."

"And Horsie."

"Yeah, and Saddler."

"Jack Dan da Cyppal – who lived by the church."

"All right," called out David waving his arms. "I think she gets the idea."

"How about the women? Do they have nicknames?" Megan asked.

"Well, now. They more or less get identified by their husbands," Tadcu began. "Like, we have two Ruths here married to men with the last name of Evans so we jus' call 'em Ruth David or Ruth Daniel. That way we know which Ruth Evans we're talkin' about."

"Don't ferget God Dammit to Hell Davis," someone called out and· the men roared with laughter. David quickly called them to order. Haydn Gwyn from Zion was missing. He would know about the letter, David thought.

"Okay, we do have some business tonight. Only one person hasn't arrived so I'm going ahead and hear the reports."

First, was the report on the recent Gymanfa Ganu that had been held on the regular Labor Day Sunday. Squire Lloyd, for the Music Committee, reported the attendance had been a usual full house and the director satisfactory. From the offering, they were able to pay all expenses and put a little away.

"Put it away!" exclaimed Thomas. "I say we take some of that money to have something done on our organ," Aside to Megan he said persuasively, "Half the time you don't know if it's gonna play for you or not. I've fixed it make-shift for years but it's just not holding well anymore."

"That's a decision for the Music Committee," said David.

"The Session should make the motion so it gets done," snapped Thomas.

David sighed. "Do I hear a motion?"

"I so move," said Thomas of his own recommendation. They passed the motion and Megan flinched a little as she observed the proceedings.

"Then, Squire, will you take this to the Music Committee?" David asked.

"I'll do it myself," Thomas insisted. "I'm at all their meetings anyway."

Megan recognized the power struggle immediately.

Tadcu then reported the manse was in good shape but that they needed to look ahead to the 125th Anniversary a year from then to have the church building ready for the celebration. David said he was a bit premature but that he would appoint a committee soon. Next came the treasurer's report from Jim.

Megan perked up. She knew from Professor Jarvis that if the harvest was good, money came in well in the fall. Spring was leaner because of the expense of planting. She was warned to be sensitive to that. Jim said there was not enough money to pay bills due, nor for repair of a leak in one of the radiators.

Before they could discuss it, David heard the opening he needed. Instantly he made his decision to read the letter.

"I have a new item of business that I believe we should consider at this point," he began.

"We haven't settled the old business yet," Robert said.

"Well, I think this may be the answer to our problems," David said with a bit of mystery. "A few days ago I received a letter from Berlin Miller."

"Why would Berlin Miller be writing a letter to us?" asked Squire. David ignored Squire's comment and explained to Megan that Berlin Miller was a lawyer in nearby Van Wert, the county seat. Then, unfolding the letter, he began to read it aloud.

"Dear Mr. Thomas,"

This is to advise you that the undersigned, and Misters Haydn Gwyn and Paul Jenkins hold in their possession as Escrow Agents, stock certificates in the name of the Welsh Presbyterian Church of Cambria, Ohio, a corporation not for profit. These certificates have a current market value slightly over $15,000. The men all looked at Paul.

They represent a gift to the church in memory of the donor's family and should represent approximately 50% of the cost of a new organ, and these certificates are being held for the purpose of starting the procedures for the purchase of a new organ."

"Fifteen thousand dollars toward a new organ!" Squire exclaimed, soaking it in. Thomas frowned.

"The escrow agents hold these certificates subject to the following conditions."

"Oh-oh, here it comes," mumbled Jim.

"Number one. That this gift shall be in memory of the donor's family."

"Who's the donor?" questioned Robert.

"Just wait," ordered David.

"Number two. The purpose of the gift is to start a fund for the purchase of an organ."

"What if we don't want to buy a new organ?" interrupted Thomas.

"Will you all just wait until I've read it through?"

"Number three. That Haydn Gwyn and Paul Jenkins be members of any committee to select an organ."

"Why them?" asked Squire.

"They're the ones that got the money," slipped in Jim.

"Jim!" scolded David. "Because they're the escrow agents, Squire. Now if you'd just let me read this through you all would get your answers." They turned strained silent faces toward him.

"Number four. That the rest of the money may be borrowed-"

"I'm not for borrowing money," said Thomas leaning back in his seat. David held up his hand.

"-or in the event that this gift and other gifts together shall exceed the cost of the organ, that the Escrow Agents in their sole discretion shall designate other use for the benefit of the church.

Number five. That the Escrow Agents shall report quarterly to said church the amount of interest received from said gift.

Number six. That in the event this gift should become a source of dissension within the congregation, the Escrow Agents, in their sole discretion, may withdraw the gift and return it to the donor. Upon acceptance of this gift and conditions, this letter must be signed by the President of your Board of Trustees and yourself as Moderator, indicating your agreement to the terms. The Escrow Agents will so inform the donor who will decide when said donor's identity shall be revealed.

Yours very truly, Berlin Miller"

"Dissension," mumbled Jim.

Stunned, they sat in silence, not knowing what to do, nor wanting to be the first to speak. Megan was wondering why David hadn't warned her about this. Was he trying to protect her? If so, why did he bring it up tonight? A special meeting could have been called later and they could have talked it over beforehand.

"I know this is a bit of a surprise," David began, "Fifteen thousand dollars is a lot of money. And Thomas has been telling us for a long time now that we're in trouble with the organ – "

"Now, David, I never said we needed a new one."

"Come on, Thomas. You're always going on about the organ," snapped Robert impatiently.

"I think this is a wonderful gift," interrupted Squire, "and a chance for us to work together to improve the music of the church. This person is a far-sighted person. Whoever it is knows that music is the main ministry of this church. We have to accept this gift. It's wonderful, just wonderful!"

Megan caught the statement that music was the main ministry of the church.

"Just a minute, Squire. Not so fast." Thomas held up his hands. "I say we get a professional in here to look at this organ before we do anything more. If we don't need a new organ, maybe we can use the money for something else."

"The letter said the money has to be used for an organ," said Jim.

"I want to know who the donor is," Robert stated.

"You ain't gonna know that right away," said Tadcu.

"It's a strange amount of money. A lot, but not enough. I don't understand this. Could I see that letter?" Jim wanted to know.

They all began talking at once. Megan could see David struggling to hear everyone and not able to take control. She touched his hand to get his attention. Startled, he leaned toward her.

"Appoint a committee to study the possibilities and bring a recommendation to the next Session meeting," she whispered. Immediately, David stood and pounded the table for attention.

"Quiet! Quiet everybody."

"How come Haydn's not here? Does he know he's named in that letter?" It was Paul Jenkins, one of the Escrow agents. Up to then he seemed to be very quiet.

"He knows Paul, same as you. I don't know why he's not here. Probably didn't think I'd be reading it this soon. Now I want to say something. I'm appointing you, Thomas, to represent the Music Committee. Robert, you for the Session, Haydn for both Zion and the Trustees and Tadcu for the church-at-large, to act as a committee to study this and bring back a recommendation to the Session. I'll contact Haydn and I'm sure Pastor Megan will sit in with you if you like." He glanced at her for approval. "If you need me for anything I'll be glad to assist. If you decide to accept the gift, I'll select a committee to lead the search for a new organ and to raise additional funds. If you decide to reject the offer, we'll notify Berlin Miller. All right? Then this meeting is adjourned."

David and Megan walked out together leaving the others talking among themselves.

"Thanks for saving me when they got out of hand," David said gratefully.

"I thought this wasn't going to be a business meeting, that I was just to meet everyone tonight and that was it." said Megan.

"I hadn't intended it to be but I got this letter –"

"This was business that should have been conducted by the Moderator of the church, David."

"I've been the acting Moderator."

"But I'm here now. If there was business to attend to tonight then I should have known about it."

"Honestly, I hadn't intended reading it tonight, but when they got to talking about the organ and the bills and all the stuff that needs repair, I suddenly felt this letter would be the answer."

"Is that the way you handle everything – on the spur of the moment?"

"No, I –"

"David, that letter isn't going to be the solution for all the church's problems," Megan went on. They were caught in this together and she wasn't sure just what that meant yet. She needed time to think.

"That's probably true," he responded, "but the offer was made with great faith and it may be the very thing that will turn this church around. There's a lot of stuff you don't know yet. I wasn't sure you could handle it."

Typical male response she thought, when trapped, counterattack. She glared at him and he smiled back knowing he had struck pay dirt. "David, I have been trained to handle this kind of situation. But the ruckus could have been avoided by talking to me first, by not bringing it up tonight, and by letting me handle it at a regular meeting."

He straightened up. "I'm sorry. Being in the field and all I just didn't think there was time." Now he was making excuses for himself.

"A person can make time when necessary," said Megan calmly.

They walked toward the manse not looking at each other. David chattered nervously and gradually came around full circle to the letter. She stopped him.

"Tonight is not the time to settle this, David. We both need time to think about what happened and how best to handle it. We need to talk and I promise we will, soon." David turned to face her.

"I do apologize for not talking to you about the letter first. I'll call in a day or two."

"Thank you. Good night, David."

"Good night," he said politely and left. The air had cooled. He breathed in deeply and cruised along slowly past barns with dim lights shining from their doors where men were feeding livestock or greasing equipment before turning in. He was relieved to have this day behind him. Relieved too, that the letter was now out in the open even though it had caused a temporary rift. He knew the news would be all over the place by tomorrow.

He knew now that he had made a bad decision in going ahead on his own, but God, what a woman. She didn't flinch an inch in the meeting but supported him and held her reprimand until afterwards. He was wrong. She accepted his apology but held him off until they both had time to think. Pastor Megan was a more exciting and capable woman than he had anticipated.

Inside the manse, Megan settled in her bedroom and began writing in her journal about the meeting. She would not be called Reverend Brown as she had anticipated but Pastor Megan. She could live with it. Maybe, this way, she would be closer to her parishioners.

There were a lot of undercurrents in that meeting. What did the gift mean for them? Do they need a new organ? Thomas hedged. Squire said yes and that the music was especially important in the church. What did that mean?

Sorting it out, David's face kept getting in the way. The very person she hoped she could get along with and he pulled a stunt like this. Confused and distracted she laid her journal aside. The breeze had died down and night was mute with the sliver of a new moon shining through her bedroom window.

"Lord," she said, "I got off to a bad start. Please help me straighten it out."

CHAPTER FOUR - EVIE AND DAVID

David rose early the next morning and slipped out of the house before his parents were up. He saddled up Duke, his rust-colored quarter horse, and headed along the back lane toward Evie's. He loved riding in the early morning and knew Evie would be up early. It was his habit to check in with her before he worked her fields, and today he planned to harvest her beans.

David and Evelyn Davies Evans had been childhood sweethearts, but when both her parents died in a train and car accident, the three children were sent to foster homes in Van Wert. To keep the land for them, John Thomas farmed it until David finished agricultural school and then gave him the responsibility of Evie's farm. A year later, Evie, then twenty-one, was the only sibling to return and was happy to keep David as tenant. Through the past nine years they planned all of the work together. Evie often helped David in the fields which caused some eyebrows to raise. Field work was considered too heavy for women. A woman's place was in the house. Chickens and vegetable gardens were the most women should be expected to do. Evie always had a large garden.

As the dew was still on the ground this early, David would wait until it was dry enough to harvest, probably around ten in the morning, so this early hour was a good time to talk. Duke took off at a gallop on the back lane along the corn. Red-winged blackbirds swooped low searching for seeds in the freshly cut hayfield. As horse and rider came around the edge of the woods, Evie's dog, Corgi, circled behind them and herded them in. Corgi was a working dog bred in Wales. Evie's tad had had a black and white sheep dog descended from the Cardigan Welsh Corgi to drive his cattle when she was a child. Keeping a real Pembroke Welsh Corgi of her own helped Evie keep her father's memory alive. The Pembroke was small and reddish-blond in color. Evie had a few sheep that she kept for wool in the little lot between the barn and house. Corgi not only herded her sheep but was an affectionate and intelligent pet and good at warding off strangers. Duke and Corgi were friends, so David dismounted to let Duke graze freely and walked to Evie's back door.

"Come on in," she called. He walked through the enclosed porch to the kitchen. She sat in the corner spinning yarn, wearing jeans and a blue denim shirt. She wore shoes with flat heels and steel reinforced toes. David seldom saw her in a dress.

Evie was a lover of nature. One time David had found her sitting in the middle of the hayfield looking up at the stars. Another time she stopped him from cutting down a tree long enough to hug it and apologize for David's cutting it down.

"They're souls too, you know," she had scolded.

David never pushed her. She'd been through a lot in her life and she was just happier communing with the earth, animals, trees and stars. It was okay with him. He enjoyed that mystery about her.

"Help yourself to coffee. I thought you'd come over this morning."

"Yeah? How come you know so much?" He poured himself a mug and straddled a chair at the table.

"Well, for one thing the beans are ready." She stopped the wheel and wrapped the yarn setting it aside and moved to a chair across the table from him. "And for another, I knew you had the meeting with the new preacher last night." David raised his eyebrows a bit as if he knew something she didn't.

"Well, how do you like her?" She waited bright-eyed.

"Okay." He blew on his coffee to cool it. "She's okay."

"Come on, David, you're grinning from ear to ear."

"Evie, that's not what I came to talk about."

"It is too. I know you're taking the beans off today. If that's all you wanted to tell me you'd have come just before starting. You're here early because you want to talk. So tell me."

"I like her," he admitted. They leaned into the table facing each other like two conspirators and he told her everything. His eyes gleamed with excitement when he told Evie how, when he had read the letter and everyone got out of hand, she helped him regain control. "I tell you, Evie, she's smooth. But she'll be a handful to work with."

"How so?"

"Well, she didn't let me get by with it."

"With YOUR reading the letter you mean?'

"Yes."

"Why?"

"Because now that she's here I'm not really the moderator anymore. She is and she let me know in no uncertain terms that she should have been told and should have handled it herself."

"Oooohh," responded Evie as they both beamed at each other. Evie watched him closely as he talked. She had always loved him and she knew she would marry him some day. But David still had the wanderlust when it came to women. He was not ready to settle down. It didn't matter. She could read him like a book and she could wait. They sat talking and drinking coffee for an hour. Then, realizing how much time had passed, David stood to leave and Evie asked point blank, "Do you have romantic feelings for her David?" Evie always came straight to the point.

David knew there was no hiding anything from Evie. "I have to admit, I'm attracted," he said raising his eyebrows. It was enough for Evie and she didn't push him.

"I've about finished canning the tomatoes. Does your mam need any?"

24

"Lord, no," David laughed. "Mam's done about two full shelves of her own."

"Just thought I'd ask. Please tell Pastor Brown I'd like to meet her."

"You can call her Pastor Megan. Why don't you just take her some of your tomato juice?" he teased.

"David, you'll see her before I will. Just tell her about me and I'll bet she'll come to call on her own."

"Bet?" he asked, grinning.

"Bet."

"Come on, Corgi, let's get Duke." David gave Evie a quick hug around the shoulders and left saying, "I'll see you around ten. Wanta pull wagons?"

"Sure," she agreed. Corgi escorted him and Duke as far as the woods, then gave a farewell bark and padded happily back to the house.

When David rounded the barn he could see that Mam had her line of wash out ahead of her neighbors and he guessed there would be a good breakfast as well. He was hungry. He brushed Duke down, checked the milking parlor to find Tad had finished milking and headed for the kitchen.

He was right. Mam had fried potatoes, biscuits with strawberry preserves, fresh scrambled eggs and home-made bacon, and was getting ready to bake an apple pie. They sat down together and he told her about the meeting and the letter, being careful not to mention Megan other than to say she'd been easy to work with. Mam was more interested in the letter.

"It's a lot of money, David. Who gave it, do you know?"

"I know, Mam, but I'm sworn to secrecy."

"I'm trying to think who'd have that kind of money to give. Is it someone from our own community?"

"I can't say."

"Or, someone who used to live here?"

David kept eating.

"It'd be someone who knows we need a new organ."

"Good breakfast, Mam."

"I'll bet Squire's excited. He wouldn't have to listen to Thomas complainin' all the time. How did Thomas take it? I bet he's happier than a rooster in a hen house."

"He's not so excited."

"He isn't?"

"No. He's actually pulling back on it. We'll just have to wait and see how it all plays out."

"What do ya mean, wait? What did they decide?"

"They didn't decide anything last night, Mam," he answered a bit impatiently. "We appointed a committee to look into it."

"A committee!" she said, flabbergasted. "All you had to do was say 'Yes, thank you very much, we'd be pleased to take your money.' What's the matter with those men?"

"Not everyone was agreeing to it, and besides, there's a lot to consider. Trust me, Mam, it'll all work out in time."

"How about the new preacher? What does she think?"

"She agrees with me. I'll be talking to her after I get the rest of these beans off. Now I gotta go. Thanks for the breakfast and tell Tad thanks for doing the milking." He left her to her dishes.

"Land sakes," sighed Betsy, "Those men can't ever get anything done. What they need is a woman on that committee. I'll bet that new pastor'll get a woman on there. Can't come soon enough for me, that's fer sure."

CHAPTER FIVE - VILLAGE POST OFFICE

In the heart of the village at the Cambria Post Office, Bryn Morgan, post-mistress, arrived at 7:30 AM sharp. She entered the back door, turned on the lights and unlocked the front door. Stepping outside to raise the flag, she glanced across the street at the store. There was a light on. She raised the flag, tapped the outside collection box and brought in the mail that had been delivered at 6:30AM from the sectional center in Lima. She took the boxes of letters, magazines, catalogues and junk mail into the back room of the sixty by twenty foot building, turned on her radio to pick up the weather and news and began sorting parcels first. Next she laid aside the flats, periodicals and letters for the rural delivery.

The town's people usually began arriving by 8:00 to pick up their mail, buy stamps or postcards, or just visit. Bryn always got the sickness reports, new baby reports, state of the village, who said what to whom, and the sagas of their lives. When she first worked there it burdened her heavily but she soon learned how to handle it. She listened attentively, asking questions, and when people began repeating the story, she excused herself saying she had work to do and walked away from the window.

At 8:15 Pete, the rural carrier, arrived and put up the mail route. Pete left at 10:00 and Bryn checked the rainfall gauge, which was still dry and began her bookkeeping.

Just then, she heard the door close. She looked up to see Squire Lloyd.

"Good morning, Squire."

"Good morning, Bryn. Looks like another great day."

"Mid-September usually is. A bit dry though." Bryn waited a minute until he had his mail and then asked, "How did the meeting go last night?"

"Fine." Squire, supposedly having descended from one of the members of King Arthur's court tried nobly to live up to the code of honesty but it was like trying to stay with a New Year's resolution not to egg on Aycee and the post-mistress. A single question could get his juices going.

"So, what do you think of the new preacher?" she asked.

"Oh, it's gonna be a duel. She took the sails right out of old Thomas when he tried to get by callin' her by her first name." Bryn's eyebrows rose just enough that he kept on with his story. "You know Thomas. He wasn't about to call her Reverend Brown, her bein' a woman and a young un at that, so he jus'calls her Megan, right to her face. It got Tadcu raving at him but she come right out and said she'd like to be called Pastor Megan. Yessiree, she took the sails right out of ol' Thomas." Squire beamed as if he'd given out the best secret in town.

"Is that right?" Bryn cooed and Squire was trapped.

"Oh, but that's not the best that happened last night." He dropped the clue so cleverly that he grinned in pride of himself.

"Really! What else?"

"Well, it's quite secret yet but it's exciting." Raising his eyebrows and he nodded his head to convey the importance of his knowledge.

"So, why did you bring it up, Squire, if you can't talk about it?" Bryn was used to his teasing ways.

"Well, you asked, Bryn, and I couldn't be rude."

"When did I ask?"

"When you said, 'Oh, what else?'" He mimicked her usual inquisitive tone.

"Humph," she snorted in embarrassment and turned back to her work. Squire pinched back a grin and walked out the door. He knew she'd ask for more when he gave her a little bait.

Across the street Aycee Sewald was perched on the pew bench in front of the store, legs crossed. Aycee had seen Squire enter the Post Office and was waiting. He wasn't Welsh. He just arrived one day. He was seen here and there until he became a bit of a curiosity to the people in the village. Then he began to sit on the discarded pew bench in front of the store. No one had ever sat on it before. It just appeared there when the church removed a few pews to put in new choir seats.

He made himself at home and when anyone stopped by the store or the Post Office, he'd strike up a conversation. Eventually, the farmers started hiring him as an extra hand baling hay. It was rumored he lived in the Livery Barn at the edge of town. Thomas, who owned the barn, said he didn't think so. But the Morrises, who lived across from the manse could see both the General Store and the Livery Barn from their house, and they said they saw him coming out of the Livery Barn early one morning.

Squire ambled across the street. He liked to feed Aycee a little meat to chew on every now and then.

"Mornin' Aycee," he said tipping his cap.

"Squire," Aycee responded as Squire came toward him.

"Seen the new preacher yet?" asked Squire.

"Yup." Aycee answered cautiously and waited.

"Whaddya think?"

"Whadda you think?" Aycee tossed back.

"I like her. When did you see her?"

"Yestiday, when she come into town."

"Yeah?"

"Uh huh. She drove a red convertible, of all things. Watched her all the way through town." He saw Squire nod his head as if that seemed feasible.

"Well, of course, I'd met her when she come to interview so I struck up an easy conversation with her last night," Squire boasted. "She's an interesting lady."

"How so?"

"Can't tell ya. Sworn to secrecy ya know."

"Oh?"

"Well, gotta get the misses some flour. See ya."

Squire moved past Aycee into the store. He hadn't exactly told the truth but he was only teasing Aycee. It wouldn't matter. Aycee snuffed his nose and waited.

When Squire came out, Aycee hopped up and grabbing him by the arm half whispered, "Listen here, Squire. If you got news, I'd love to know what 'tis. Promise I won't tell a soul."

"Aycee, you know I can't do that." He pulled away.

"I promise, Squire. I know you know somethin' about that preacher lady."

"Well, actually Aycee, it ain't about her. It's about a letter."

"Letter?" Aycee stood nose to nose with Squire now, his curiosity really aroused.

"Yeah." Squire paused just long enough to whet Aycee's appetite. "There was a secret letter that David read. Didn't say who it was from but it was real interestin'." He turned and walked toward his truck.

"A secret letter?" Aycee hop-skipped a few steps to catch up.

"Yup. Now Aycee, that's all I can tell you." He opened the truck door and set the sack of flour on the seat and closed the door. Aycee grabbed his arm again.

"Come on, Squire, what did the letter say?"

"Can't say."

"Who was it from?"

"Can't tell ya," Squire broke loose and walked around to the driver's side.

"Squire?" Aycee pleaded looking through the window.

"Nope." He climbed into his truck and looked back at Aycee. "Already told too much," he said and making a U-turn, drove north out of town wondering why he loved to tease people so. Especially Aycee, poor soul. He always seemed so vulnerable.

Aycee watched until Squire was out of sight and trotted across to the Post Office.

Bryn had her head in her books when the front door opened and slammed shut with a louder-than-usual bam. She leaped out of her chair knocking it over, and moved quickly to the window to see who was there. Aycee was already peering into the opening so that their noses nearly collided. Startled, they both leaped back yelling at the same time.

"Aycee, what in the Sam Heck are you doing?" Bryn asked, more than a little perturbed.

"Bryn, oh, I'm so glad you're here."

"Of course I'm here. Where else would I be?"

"I could hardly wait to tell ya'."

Bryn frowned at him over her bifocals. She was getting impatient. He was always wanting to gossip about somebody. He just sat most of his day away on that bench watching and listening. She picked up her chair.

"Well, don'tcha wanta hear what I have ta say?" He looked a bit rejected.

The Post Office Employee Manual stated that the post-mistress must be polite and greet customers in a pleasant manner at all times. At this moment Aycee was not a customer so she didn't feel obliged but he was certainly keyed up about something, so she guessed she'd better listen. She turned back and stared at him. He took that to mean she was ready and proceeded.

"I guess you knowd that preacher lady drove into town yesterday."

"Everybody in town knows that, Aycee."

"Well, I knowd they was gonna have a meetin' last night so I jes kind of meandered over that-a-way about the time they was a comin' out of church, and you'll never guess what I heard." He stood there beaming full to the brim of his hat. His eyes were practically bulging out of his head, Bryn thought.

"Well?"

"Well, I didn't want nobody to know I was there so I scrunched down under them bushes by the front porch. I had dark clothes on so's nobody could see but I jes thought I'd catch a little idea about if'n they liked the new preacher, ya know. But then, they was so busy talkin' and excited-like that I won't have needed to worry about 'em seein' me."

"Wait a minute. Are you telling me you were hiding in the bushes at church?" Bryn was astonished.

"Yeah," he slurred. "You wanna know what they was a sayin' or don'tcha?"

"That's eavesdropping, Aycee."

"I know that. They weren't no harm done."

"Someday you're going to get caught at your shenanigans," she scolded.

"Do you wanna hear or not?" He asked perturbed.

"Well, get on with it."

"You're never gonna believe this but I reckon you'll hear it soon enough. Jus' remember I told you first."

"Aycee, get on with it!" Now Bryn was impatient.

"All right! They was talkin' about money."

"Money?" That surprised Bryn.

"Money. Lots of it. Like thousands of dollars, and they was a sayin' things like 'I wonder who'd have that much money to give,' and they was mad at Thomas about somethin' and then I heard somethin' about a new organ."

"What?"

"It's true. I heard every word myself. Not only that, Squire was jus' talkin' to me and he said —"

The door opened and in walked Paul Jenkins. Aycee hushed up and slid over to the corner pretending to be looking at a book in the little library there.

"Morning, Paul." Bryn spoke first.

"Morning, Bryn." Paul walked business-like to his mail box. He generally was pretty tight-lipped but Bryn was such a good listener and he was brimming over with news of the Session meeting last night. He opened his box and drew out some official looking envelopes. Bryn couldn't wait.

"Did you meet the new preacher last night?"

"You mean Megan?" He tossed the name out casually as if he had known her forever. "Yes, indeed. She's a pretty smart lady. She didn't chair the meeting though," he was quick to explain. "She just met everyone and sat in to see how we do things. David still ran the meeting." A little piece of Paul still didn't want to give in to a woman.

"How do you like her?"

"Seems quite pleasant. I think we'll have to wait and see how she does." Bryn waited. She knew there was more to come. Paul shuffled through his mail and then looked up as if remembering something.

"It was an interesting meeting," he added.

"Oh? How's that?"

"David had a letter he read that caused some excitement."

"Really?"

"In the letter an offer was made to give the church some money, if we would use it to buy a new organ."

"Really!" She glanced at Aycee whose eyebrows shot up. Behind Paul's back he tipped his head as if to say, 'I told you so.'

Paul went on. "We've got a committee lookin' it over to decide whether or not we'll take it."

"Why wouldn't we take it?" Bryn asked, surprised.

"As I understand it, the money has to be spent just for an organ and even though it was a large gift we still might have to raise more money." Then spotting Aycee listening he decided he'd already told more than he should have and stopped talking.

"How much money?" Now Bryn's curiosity was aroused.

"I can't disclose the amount just yet. Sorry, I have to go." He made a quick exit, nodding at Aycee. He hadn't intended to tell as much as he did and he felt guilty. He knew the news would fly now.

"Didn't I tell ye?" Aycee hopped up and swung out the door to follow Paul.

When Aycee Seawald first appeared in town he had settled himself in the abandoned one-room schoolhouse a mile east of town. For a while he'd slept in the livery barn at the south edge of town while he was fixing up his other place. No one knew that. He especially didn't want Thomas, who owned the livery barn, to know that's where he'd been; so when he heard the rumors that he'd been seen coming out from there, he went right back to his schoolhouse home. He spent his days mostly around the Post Office and talked to people as they came in, to get acquainted. Soon some of the farmers began hiring him to do odd jobs but when he wasn't helping with hay baling, he spent so much time on the bench in front of the store that the storekeeper began to complain to the village Council. So Squire, who was the Mayor, put Aycee to work in the cemetery, mowing, trimming and digging graves. He seemed happy with the job but still made it his business to know everything that was going on. If people didn't offer information, he'd ask. 'I know it's none of my business. I'd jes like ta know,' he would say. If he got information, he'd tell. If he couldn't get any, he imagined it. It seemed to him that everyone had more exciting lives than he. He'd found in Bryn a crony, although she generally managed to stay a little more tight-lipped.

Aycee couldn't control himself. Whenever he suspected something he got on a high. Bryn knew he was a goner on this one. He'd snoop around like a hound dog and bring everything he found into the Post Office for approval. Bryn never complained. To her, he seemed like a decent enough fellow, just down on his luck. And sometimes, like now, he'd hit pay dirt. He seemed harmless.

Bryn went back to work. During the day others stopped by and Bryn sorted out fact from fiction and straightened out others who didn't have the whole picture quite right. She finished her book work, had her lunch, and when Pete returned from his run, told him the story. Of course, Aycee was in and out to catch up with any new developments during the day and Pete had picked up a few remarks on his route. So the news was definitely on a roll. Bryn would pick up more from her twin sister, Bronwyn, when she went home. Bronwyn was the village telephone operator.

Back at the manse, Megan had spent the morning studying and writing in her journal. She had been too wound up, the night before, to focus. This morning she recalled clearly the progress of the meeting and put her impressions down, along with a list of things she wanted to look into. Then she worked up a draft of her first sermon.

The moving van wasn't due with her belongings until Saturday, so she decided to walk to the Post Office and get acquainted. As she stepped out the front door, Mary Morris from across the street came toward her with something in her hands.

"I thought you could probably use a nice casserole about now," she said.

"How nice! I could, thank you. I guess you saw me come in yesterday." Mary Morris nodded. They chatted briefly and Megan took the casserole inside and started out again. As she approached the Post Office she noticed Aycee, whom she had not yet met, sitting on the bench in front of the store. He caught her eye and grinned. She thought she noticed a tooth missing. She smiled back, walked on into the Post Office and introduced herself as Pastor Brown.

"Is the mail delivered or are we to pick it up here?" she inquired.

Bryn introduced herself and explained the system. Aycee slipped in trying to be invisible in the library corner, but Bryn didn't let him get by with it.

"Aycee, have you met Pastor Brown yet?" and then to Megan. "This is Aycee Seawald. He is the caretaker of the cemetery. For a little compensation he will do work for you around your house."

"You can call me Aycee, Ma'am," he said quite politely.

"I'm pleased to meet you, Aycee." Megan held out her hand and he stepped gingerly over to shake it.

"I'll remember if I need something. Mr. Williams has taken good care of things for now. Do both of you attend church?"

Aycee shook his head negatively and Bryn answered, "I do." Before Megan could ask more, Bryn asked how the meeting went the night before.

"Of course, it was my first meeting so I just sat in, but I met quite a few people and I thought things went well for the most part."

"News is that someone gave money for a new organ. Is that true?"

Taken by surprise that word had traveled that quickly, Megan phrased her answer carefully. "Yes, a letter was read in which an anonymous person offered the church money to start a fund to buy a new organ. The church must decide if they want to accept it. David appointed a committee to look into it."

"You say it was anonymous. So, no one knows who it is then?" Bryn was sure Megan knew something about the giver.

"I'm sure the lawyer knows but the donor is not to be disclosed just yet."

"Seems to me that something as important as that should come up before the whole congregation." Bryn was pressing.

"No doubt it will in time. Right now a committee must get more information in order to be able to present it."

Bryn decided to stop pushing. She didn't want to alienate the new preacher.

"Well then, I hope to see you both in church next Sunday." She left and walked across to the store.

Aycee watched her through the front window, then turned with a pinched up face to look at Bryn. He opened his mouth as if to say something but she beat him to it.

"Gotcha, didn't she?" She beamed.

Aycee, tongue-tied, turned back to the window.

"You know, it wouldn't kill you to go to church some Sunday." She watched for his reaction. But Aycee was so shocked he had nothing to say. He waited until he saw Megan head home, then scooted out the door and off in the opposite direction.

It was four o'clock. Bryn determined how much business she had done for the day, sent a registered deposit to the bank, straightened the books, closed the window, took down the flag, locked up the safe, and left. She lived just a block away so always walked to and from work. At the end of the street she saw Aycee heading into the cemetery instead of his schoolhouse. *I thought he was going home. Oh, well, he must have some work to do in the cemetery.* She was anxious to hear what Bronwyn had learned over the phone lines.

CHAPTER SIX – CEMETERY

When she reached the manse, Megan put her groceries away and tried to keep her mind off David. Already the news of the letter was spreading fast. If he didn't call her by tomorrow she would try to see him at his home. It was important they talk before she met with the committee concerning the organ.

Meanwhile, she looked for but did not find the record book at the church. She guessed Robert Jones must have it at his home so gave the phone a quick crank. Bronwyn's voice quickly came over the line.

"Oh," said Megan, startled. She had not used a country phone before. "I'm trying to reach Robert Jones and I don't seem to have a phone book here."

"Which Robert Jones did you want, the one on Mendon Road or Route 116?"

"I'm not sure. This is Pastor Brown. All I know is that he is acting clerk of the Session at church."

"That'd be Bob Jones on 116. This is Bronwyn, the telephone operator. I'm glad to meet you, Pastor. Anytime you need help, just call me, for anything."

"Pardon me for asking, but isn't this an out-dated telephone system for these days?"

"Yes, Ma'am. The telephone company has been sayin' for almost a year now that they were going to install dial phones but nobody's seen any action yet. I'll ring the Joneses for you."

Megan heard three rings followed by one short and then a woman's voice answered. Megan introduced herself and asked to speak to Bob Jones. The woman was his wife and explained he was in the field but she would give him the message at supper. Megan explained what she needed and apologized for not remembering he would be outside. She hung up berating herself.

Her next goal was to get a bite to eat and walk to the cemetery before sunset.

She walked through the village and north on Route 116 a short distance through an arched gateway and back to the older part of the cemetery. The leaves of the huge, old oak and maple trees had started to change color. The grounds were well kept. Wandering through the old grave sites she got a sense of history and place. Names like Jones, Morgan, Morris, Evans, Thomas, Richards and Jenkins were repeated many times and she wondered how they kept families straight. She understood now a remark someone had made about being careful what you said about people because they were all related.

She walked across a grassy area toward two war monuments. The veterans listings were surprisingly numerous for such a small farming community. She noticed no Vietnam Memorial had been placed yet and wondered how many young men from the community were serving in the Vietnam war. The men she had met were all older. Perhaps David knew. She spotted a small bridge crossing over to a newer part of the cemetery and stepped up her pace to see it before sun set.

Unseen by Megan, Aycee had been putting his tools away when he saw her arrive. Curious, and not wanting to confront her, he hid behind the small shed and watched her through its windows. Watching her at the monument he wondered if she knew someone from here who had been in the war. Then he thought maybe she had been in love with one of the soldiers. He just couldn't fathom why a smart, young chick like her would be a preacher in a little podunk town like this one. Heck, these days she might even be a spy. Who knows? By golly, he convinced himself, I betcha that's it. She ain't no preacher. That's all jus' a cover up. She could be workin' for the FBI or the CIA or one of them sneaky groups. The idea struck him so profoundly, that he leaned against the shed wrapping his arms around himself and rocking back and forth. Thinking about it made him break into a cold sweat. *This woman could be dangerous. I gotta be careful. She can't know I've seen her.* He held his breath as she walked past the shed and headed across the bridge.

Aycee watched for his chance, then dashed from tree to tree staying a distance behind her but closing in to where he could still see her.

Megan crossed the crude flatbed bridge with no railings, just wide enough to support a hearse or mower, and walked through the stone markers. She noticed they were mostly new and waiting for bodies. Everything but a death date had been engraved on them and they were of impressionable sizes, which surprised her.

She sniffed in the fresh scent of hay from an adjoining field and moved quickly from grave to grave, trying to see as much as she could before sunset. But the sky was so magnificent she had to stop and gaze up at it. Varying shades of pink and gold clouds were being drawn toward the sun. She imagined a hand with a paint brush stroking in the colors. Looking back toward the village she saw the row of Main Street's white frame houses aglow with golden windows. It was the wide open space of field and sky and being able to see it all in such vivid color that impressed her.

As the light faded, it became harder to read the markings on the stones but there was one that looked like a poetic phrase. Curious, she bent down to read it.

Twenty feet away, Aycee, lay in the tall grasses on his stomach on the bank of the ditch below the bridge. She was a mysterious silhouette against the vivid pink afterglow as she bent over the stone to read. It appeared to Aycee as though she had found what she was looking for. *I knowd it. She's lookin' fer somethin' specific.* He watched, holding his breath while she took paper and pen from her pocket and wrote something down. His chest pounded with excitement. Then, quickly, she stood up tucking the paper in her pocket and headed back across the bridge. Aycee scooted under the bridge, out of sight. He lay still holding his breath as her footsteps clacked directly overhead. Without looking back she walked to the gate, so he was sure she hadn't seen him. When she was far enough away, he crept up the bank and, keeping a safe distance between them, followed her home. There, he hid in the church shrubbery crouched in a sitting position and waited until her lights were off for the night.

Satisfied, he crawled out and walked home on the vacant country road with only the stars overhead, his chest exploding with excitement. Wait 'till Bryn hears this, he thought. He'd tell her first thing in the morning. He laid down on the bales of hay stacked into the resemblance of a bed and, covering himself with the light cotton blanket he'd gotten from the Red Cross, quickly fell asleep.

The next morning, Bryn had no sooner arrived at the Post Office when Aycee pounded on the front door. Now what? He could at least wait until I unlock the door, she thought. Irritated by the banging, she frowned through her glasses at him through the window.

"What?" she asked curtly as she opened the door; he was already spouting off about Megan.

"Hold up! Now calm down and start over. What is the problem?"

"I knowd there was something strange about the church a hirin' a woman preacher and now I'm dead sure of it. You know what I think?" He was standing nose to nose with Bryn and she felt uncomfortable. She backed off and reached for the flag.

"What?" she asked obligingly. Aycee followed her every move. Then leaning close to her ear whispered, "I think she's a spy."

"A spy!" Bryn exploded backing off again. Aycee shushed his teeth and hands at her.

"You think Pastor Brown's a spy?" Bryn was unable to imagine what he was trying to tell her.

"I do. They's all over the place these days what with the FBI and CIA and all that, and then that there war a goin' on in Vietnam. But listen here. I was at the cemetery last night finishin' off some work when I seen her come into the cemetery."

"Pastor Brown?" asked Bryn, trying to keep it all straight while walking outside with the flag in her hands.

"That's right, Pastor Brown," Aycee snapped at her impatiently. "She was walkin' in the cemetery."

"So?" Bryn had the flag attached and started to pull it up the pole.

"So," he rebutted as if she ought to know everything he was thinking. Then he saw she had the flag on up-side-down. "Hold it. Hold it. You got the dang thing on up-side-down." He reached for the wire and brought it down, knocking Bryn to the side.

"Aycee," she spoke angrily. "That's my job and I'd have done it right if you wasn't yackin' in my ear. Why didja have to come barreling in here so early in the morning anyway? I don't even have my chores done yet much less opened up."

"Well, I had to tell ya what happened, that's all." He fumbled with the clasp. "How do ya get this here flag unhooked anyway?" The sound of their voices attracted the storekeeper across the street, and Bryn saw him watching from his window.

"Calm down," she said in a lower voice to Aycee. "Here, give it to me." She took the line, unhooked the flag, turned it around and hoisted it up with ease. They exchanged looks and Aycee started to pace.

"I declare, I've never seen you so worked up," said Bryn. "Come in here and tell me what happened." Aycee followed her in. Bryn went into the back room so the window was between them while he talked, in case anyone came in. She was trying to keep things under control. By this time he had calmed down a little but continued to pace back and forth past Bryn's window. "I seen her come and I follered her. I couldn't imagine what she was a doin' there."

"It's a nice place to walk, Aycee. She probably was just taking a walk."

"No, Bryn. She was up to somethin'. I could tell." He continued his story describing all that had happened and trying to convince Bryn that what he now believed was true. When he told her he hid in the ditch she snorted out a tone of disgust but let him continue. Then he told her about her copying something from the gravestone and Bryn asked, "Which gravestone?"

"Dang it. I ain't sure. It was gettin' dark and she suddenly was a comin' right at me and over that bridge. I didn't have time to go look. I had to follow her home."

"What for?"

"For security."

"Is that all?"

"Ain't that enough? It makes me s'picious."

"Aycee,I think your head's whipped right up out of your hat."

"But what about that there stuff she copied? Folks don't usually do things like that in a cemetery."

"Who knows? It's not our business anyway." She turned away.

"Now you jes listen here. I'm warnin' you she may be dangerous. She coulda been sent here to get rid of somebody. Bryn, we jes don't know. I heerd tell that some of them FBI agents is trained to kill folks jes like that!" He snapped his fingers in her face and jutted his chin out.

"Aycee, you're makin' me nervous." She moved a mailbag and began sorting. "Go on, get out of here. I've got work to do and so do you."

He stood a minute thinking and then snapping his head up said, "That's right. I do," and marched out.

CHAPTER SEVEN - MOVING DAY

As Megan came down the stairs the next morning the telephone rang.

"Good morning," she sang into the receiver feeling happy.

"Mornin'." Tadcu's distinct voice was readily recognizable but she soon learned no one in the community identified themselves on the telephone. "I called to see if now would be a good time to bring Haydn Gwyn over. He missed the meetin' Wednesday and he's a mite anxious about Zion's Sunday service." Megan remembered she was to preach for another small church in the community.

"Of course. I'll make coffee." She had it ready when they arrived in exactly ten minutes. Haydn Gwyn moved as if he'd been riding a horse too long. She judged him to be just under six feet and somewhere around 45 years old. A toothy grin slightly over-touched his lower lip and a tiny cleft showed in his chin. His long Roman nose and Celtic blue eyes made him quite an attractive man. He was spanking clean, smooth shaven and polite. He sat at the table and took his coffee with cream and a heaped spoonful of sugar. They got acquainted and Tadcu left saying he had some errands and would check back later. Megan invited Haydn into the study.

"The moving van should arrive tomorrow with my things," she apologized, "but I think we'll have plenty of space to work on the desk."

"They did a nice job on the floors," Haydn observed. He laid out his papers and Megan carried in an extra chair from the kitchen. "Tell me about the Zion church and people," she began.

He spoke as if every word were thought out carefully. "We have only twenty-five members, counting the children, of which there are two, but we only average eighteen in attendance. Three are in Vietnam." She had believed there were more members in Zion but quickly calculating the attendance percentage in her mind, was impressed.

"The building is built on land originally loaned by a farmer named Cook. When he died the land was turned over to the church, so we rightfully own the land and the building. Back when they built it there were more families that lived in that area and they felt it was too far to drive their buggies to Cambria. Especially in the winter. That was their reason for starting the church. But Cambria's pastor has always served us, too." He paused. It seemed to be all he was going to tell about Zion, but she waited and he continued. "I know some folks feel it's a burden for the pastor to preach at both places because we're so small. We were told you didn't mind making the trip." Megan nodded in agreement. "So, we do look forward to hearing you preach this Sunday."

"Of course," she assured him quickly. "I've been counting on it." Slowly, she began to realize that she should have been responsible for checking with the Zion people. She apologized and, with that straight, they communicated enough to set everything up for the Sunday worship. When they finished, Megan remarked about the letter David read at Session meeting. He nodded, affirming he'd agreed to be an escrow agent for the process.

"Perhaps you could tell me if I am to know who the donor is."

Haydn was surprised. "You don't know?"

"No. It came up rather spontaneously at the end of the meeting. I'm not sure if David planned to tell me or if he even knows."

"He knows. You should know too. The person's name is Evie Evans. She's single, about twenty-eight, lives over by David's. Matter-of-fact, he farms for her. She's a niece of Thomas Evans. You probably met him at the meeting."

"I did meet him. He's the Choir Director."

"Our folks just call him a Chorister because he leads hymn singing, but he does direct all of the music at Cambria church. We don't have a choir. No offense meant, mind you, he just is a very directed individual."

"Yes. You said the donor is his niece. Does Thomas know she's doing this?"

"Oh, no. Berlin Miller, Paul Jenkins, David and I are the only ones who know, and now you; so it must be kept that way until Evie decides to tell."

"Of course. Do you think it would be acceptable for me to visit her?"

"I think she'd be most happy to meet you. The last I talked to her she was quite excited over the prospect of a woman pastor. But you should know, she doesn't attend either church."

"Oh? What else do you know?" Megan asked him.

Haydn thought a moment. "Some years ago her parents were killed when a train hit their car. They stalled on the track and couldn't get out in time."

"How horrible."

"Yes. Fortunately, the three children weren't with them at the time. So, they were all placed in foster homes. Evie is the only one who came back to the farm."

"She lives alone?"

"Yes."

"It must be hard for her."

He paused, thinking. "Not really. She's pretty independent."

Just then Tadcu pounded at the back door.

"Come on in," Megan called.

"I'd best be going. I hope David won't be too upset by me telling you all this." Haydn picked up his notebook and followed her to the kitchen. Tadcu stepped aside as Haydn squeezed by him in the doorway saying, "See you Sunday, Pastor. We'll have everything ready." He turned to Tadcu, "Much obliged," he said and left.

"Sit down. Can I get you some coffee?"

"You know, I'd rather have a cup of tea if you have it," he said politely. He had on a fresh pair of overalls over a neatly pressed blue work shirt. He hung his cap on the kitchen door handle and sat down with a little groan.

"Well now, how can I help you?"

"You've already done quite a lot. May I pay you for the food?"

"Oh, my no. That there's a part of the church expense. It's all taken care of," he insisted.

"Then there is nothing I need until the moving van comes tomorrow, so why don't you tell me a little about yourself."

"What's to tell?" he teased a bit, knowing full well he had oceans of things he wanted to tell her.

"Don't give me that. Your accent tells me you must be true Welsh. Have you lived here all your life?"

"Pureblooded," he said proudly, "and yep, I've lived here most all of my life."

Megan was beginning to understand that being pureblooded was important to them. "But you were born in Wales," she guessed, propping her arms on the table.

"I was," he began, then poured out his story, hungry for someone to listen. "My tad raised sheep. Folks in Wales called him Bigul, shepherd." He paused. "That's kind of what you are for the folks in this here church." Megan was reminded of the window and smiled at the comment.

"We lived up in the Cambrian Mountains which is in central Wales. Cambria is a name that came from the Cambrian Age way back in Roman times when the Celts settled mostly in Britain and Wales. Wales survived a lot of wars."

"Folks 'round here argue 'bout which is better, north or south Wales. I don't get into that because I come from the middle. The miners and sheep herders lived in the mountains. In the south-east the soil was good enough for farmin', but up in them mountains you could only raise sheep. If you were from the south you were considered to be a little lower class, I guess. That is, if you were talkin' to someone who come from the north. In the north was the universities, theaters and such." He took a sip of tea. "You know, I do prefer tea to coffee."

"It will be better when I get a teapot." She apologized for making it with a tea bag.

"Anyway," he continued, "I was little but I can remember goin' fishin' with my tad in the Severn river. Each year when the salmon was comin' up stream we'd go watch 'em leapin' clear out o' the water. We'd catch us a couple and take 'em home for Mam to bake. No fish around here like that." Megan thought of the Lake Erie perch her father used to bring home.

"They spawn there, ya know. Come up the Bristol Channel right into the Severn River. It's a sight to see."

"When did you come to this country?"

"My parents and my brother and I come over on a ship when I was eleven. In 1892. My grandparents were with the first settlers back in 1845. See, that was right after the US Government had bought the land from the Indians. The

Wyandots left and five of our families came over. It was pretty tough livin'. The land was swampy, forest so dense they had to hunt to make a livin' so they only stayed seven years before they went back to Wales to have my tad. They intended to come right back but things never worked out until my tad and mam decided to come. By that time I was eleven and Edwin, my brother, was nine. My tadcu and mamgu must of been in their sixties. Anyway, we come over together on the ship. I'll never forget driving that mule-wagon from Philadelphia over the Alleghany Mountains all the way to the Ohio River. There we took a barge down the Ohio River to Cincinnati where we got off and made our way north. My tadcu remembered the way. By that time they was a good sized community of Welsh folk here, and they'd found the land so rich that they'd started to farmin'. Land was available so that's what we decided to do. We built a cabin 18 feet square. We'd hear the wolves a howlin' at night and then we'd farm by day. In the early 1900's they found oil but it soon run out and we all went back to farmin'. I've lived here ever since, married, raised my own family." His eyes glistened with a touch of tears.

"That's a wonderful story," Megan said feeling very privileged. "I admire people who leave the places they've known and go to far-away lands. It took great courage for your family to leave Wales and come to America, not knowing what was in store for them."

"Hardships, lots of hardships." Tadcu spoke softly, "and yet, we was a family and we done everything together. That's how we made it. We'd come lookin' for a church family. We brought our hymns and sang 'em and that's what we found after all, our own people, our own community in a free land."

"Have you ever thought about returning?"

"Back to Wales? No. I'd never go back. We made this our home. I'll stay here 'til I die. Then I'll sing from the grave – 'A clean heart forever singing, singing through the day and night.'" He burst into song.

"Singing with your wife," suggested Megan remembering the gravestone.

"Yes," he paused, wondering how Megan knew his wife was a singer. "One should never take anyone for granted, 'specially your church, 'cause a lot of people broke their hearts to get it for you. Right now we're losing ground to the Catholics. Our people, they're thinnin' out." He broke off into another mood. "There's a difference between a Frenchman, an Englishman and a Welshman. Do you know what that is?"

"I've no idea." Megan noticed a twinkle in his eyes.

"The first thing a Frenchman done when he come to America was build a trading post. The Englishman, he built a fort, but the Welshman — built a church." He stood up, grabbed his cap from the door knob, pulled it on and gave it a pat. "Thanks for the tea."

"Thanks for the story. It means a lot to me."

"Me, too," he said and walked off toward his truck in the parking lot.

Megan watched him from her window, touched by the story, but more by the man. She had so much to learn of these people. She decided Sunday she would ask David if she could come see his farm. After that, she would visit Evie Evans.

Saturday, the moving van arrived two hours late. A group of onlookers gathered quickly in the parking lot. As might be expected, Aycee was with them. Moving vans seldom came to their village so were an object of interest.

"Looks mostly like stuff a college kid would have," said someone.

"Yeah, but she's obviously lived in her own apartment or brought stuff from her folks' home, because there's some good sized furniture there," added another. Their curiosity and observations prompted Aycee to enter the conversation. "Looks to me like she's not plannin' to stay long."

The observers turned to stare at him. "Why's that, Aycee?" one of them asked.

"She don't have near enough to fill all them rooms in that house."

"Well, she's just out of college. What didja expect?"

"Still, I betcha she ain't stayin' long." He squinted his eyes.

"You know somethin' we don't know?" asked Jim.

Squire Lloyd and Paul Jenkins pulled up in Paul's pick-up. "What's goin' on?" asked Squire. He felt it was the Mayor's business to know what was happening in the village.

"Pastor's movin' van arrived."

"Aha." The two men entered the conversation.

Aycee spoke again. "It seems mighty strange to me that Cambria Church would hire a young un like her to be pastor."

"It ain't strange, Aycee. It's just that we couldn't get no one else." Squire had served on the pulpit committee. "Pastors now-a-day don't like to take on two churches, and you can't find a Welsh one, anymore than you can find a cookie in a pickle barrel. Besides, she was cheap and eager."

"That's the curious part," said Aycee. "Seems too eager, like she knows somethin' we don't know."

"What are you getting at, Aycee?" asked Paul.

"Did you all ever think about lookin' into her past?"

"What's to look into? Richard Jarvis recommended her. That's all we needed to know."

"Well, don't it seem just a bit strange to you that both her and the money come at the same time?"

"Explain what you just said," barked Squire.

Now Aycee had their attention. He could put on a good act when he wanted to. He knew if he was to get his point across he had to do it now. "Well, suppose she ain't a preacher, but a spy for the government."

"Spy!" they all said at once half laughing.

"You know, one of them ordinary folks that the gov'ment sends out to do their dirty work."

"What gives you that idea?" asked Squire. He wasn't about to miss a chance to lead Aycee on.

"I been watchin' her. I seen her in the cemetery."

"So?"

"She wrote somethin' down."

"When was this?"

"Thursday night."

"After dark?"

"Sunset. I follered her home."

"Seems harmless to me," said Paul.

Everyone was watching Aycee now, forgetting about the moving van. "Mmm," mused Squire, "but we don't know for sure do we, Aycee? You may be onto something. I think you'd best keep an eye on her for a while." He looked slyly over at Paul who was shaking his head.

"You bet, Squire," Aycee's excitement was spurred again. "You know the gov'ment could a sent that money to help support her."

"No," said Paul quickly. "I know right where that money came from and it sure isn't the government. You can forget that right now." Paul was not about to get tangled up in that kind of mischief.

"How do you know?" challenged Aycee.

"I can't tell ya. I just know."

Aycee snorted. Now the men began supposing all kinds of bazaar scenarios, laughing and letting their imaginations get out of hand. Aycee couldn't make sense of what they were talking about, and thinking they were half crazy, huffed off down the street. The guffaws bellowed out as soon as he was out of ear shot. The movers finished their task and people went back into their houses.

Megan was facing the task of unpacking boxes when Tadcu appeared at her door with several people from Zion carrying dishes of food and offering to help. She learned the churches took turns in helping each new preacher get settled, something like a house warming, but instead of gifts they brought food and worked.

The men moved boxes and placed furniture, hung curtains and pictures, and unpacked books and placed them on the shelves.

The women went straight to the kitchen to organize food, then began unpacking, washing dishes and putting them away under Megan's direction. Fortunately, she had had two days to think about where she wanted things, and it went very smoothly.

The few youth went outside under Tadcu's watchful eye to trim bushes and mow grass. They worked most of the day, coming in only for snacks or drinks of water. By five o'clock, they cleaned up and ate and laughed and told stories about the good old days. Megan learned a lot by listening, recognizing it was their way of introducing themselves.

As the air cooled down in the evening, Tadcu brought in wood and built a fire in the living room fireplace. The crackling sound drew people in and Haydn's wife, Grace, slipped onto the bench of Megan's Spinet piano and began playing hymns. Like bees homing to their hive, they came, their robust voices beautiful in minor harmonies. Megan had never heard hymns sung like this before. Their souls came alive and the expressions on their faces moved her close to tears. They went from rousing marching songs to softer ones of longing and on to ones of devotion. As their voices softened and the fire faded, Megan sensed the deep ties they had with one another.

"I don't know how to thank you. This has meant so much to me."

"Nothing to it," said one.

"It was fun," added a youth.

"I feel as if I have been brought to a very special place."

They applauded and Haydn said, "I think Megan would probably like to get some sleep before her first Sunday worship with us." They gathered their belongings and each one welcomed her as they filed out the door and went their separate ways.

When they had all gone, Megan went to her piano. Touching it lightly she spoke aloud. "I'm so glad you are here. We have made some new friends, a whole new family of people who love music as we do." She sat down to play a little, herself. Her fingers were at home on the keys as she played Debussy's "Clair de Lune" and Beethoven's "Moonlight Sonata." Then she opened her hymnal and played several familiar hymns, ending with "Abide With Me."

Afterwards, she curled up in her big Ottoman chair to watch the last flickering embers die. She didn't know which was more full, the house or her heart. Strange, she thought as she climbed the stairs to bed, my first sermon was to be about singing a new song in a strange land, and today I heard it for the first time.

Outside, hidden in the bushes beside the church, a lone figure watched until her lights went out.

CHAPTER EIGHT- DAVID'S BARN

Early Sunday morning Professor Richard Jarvis phoned from Princeton to ask Megan how she was getting along and to wish her well with her first sermon.

"What is your text for this morning?" he asked.

"John 10, The Good Shepherd."

"That fits you, Megan. I'll pray for you."

"Thank you for calling, Dr. Jarvis."

"I wanted to. It's been good to hear you're getting along so well. Incidentally, I think we could drop the *Doctor* now. Please call me Richard."

"I'd like that."

"Good. So go preach one of your exciting sermons and we'll talk again soon."

Following the service, David introduced her to his parents, John and Betsy Thomas, who invited her to stop by to visit during the week. Megan was grateful not to have to make the request herself. She was excited to see a real farm for her first time and hoped there would be time to talk with David and work things out. She arrived promptly at the designated time.

"Come in, come in," repeated Betsy happily.

"What a pretty skirt." Megan noticed the floral fabric.

"Oh, thank you. I made it out of a feed sack."

"A feed sack?" Megan was surprised.

"Oh, yes. Farm women sew lots of things from them."

"I always thought feed sacks were burlap."

"No, chicken feed comes in a heavy cotton. They just started putting designs on them. I suppose it's a gimmick to get farm women to buy a certain kind of feed. Who knows?"

"Well, I'm impressed." Megan liked Betsy immediately. Her hefty build and rosy cheeks showed hearty eating and muscle strength.

Betsy placed tea and cookies on a small coffee table in front of the sofa. Mary Morris had told her that Betsy Thomas made the best apple pies of anyone in the church, so Megan had been primed for a piece of pie.

Offering the cookies, she said, "I just baked these fresh this morning. John's getting spruced up and David should be along soon. He had some errands to run in Van Wert. I reminded him that you were coming, so I'm sure he'll be along. He thinks very highly of you, Pastor Brown."

"Thank you, but please feel free to call me Megan or Pastor Megan."

Betsy smiled shyly and said, "Here's your tea. Would you like cream or sugar? Maybe lemon?" She poured the tea and began talking again.

"We are so happy that you're here. You know, there was a lot of talk about you before you came, but I just knew you'd be what this church needs. I just bet that, being a woman, you'll shake up some of these know-it-all-men." Their eyes connected in a knowing look and Megan smiled. Betsy continued. "You know, I think women are just natural nurturers, don't you? People are hungry for your kind of sermon and I heard people commenting afterwards that they'd never heard such a good sermon from so young a person. I know I never heard a sermon as good as yours."

"I'm glad you found it inspiring." Megan was amused.

"I did. It was perfect for the occasion, don't you know? And your language was so poetic. Like a breath of fresh air." She paused and looked at Megan in admiration. Then, embarrassed, added, "I'm sorry. I went a bit overboard. I haven't given you a chance to say a thing."

Megan saw a true soul mate in this woman. "I love your cookies," she said, changing the subject. "How do you make them?"

"Oh, that's easy. You just mix everything in a pan and pop it in the oven. I'll give you the recipe." She folded her hands in her lap and waited for Megan to speak.

"Thank you. How long have you lived in Cambria?"

"All my life. I moved into this house when John and I got married. This was his family's home."

"And where was yours?"

"Our farm adjoins this one to the north," she pointed through the north window.

"Our families were neighbors," added John, entering the room and walking across to shake hands. "I was born in this house and lived here all my life. Betsy and I were childhood sweethearts."

"And it looks as if you still are." Megan could see obvious affection for one another.

"Yes, well you marry someone older than you and they'll be the boss," he said glancing teasingly at Betsy.

"All who believe that can stand on their head," chirped Betsy back and they all laughed.

"There's been a lot of living in these two farms," John went on, "and a lot of changes through the years. Betsy's sister still lives in their old farm house but we own and farm both places. Betsy couldn't have any more children after David, so some day all of this will belong to him; lock, stock and barrel, you might say."

"What a wonderful inheritance." Megan knew she had said the right thing. They appeared eager to tell about themselves. Betsy kept the house, the garden and the chickens and drove errands for the farm work when needed. They watched the markets and sold crops at the right price, and were faithful to the land and its needs.

"It was the hogs that got us through the depression," John boasted. "I was able to save money when most people were scraping the bottom of their barrels.

In fact, we not only saved our land, we were able to put aside money for David's education."

"Where did David go to school?"

"He has a degree in Agriculture from Ohio State University. He was the first from this community to get one. A degree, that is. Lucky for us he didn't have to go to Vietnam but I guess they figured I was getting too old to farm and he was needed here. I'm mighty proud of that boy. It won't be long before Betsy and I can sit back and let him take over."

Megan smiled. "How many men are gone from this community?"

"David could tell you. A lot of the older men are working harder than they would have if their sons hadn't been drafted. Seems so senseless. They're needed more here than there."

"Now, John, I don't think we want to talk about the war," spoke Betsy uncomfortably.

"I'm sure you feel fortunate that David didn't have to go. He seems very capable. I'll be needing someone to guide me through this Welsh culture." They smiled proudly and she suddenly blushed.

Just then the screen door slammed and David came quickly into the living room.

"He's always in a hurry," Betsy whispered. They excused themselves as David came into the room.

"I told them beforehand that we needed to talk business," David explained.

"I like your parents. They're very proud of you."

"They were pretty impressed with your sermon Sunday."

"Thanks. I told them I would need your help in understanding the Welsh culture. Incidentally, this is my first time on a real honest-to-goodness farm. I wonder if you'd be kind enough to show it to me."

He sat down next to her and helped himself to a couple of his mam's cookies. "I'd enjoy doing that. Ours is probably the most impressive farm in this community. I don't say that to brag. We're very fortunate. I give my parents a lot of credit."

"They said some day soon they would be turning it all over to you. Are you looking forward to that?"

"I am. I have a lot of ideas I learned in school that I think my tad's not sure of. If they turned it over to me I could try some of them." He offered more cookies to Megan. "Take a couple with you. If you're finished with your tea we could walk out to the barn."

He led her through the kitchen and out the back door. Megan spotted two fresh pies sitting on the stove, which reinforced Mary Morris's comment but didn't satisfy her cravings provoked by the smell of apples. The screen door slammed again behind them and they walked to the chicken house.

They entered the door to a flurry and fluster of cackling hens and a rooster reluctantly took roost on a rafter. Megan stepped back in alarm. Smiling in amusement, David recited a poem.

"Said the little red rooster to the little brown hen, 'You haven't laid an egg since heaven knows when.'
Said the little brown hen to the little red rooster
'You haven't been around as often as you uster.'"

Megan burst into laughter which set off the hens again. David shushed them into calming down, then told her to reach in under a sitting hen. Bravely, she reached and was thrilled to find and pull out a warm egg. On the way to the barn he told her about the economics of chickens and eggs and how his mam had paid for a good part of his education.

The large white barn with green roof and a matching green silo glared in the sun. David pulled the heavy door, opening it on its track, and they stepped inside to the stillness and the sweet smelling fragrance of freshly baled hay. To David, the barn was security. For Megan, a whole new world. Never had she smelled such fragrance. She breathed in deeply and looked up through the rugged rafters into the full mow.

"Ohhh," she sighed softly, the sweet stillness touching her deeply. Sunlight streaked in long rays through the roof windows to where they stood and she heard only the breathing of Duke from a nearby stall.

"I love this barn," said David in a quieter voice. "The beams were made from giant pines, topped and hewn to 14 inches square. See here, the ax marks — and here, the oak dowel pins holding it all together? They don't make many barns like this anymore."

"Amazing," Megan's voice softened to match David's. "I had no idea a barn could bestow such a feeling of sacredness."

"Sacredness?" The word surprised him. "Yes, you could call it that." David gazed upward with her, thoughtful for a moment, and then spoke. "Dean Hughes, a Welsh poet, said it this way: 'Monument to the past, feast for the present, song for the future.'"

"Beautiful," she said surprised at him. So he knew poetry.

Only slightly embarrassed to expose himself he moved quickly on. "And here is the tongue of the anchor beam, mortised and pegged, as it passes through this post." Megan nodded, but this time she was not as impressed, knowing little about barn structure. David, however, was in his element, the Welsh pride in him oozing out.

"This is a well-built barn. You'll see a few uncared- for-ones here and there where farmers sold out to urban sprawl but in this community, you'll only see serviceable and well kept barns. They are a part of our culture."

He's either trying to make an impression or is totally immersed in his culture, thought Megan. Her hand touched one of the posts.

"Surprisingly smooth," she commented.

"They soften up from the rubbing of hay and straw bales."

"What's the difference between hay and straw?"

"Easy." He walked to a corner and picked up some loose straw from a pile.

"This is straw," he said handing the dry yellow stems to her. "It's the left over stems from wheat and oats after the tops are harvested. We use straw for bedding the animals. Up there," he pointed to the haymow, "in the bales, is hay. Hay is dried grass grown from special seed like alfalfa or clover. There's a whole science to hay, what kind to grow and its different uses. It's basically used as food for animals." He led her then to the loft ladder.

"Come on up," he said and climbed deftly up to the first mow. She followed, glad she had worn slacks. At the top, a whir of pigeons took higher roost. She spotted four perched on a high beam. Now she saw a broader expanse of hay bales stacked to the ceiling. David pulled up a trap door in the floor to show her where they dropped the bales into the cow mangers below. Then they sat down on the bales to rest.

"This is a great place to get away and think. I used to build tunnels with rooms at the end of them, way back under the bales. It was a wonderful hiding place. I don't think my folks ever knew where I was."

She listened as he seemed lost in memories, his face tan and expressive, his eyes shining with happiness. She imagined him lifting the heavy bales easily with his strong arms. She felt comfortable with him at this moment, as though she had known him for years. How had that happened?

"How different our child-hoods were. I lived in a small town where I rode my bike everywhere. I played in a school playground. There were always other children to play with. I can't imagine growing up almost alone."

"I had the pond to swim and fish in. Sometimes my friends rode their bikes over to swim. In the winter we played ice hockey. My best friends were those in the youth group at church. We don't have a youth group anymore." Megan noted the remark.

"Megan, I've been trying to find a way to tell you that I'm sorry we got off to a bad start. I know I should have found the time to talk over the letter with you and let you handle it."

"We don't just find time, David. We make it. To get anything done one has to be intentional. It's what we give priority to that matters." She was hearing Professor Jarvis's words coming right out of her mouth.

"And I didn't give you credit for being able to handle it."

"No," she agreed. "Why was that?"

"Scared, I guess. I wasn't sure how to act around a woman preacher."

"Perhaps, you made some assumptions about me." It came out like a question.

"Assumptions?"

"Yes, that as a woman, I wouldn't know what to do."

"Now wait a minute. I admit I had doubts about you but that was because you were unfamiliar with our procedures, not because you're a woman. I don't think that influenced my decision about reading the letter."

"I hope that's true, David. I just know I was taken back when suddenly the meeting included business when I hadn't expected it and hadn't been warned. It felt like you didn't think I could handle it."

"I'm sorry. I had no idea you felt that way. You were so helpful to me. I admired that. How can I apologize?"

"I want to be a good pastor for Cambria, David. I know I will make mistakes. I have a lot to learn and I'm counting on you, to help me know what's important to this congregation. The hardest part of that is that I am a woman and a lot of people don't know how to deal with that."

"I know. There are several who still think it's a man's place to be the pastor."

"And a few women too, no doubt. David, how do you feel about it?"

"I probably could adjust easier if you were a middle-aged, motherly type, you know what I mean?"

"Oh, thanks," she whipped back but knew there was sense to what he'd said.

"I'm serious," he pushed it. "You just don't fit the image of a preacher that most people have. I know some of the older women are used to and probably would prefer having a man. The younger women will probably love you right off. Men? Well, the older men will think they have to tell you what to do, like a daughter, you know; but it'll be the hardest for the younger men because we don't know how to act around you. Face it, you're beautiful and you're young."

Megan breathed deeply. She was about to speak when he interrupted. "What I'm trying to say, Megan is — well — what young farm guy is gonna come pour out his soul in your lap? It'd be like admitting he was a weakling runnin' home to Mama."

"Come on, David. Men do that all the time." She was determined to get her point across.

"If not that, they'd be flirting with you all the time, seeing how far they could go with you and talking about it behind your back."

"I would hope they'd give me the same respect I'd give them. I'm not about to walk around flirting with every young man that makes a pass at me. That is not what I'm here for. And that goes for you, too, David. I respect you as a leader in the church and a capable helper to me, but I will not flirt with you or play games."

"Well, I guess you won't have to worry too much. Most of the younger guys are off to war. Those of us who are here carry heavy burdens of work and we really don't have time to play around." David quickly covered his own feelings of excitement when he was around her.

51

"Good, because right now I could use a little kindness." She hadn't wanted to show weakness and wondered why she had said it.

Relieved, he said, "Now that we have that settled, let's go see the rest of the barn." He offered her his hand to pull her up and then changed mood and posture. Continuing his guided tour, he built up the image of his family and himself. He wanted her to like them. He described the milking process, explained the different kinds of cows, talked about how his father had spent money remodeling the barn, showed her the milking machines and explained the challenges of the modern farmer to her.

"A century ago 85% of the people in this country were farming. Now only 20% of our land is agricultural. Fewer farms means we have to grow more food for a growing population. We have to find new ways to save time and produce more crop on less ground. That means mechanization and that means larger farms and as richer farmers buy up more land fewer people are farming."

"You sound as if you really know this stuff." She was fully convinced.

"I'd better," he replied.

On the lower level tools and pitchforks were hung on the walls on one side, and on the opposite side was the horse stall where Duke slept. Bridles, old harnesses and double-trees hung on the wall. David explained they were from the days when they farmed with horses. Just then some beautiful little birds with orange breasts and forked tails swooped down over their heads and back up to the rafters.

"Barn swallows," he said. "They nest up there. They like people." They stepped outside and he pulled the door shut. Megan noticed a horseshoe hanging above it.

"For good luck?" she asked pointedly.

"To ward off evil spirits. The belief is that witches have a passion for mathematics and curiosity. If a witch sought to sweep through the barn on her broomstick and was confronted with a used horseshoe, she was forced to turn about and have no peace until she had retraced and counted all the hoof prints made by the shoe."

Megan was laughing at him now because he was telling this so dramatically it was like a spoof.

"The more worn the shoe," he continued "the longer it took to track and count all the hoof prints to satisfy her compulsions, and she could not complete her impossible task before morning arrived so had to return to wherever she had come from. Each night she would have to start over and thus would never complete her task, even in the long nights of winter, to get through the door to the cattle." He leaned toward her with a mischievous look and took a bow.

"David, I believe you are a story teller," Megan said laughing.

He shrugged his shoulders. "All the Welsh tell stories." He moved around and walked ahead of her. His nervousness had gone. He was feeling secure and sure of himself again.

Keeping pace behind him she said, "I used to drive through the Pennsylvania Dutch farming areas on my way home from Princeton. There they paint Hex signs on their barns. I suspect their explanations would be similar to your horseshoe one."

"I don't know about Hex signs but actually, the Moravians were the first to paint on the sides of their barns, and usually it was a full country scene with pictures of many farm animals. They believed the painted animals would absorb any witchery rather than the animals inside." Once again, Megan thought she caught an egotistic tone in David's voice. She caught sight of a little twist in his lips that gave her the impression that he believed he had impressed her.

Not to be outdone, she stopped and said, "David, I think you should have a Distlefink."

"A what?"

"A Distlefink."

"You're joking."

"No, I'm not. Someday I shall get you one."

She marched past him and leaning on the fence turned casually toward him. "Now, tell me about Evie Evans."

Without blinking he asked, "Have you met her?"

"No, but I think I should. Haydn told me she is the one who gave the $15,000 gift."

"Yes, I should have told you that."

"I was a bit embarrassed to admit I didn't know about it. What can you tell me?"

"Evie's real name is Evelyn Davies Evans and she lives on the other side of the woods there," He pointed south east in the direction of Evie's farm. "She is the niece of Thomas and Cridwyn Evans. Thomas and her tad were brothers."

"I met Thomas at the meeting and Cridwyn is the organist, right?"

"Right. Their farm," he stepped up to her and turned her in another direction, "is that one over there." He pointed north east and Megan could see the tops of their buildings over the corn. "Did Haydn tell you about the accident?"

"Yes. That must have been a very hard time."

"It was. Evie was in my class in junior high school.

She was the youngest of three. They were all placed in foster homes in Van Wert. When they came of age they were given the choice of coming back to the farm or not. Her brother never was interested so he studied in a vocational school. He worked in a factory before he went to Vietnam. Her sister was married right out of high school and lives on a farm up north, near Napoleon."

"So Evie was the only one to come back to the farm?"

"Yes. There was money laid aside for her from her parents' estate. My father had farmed for her on a share crop basis and the money that was left over was put into a savings for her. I think she must have given about all of it to the church. When I graduated from Agricultural school and returned home, I took over the farming of her land." He studied Megan's face and then said, "We're very good friends."

"I understand she doesn't attend church," said Megan.

"No, and there's no use in trying to get her to come. She remembers the church like it was when we were kids and she wants to know what's going on, but has no interest getting involved in any way."

"Then what's her reason for giving such a generous gift?" The question was unexpected and David paused.

"She knows Thomas is unhappy with the organ. I think he's troubled about the way he handled things in the past. But that's just my opinion. He also believes the hay-day of music is over in the church and that upsets him. I think she hopes this will make him happy again."

"But he wasn't a bit happy about the gift."

"You gotta understand, their whole family is wrapped up in the music of the church. All she ever hears from Thomas is that if the music dies the church will die, and that would kill all of them. I think that's why she gave the money. She hopes it will save the church."

"It's that important?"

"I'd say so." David plucked a blade of timothy grass and began chewing it.

"Thank you, David. You've been very helpful."

"Megan, I wasn't deliberately keeping things from you. There are a lot of things you don't know yet. It will take time. All I can say is, I'm sorry if I've caused you concern. I'll really try to be more helpful in the future."

"It's all right, David. I can't possibly learn everything in the first week. I really should be going now. Thank you for a really nice visit."

"Oh, wait. I think Mam has something she wants to give you." They walked back toward the house just as Betsy came out of the door with a package.

"I saw you heading toward your car so I figured you'd be going home now and I wanted you to have one of my freshly baked pies." She handed it to Megan whose mouth dropped wide open.

"They're pretty good pies," said David.

"So I've heard. Thank you, Betsy. I know I will enjoy this very much. And don't forget to give me the cookie recipe you promised."

"It's in there," Betsy said smiling at her response. David walked her to her car. It crossed his mind that he ought to tell her to get a different car for winter, but his instinct said to wait.

She drove out the lane, top down, absorbing the wonderful scent of freshly baked apple pie.

Already, she was anxious to meet Evie. She had seen a protective look in David's face when he talked about her and suspected they were a little more than childhood schoolmates.

CHAPTER NINE - MEGAN VISITS EVIE

Lost in a whirl of thoughts, Megan's morning slipped by. She was to visit Evie at two and it was already one. She tidied up her desk, ate a fast lunch and made a quick walk to the Post Office. Aycee was asleep on the bench, his head slouched to one side. Bryn was busy in the back room of the Post Office so Megan was able to get her mail and depart quickly.

At home she rolled the top down on her convertible to enjoy the warm sunshine and drove to Evie's. As she drove in, she noticed a few large sheep and two horses in a small pasture by the barn. She pulled up near the walk to Evie's back door. Visitors, she had learned, were welcomed through the back doors in this community. They led to kitchens where people sat over cups of coffee or tea with freshly baked pie or home-made cookies. Food kept people longer, and visiting built community.

Stepping from her car she was greeted by the boisterous barking of a bright little dog. Keeping his distance, he moved back and forth barking her toward the house, then ran off in another direction. As she neared the house she heard barking again, and a voice.

"Hello!"

Turning in the direction of the voice she saw Evie in jeans, a white short-sleeved shirt and a large-brimmed hat. In one tan arm she held a bouquet of flowers and with the other she was waving a pruning shear. Megan could have sworn the dog was smiling at her. For a split second, the sun shone like a spotlight on them. A few white clouds nested in the rich blue sky and the flower garden in full bloom made a stunning backdrop. It was an image Megan would remember.

"Evie?"

"Hello," Evie said again. "I was just getting some fresh flowers before you came in. Are you always so prompt?"

"Yes," answered Megan truthfully, watching Evie stride toward her.

"I've been so anxious to meet you. This is Corgi. He's friendly. I hope you like dogs."

"I do." Megan reached down to pet him.

"I've heard so much about you from David. He keeps me up-to-date. When they found you I got excited. I think women are better suited for the ministry than men, anyway. What lovely hair you have. Here, you should wear a daisy in it." She pulled a fresh, white daisy from her bouquet and handed it to Megan. They laughed and talked easily as she led Megan through the freshly painted, enclosed porch into the kitchen. Still talking, she whipped off her hat, and gave it a quick toss. It landed perfectly on a hook by the door. Megan laughed spontaneously at the accuracy of the toss.

"How long did you practice to accomplish that?"

"I don't tell," she beamed.

Freshly baked cookies were cooling on the counter. A round oak table took up the middle of the room and gleamed as though it had recently been refinished. It was set for tea for two.

"Corgi, go lie down," Evie commanded and the dog obediently settled himself by the door. "Make yourself at home, Megan. It'll just take a minute to fix these flowers for our party."

"Party?"

"Yes. You and I are having a get-acquainted party."

"And here I thought I was making a parish call. I do like your idea better."

"Of course. We are going to be great friends."

Megan suspected Evie was right but asked, "How do you know that?

"Because I need a friend like you and I suspect you could use a friend like me."

"You're very perceptive."

"I know." She grinned, warmly content with herself. Megan watched her move about the kitchen easily and efficiently, dropping the flowers into the sink, lifting the almost empty teakettle off the coal stove, filling it from the hand-pump and placing it back on the stove.

"You probably are wondering how I manage with this old-fashioned kitchen. This is the way it was when I left it. I loved it then and I'm not ready to part with it just yet."

She reached into a cabinet and brought out a squatty green vase, into which she began to arrange zinnias, marigolds and daisies in that order, knowing just where to place each flower.

"I'm impressed that you still use a coal stove."

"I love it. It bakes better than an electric one and I always have plenty of wood to burn. Too, I think it makes a cozier atmosphere."

"Who chops your wood?"

"I do," came the quick reply. Amazed, Megan wanted to know more about this person. She watched every move as she finished the splashy bouquet and placed it in the center of the table where it caught the afternoon sunshine. Her delight in the end product was evident when she proclaimed, "There! Flowers do lift one's spirit."

When everything was ready she sat down across from Megan, her face flushed with excitement. At close view, Megan could see her pale blue eyes and dark eye lashes. A darker blue circled the outer rims of the pupils. Lovely, she thought to herself.

"Your tea cup was my mother's favorite," Evie told her as she poured the tea. "I remember when she came in all tired from the garden, she'd make herself a cup of tea in that cup. 'It soothes the body,' she'd say; and she would sit and do nothing until it was gone. I understand that now. I guess I've kept her alive by doing some of the same things she did."

"How is it to live alone with those memories?"

"I love it here. It's home and I couldn't wait to get back. I cried a lot when I first returned. There was a lot of fixing to do, but I loved doing it."

"There are obvious signs of that love everywhere, Evie; the freshly painted door, the refinished table, even the wood pile is the neatest I've ever seen." They laughed.

"It was as if my parents were right here next to me guiding me in what I had to do. It was a wonderful way to grieve. I don't think I ever did that when I was a child." She looked down at the table.

Megan reached across to touch her hand. "You are a brave woman."

Evie's eyes filled with tears. "I'm sorry. I didn't intend to cry."

"Only actors make tears by intention. It's all right. I believe the spirits of those we've loved often stay around to help us when we need them."

"Oh, I do too." Evie was touched. Megan was all she had hoped for. "How do you like Cambria so far?" she asked.

"Quite honestly, it's taking some getting used to. I grew up in a small town called Medina. I rode my bicycle everywhere and knew most of the people in town. My father owned a hardware store and everyone knew who I was. At college it was the same. At Ohio University and even Princeton I got acquainted all over town in a hurry. Here, to see the church members I have to get in my car and drive several miles. I'm slowly getting acquainted with the people and even more slowly trying to understand why God brought me here. I'm trying to visit every church member in their home."

Evie gasped, "Oh, my! Megan, you can't do that." She had very naturally used Megan's given name and Megan liked it. "With over two hundred people, you would have to visit someone everyday," she went on. "Two a week would be plenty, I think."

"But it's important to me that I get to know everyone in their own surroundings."

"I can understand visiting nursing homes and hospitals but house calls too? Don't you see most of the people in church every Sunday?"

"I was taught that it's an important part of ministry. If I visit in their homes, I learn more about them and can build trust. Then, when people really need me, such as in sickness or death, they won't hesitate to call on me."

Evie shook her head in amazement. "You are too good to be true."

"And people must feel free to visit me at the manse and be comfortable about stopping by. May I say something confidentially to you?"

"Please do."

"I find a strong resistance in the men, as if I'm expected to please them. They almost seem to be daring me to prove myself."

"God, yes. They are the ultimate superior clan. They're as stubborn as mules."

"I don't mean to be unappreciative, Evie. Tadcu and David are both very helpful and kind, but Thomas is so difficult, Squire seems all on the surface. I sense his suspicions of me. Jim is so quiet and reserved, I don't know what he's thinking and Haydn seems very reluctant to open up to me at all."

Evie nodded in understanding. "They've been their own closely knit family for so many years that I think they are always cautious about newcomers. In this case, you are very different from what they've been used to. Up to this point we've always had Welsh males as ministers, so of course, you are interesting to them, as well as a bit of a threat. Eventually, they'll come around, and when they do they'll be behind you all the way. I've seen it happen with others."

Megan was both grateful and amused at Evie's judgment. "What do you do, just sit out here on the periphery and watch humanity from a distance?"

"I just know people. But tell me. What is your goal for Cambria?"

"First, I have to find out what people expect of me. I know David's nervous working with a woman minister for the first time."

"Be firm with him, Megan. He is to be trusted, but I warn you, he's a flirt and a tease."

Megan decided Evie had a good understanding of people. "I guess the main thing that I'd like to do, because I feel it would benefit both churches, is to get them to come together."

Evie tightened her lips and Megan knew she may have stepped on a hot potato. "The environment is the thing, Megan," Evie began cautiously. "If you can create a healthy environment, ideas can be planted and anything will grow. Crops or the souls of people. The seeds are there. But they need nourishment. Lots of nourishment." Evie stopped with that and Megan realized that there was a lovely mystery about this woman. She hadn't said no, it wouldn't work. She had said to create a healthy environment.

"I suppose I should explain to you why I don't attend church," Evie broke the silence.

"Evie, you are reading my mind. You would be such an asset."

"As a child I went regularly with the family. I sang in the Youth Choir which I loved, and attended all the Youth Group meetings and activities." Again, Megan took note of the mention of the Youth Group. Evie continued. "Church was at the core of my life. When I went to the foster home the family didn't belong to any church. So, to try to make me happier, they gave me books to read about religion. I read about other faiths and gradually formed a spiritual time for myself that brought me some peace." There Evie stopped to study Megan's face, then broke into a smile. "I know I can trust you. We're about the same age and both of us are finding our own ways into a new community. It is new for me, because it's different from when I lived here as a child."

"Go on."

"I'm not ready to sit in church. I probably worship the earth more than God."

"And who made the earth?"

"God, of course. It's just that I feel more at home in the garden than in the church building."

"Why is that, Evie?" Megan wanted to know that for herself as much as for Evie.

"It's peaceful. I don't have to listen to people. It feels closer to God, somehow. It's quiet and I can hear God speak."

"That's a very important part of our faith, listening, and being able to hear God speak to us. I will be allowing moments of stillness in our worship service for that very reason."

"I have a devotional booklet I read, I keep a journal and sometimes I burn candles and play music."

"I see nothing wrong with any of that. I do those things, myself. I have always believed that no one church has all the answers. Remember, God comes to each of us in different ways. But there is another part to our lives of faith and that is a loving and sharing community. Being in community is a vital part of our loving God and serving God's people. Remember, the two commandments Jesus gave were to love God and love your neighbor like yourself."

"Oh, Megan. I sometimes long for that but I don't think I would fit in anymore. They'd all feel sorry for me and I don't want to deal with that. I want to get on with my life and I sometimes think they're all living in the past."

"There are people who find it helpful to separate themselves from church for awhile. Perhaps, in time, you'll feel more like being in the spiritual community. For now, I'd say you've made a very big effort toward the community just by giving the gift you have."

"Thank you. Oh, I hope they don't fight over it."

"You were very wise to have that phrase about working together in harmony written into the contract." Megan stood to leave.

"I've heard Uncle Thomas isn't happy about it."

"That's his problem, Evie." Megan looked at her watch. "It's nearly four o'clock already. Where did the time go?"

Evie ignored her comment. "He used to be such a happy man."

"Maybe you should tell Thomas that it was you who gave the money."

"No. Not yet."

"Happiness often has a touch of sadness in it. For us, the happy part is that you and I are going to be good friends."

"Yes," Evie agreed. She walked to Megan's car with her. "I love your car."

"Thanks. It's probably all wrong for here, but it was a right choice when I got it. Thank you again, Evie, for the wonderful visit."

Driving home Megan felt energized. Meeting Evie had given her life a new thrust. She knew it would make all the difference.

At home, she parked her car and entered the manse, her mind focused on her afternoon. She did not see the lone figure peering from the basement window of the church.

CHAPTER TEN - DEFINING THE CALL

Meeting Evie gave Megan's life a new thrust. Still, she had no focus. She was concerned with many things: the organ committee, visitations, her installation service, and finding a way to work with Thomas and the music. She made a list of needs for the Zion building and repairs needed at Cambria, but when she talked to Jim about accumulated bills, he said there was not enough ready cash to pay them. He assured her that by November they would have the funds.

"November!" she exclaimed. That they had not budgeted to pay all bills within a month was, in her mind, irresponsible. "And what about the cost of my installation service?"

Jim had not planned for that. It had been a long time since the church had had one.

"I was planning on inviting Professor Jarvis." She heard herself almost pouting.

Jim, trying to find a way around it said, "He's always had a special interest in Cambria. Maybe he'll be pleased enough to participate that he won't charge us."

The comment, although sincere, was thoughtless in Megan's mind and it made her angry. She asked to see the books. When she finished looking them over she was even more discouraged but said no more to Jim. After all, he wasn't responsible for the raising of funds. Instead, she let the problem rest for a while and drove over to the nursing home in Spencerville.

Hattie Jenkins was ninety-eight, a jovial, warm person with great wit. Megan delighted in her immediately. Hattie's large eyes, framed by her pure white hair, loomed large on her face of soft clear skin that sagged softly about her jaws. She told Megan the story of how she, a non-Welsh, married a Welsh man and became a part of the community.

"His marrying me broke the pure-blood strain," she laughed. "Strange, I never dreamed when I married him that I would become so involved in the community. We lived in his family home all our married life. When he died I sold it so I could come here to live." She told Megan of the importance of music in the church and urged her to start a youth choir.

"I've worried about Cambria Church," she said, "but I have great hope now that you are here. I always said our church should try a woman minister."

"You are a woman ahead of your time," said Megan. "I want it to be a good experience for them, but I'm afraid there are some who aren't happy about me."

"How so?"

"David tells me there were some who voted against me."

"Did you expect an unanimous vote?"

"No, but neither do I want enemies."

"If you're a pioneer, which I sense you are, you will have enemies. You have to be tough," said Hattie simply.

"I just have this fear that I will fail at what I've been sent to do."

"And what do you believe you've been sent to do?"

"I, ah, I haven't clearly defined that yet." Megan stuttered. "I have to find out what the church needs. What I want to do for myself, is prove that a woman can be just as good at ministering as a man, and —"she hesitated.

"You want to be loved." Hattie finished it for her.

"Is that so bad?" Megan blushed. She felt it a selfish wish.

·"Never fear. That's what the people want, too, to be loved. My dear, you are young, but intelligent. The Good Shepherd is in the window watching over you. Look up at the window before you begin your sermon each Sunday and you'll be all right."

"I know, we've already met."

Hattie reached out her hands to Megan. "Now, say a prayer for us, dear, we could both use one." She bowed her head and waited.

How good it is to grow old and wise, thought Megan as she walked to her car. But she drove home worried because she hadn't clearly defined her mission. At home, she sat down at the piano and played the sadness out before retiring.

Wednesday, before the choir held its regular practice, Megan slipped into the sanctuary to sit quietly. From the central pulpit she looked up at the domed ceiling and at all the stained glass windows with family names and at the wooden organ pipes in the corner. She looked at the huge painted cross on the wall behind her. She imagined a new wooden cross on the wall, new shining organ pipes in place of the old ones, new carpeting, a full and happy chorus of singers, a youth choir and a youth group; Zion and Cambria people sitting side by side and hundreds of happy people singing, singing, singing! Tears welled up into her eyes and she looked up at the window of the Good Shepherd and she knew she had recognized the design of her call. 'Anything that touches your heart deeply enough to bring tears should be paid attention to,' Richard had said, and she realized she had nested in. She knew it was their dream as well but they had lost touch with it. She would work hard to make their 125th celebration memorable and exciting, one of pride and praise. For the spiritual heritage of these liberty loving pioneers who left their homes and native land to sail an ocean to preserve their faith and mellifluous language; for those who had established homes and this church in a place of wilderness and kept it alive for over a century; and for their strong sense of identity through their spirited music; she must dedicate her labor and her love. Yes, this was the work she was called to do. The only question was how.

The wind whipped the heavy door shut with a bang!

"Hello! It's getting right gusty out there," said Cridwyn. "Cooling off a bit, too. Are you going to sing with us?" She took off her jacket and hung it on the rack in the vestibule.

"No, I've just been thinking. Cridwyn, you've worked with young people haven't you?"

"Sure, what are you thinking?"

"How about starting a youth choir for us?"

"We used to have one but they all grew up and left."

"There seems to be quite a group of youth right now. I was hoping to get a choir started."

"You're right. It's time. Problem is, the parents have to either bring them to church after school or they have to ride the buses in and then have their parents pick them up afterwards."

"Is that so hard?"

"Nope. We've done it before. If we get the parents behind us it'll be fine."

"When can we start?"

"If you want to announce it this Sunday, I could start next Wednesday."

"Great. If it works and they want to begin meeting as a youth group as well, I will be glad to help start that. I saw Hattie Jenkins yesterday and she suggested it."

"She would. How is Hattie?"

"I'd say she has a lot going for her."

Just then Thomas arrived grumbling indiscernibly. He plunked down his music, dropped his jacket on a pew, and rolling up his sleeves marched past both of them without a word and crawled through the small door behind the organ.

The women looked at each other and waited.

"Turn on your organ," he yelled at Cridwyn. She grimaced and quickly turned it on.

"Should have been warmed up by now," he added. They waited tensely silent.

"Play an E," he yelled. She touched the key but there was no sound.

"Just as I thought. Damn thing is on the blink again."

Embarrassed, Cridwyn explained quietly, "He can generally get it to work by tightening the air lever."

"Okay, try it again," came the call.

She touched it again and the tone came forth. They exchanged relieved glances and Thomas came back out bending to keep from hitting his head.

"You're a Godsend, Thomas," said Megan. "Would you show me what you do in there?"

"Good Lord, woman! Have you any idea how filthy it is back there? I wouldn't think of takin' anyone in there."

"Why can't we clean it up?"

"Can't do that. Disturb everything."

Not wanting to get into another argument with him she backed off, but did ask if she could come visit them in their home the next afternoon. Cridwyn responded with a gleeful, "We'd love it!" Thomas's head gave a quick jerk. Megan was not wasting time. She had to understand this man better.

Home at the manse, she lit a fire and made herself a cup of tea. The organ committee had gathered their vital information and were ready to ask the congregation to vote to accept the gift. If the vote went through, they would have to raise a lot of money. It could either split the church possibly causing it to die as some thought, or it could stimulate a surge of energy that she hoped for. They needed that vote of confidence in themselves to rally them together.

Megan began playing with figures. How much could they expect to raise themselves, how much could they campaign other sources for, and how much might they have to borrow? The totals looked manageable. I believe they can do it, she told herself. Now, to make them believe it. She would talk to Thomas tomorrow and she would pray about the meeting, but for tonight, she had to make one step forward in faith. She put in a long distance call for Richard and invited him to preach at her installation.

The next day on her way to Thomas's, Megan thought about what she had to find out. Why was Thomas, who loved and directed the music of the church, who had dealt with the failure of the organ for months, and whose wife was the organist, so against getting a new organ? She knew communication would be difficult but she was determined to get at the root of it.

Driving up the short lane, she noticed their house was the newer style ranch house, and guessed correctly that Evie's house had been the original homestead. The barn was the popular red built, she imagined, when farmers would raise one in a day. David had said Thomas's barn had a salt-box roof. Ohio was full of them. She had learned that farmers painted barns red because red paint was cheap. Still, it was a barn with character, she thought. She told him that when he answered the door.

"That's nice to say," he responded surprised. "Most people think our house looks better than the barn, and you know what that has to say about us."

"Well, your home is lovely, too."

"Would you like to see it? We'll give you a tour," insisted Cridwyn. She was standing right behind Thomas when he opened the door.

They walked through the house together with both of them commenting about their possessions. Megan was surprised to find a full, finished basement in the house with a laundry area, sizable pantry, even a pleasant room with couch beds and a fire place. There was a stack of *Ohio Farmer* issues, a hand carved merry-go-round, and an old Victrola phonograph with a stack of 78 rpm records on top. On the walls hung a portrait of a young boy, a certificate faded beyond reading, pictures of groups of men standing as a choral group, and an aerial view

65

of the original farm house and out buildings. From all this she learned things about them that she wouldn't have known from just working with them in the church. Now, she imagined Thomas spending time in that room reading, carving, listening to music. When she asked if he spent a lot of time there, he became tight-lipped and reserved. She saw that this very private, and perhaps sentimental, man was not ready to open up his life to her. Not yet.

They ended their tour in the living room that held their family treasures: fine furniture, cut glass collectibles, a grandfather clock that chimed the quarter hour, "The Farm" by Louis Bromfield, the latest issue of Ydrych, a five octave walnut pump organ and stacks of music.

"This is a well lived-in room," Megan commented.

"Lots of history here," added Cridwyn.

"Do you have music in your background?" asked Thomas, turning the questions in her direction.

"I took some piano lessons and sang in the high school choir, and also the youth choir at my church. At Ohio University I met a young man who was a very fine organist. Among other things, he taught me a great deal about church music." She thought it best to hold back her experiences with Charles in Africa and Selma. "I studied in the chapel while he practiced the organ."

"Ohhh," cooed Cridwyn, implying how romantic.

"I find it most unusual in a young woman to pursue the career of a minister. What ever made you want to be one?" asked Thomas.

"Women have always been called to the ministry. Only recently have our churches begun to recognize their gifts." Thomas said nothing so Megan realized she hadn't answered his question. "For me, the seed was planted in childhood when I admired my childhood minister enough to try to mimic him. At twelve, he told me I could become anything I wanted to be. Then, during the two years I spent in the Peace Corps in Africa, I taught children Bible stories." She noticed both raised their eyebrows in surprise.

"Peace Corps," they both spoke and nodded together. Megan continued.

"Then when I returned from Africa I joined a small college church and that's when I felt led in the direction of the ministry." They seemed impressed.

"Very interesting," said Cridwyn. "Your parents must be proud." Megan caught an expression on Thomas's face which she interpreted to be critical of Cridwyn's comment.

"Actually, when I announced to my parents that I had been accepted at the Princeton Seminary, my father was upset. I had not consulted with him, believing I was old enough to make my own decisions. He was hurt and angry and refused to help me financially. I was left on my own to get through, which I did. I knew what I wanted and I worked hard for it."

"Really!" Again Cridwyn was impressed. Thomas's face went red and a tight little smirk disclosed an attitude.

"So now, here you are in this small country church with your big ideas and you think you can save us all from damnation." he blurted out through an obstinate smirk.

"Thomas, what an awful thing to say." Cridwyn was shocked and ashamed.

"Sit down," he commanded. The women sat and waited tensely. Would he reprimand her? Would he lecture her on the audaciousness of women to assume they could minister? Would he take her father's side?

"Pastor Brown, if you feel I was rude, I apologize, but I'm sure you know by now how I feel about women trying to be ministers. Their place is in the home. Men are experienced for the ministry. They have the respect of the people."

"Oh, Thomas," interrupted Cridwyn.

"Shut up, Cridwyn," he said and turned back to Megan. "I voted against your coming because I knew a woman in the midst of men would cause problems. To begin with, you don't understand our Welsh culture; you know little of farming, and I question, lacking experience, how much you really know about the Bible. Yes, you may be a good preacher but we called for a pastor. We need a man who can talk to men and help us solve our problems."

"I can help anyone solve problems," inserted Megan.

"It's my strong opinion that you will have a hard time here, you will have wasted our valuable time, and most probably, our church will have died by the time you leave."

"I'm sorry you feel that way, Thomas. You know nothing about me or what I am capable of doing, yet you judge me only by my gender. I hoped we could make a step toward understanding each other today so we could work together toward the same goals but you won't even give me a fighting chance."

"Young lady, your goals are nothing like mine. I have a lot on my heart which I don't intend to burden you with because you wouldn't understand."

"That's an unfair assumption."

"All right, then. I'll tell you what I think. I think it's unwise to get ourselves in debt just to get a new organ." That was what she had come for. Megan listened. Cridwyn folded her hands hunching her shoulders in embarrassment.

"This is your first church. You are inexperienced in a farming community's church finances. I am experienced. I've been with this church all of my life and I know how the people think. I grew up here, sang in the youth choir and the church choir and when a Male Chorus was established I sang in that. I was taught by one of the well-known musicians of the time."

"He no longer lives," interrupted Cridwyn. "His teacher, I mean." Megan nodded. Thomas was irritated by the interruption.

"Thirty-eight years ago, I became the Director of Music at Cambria church. It was the honor of my life and I have loved my work. I shaped the music program of Cambria."

"Thomas's singing groups won many prizes at competitions," Cridwyn added proudly. Megan saw she consistently tried to smooth things out for him.

"That's right. We have those scrapbooks over there filled with certificates but I won't bore you with those. You had to live it to appreciate it. Suffice to say, we had our day." Before Thomas could breathe Cridwyn spoke again. "Music is so important to the Welsh people, Megan. They sing from their hearts and their voices soar with – "

"Don't get carried away, Crid. I would appreciate your letting me have my say first. Then if you ladies want to talk, I'll make myself invisible." He stared at her and Cridwyn apologized and folded her hands in her lap.

"As I said," he continued, "it's been thirty-eight years that I've led the music of this church. I know what does and doesn't work where the music is concerned."

This time Megan interrupted. She thought he needed to be thanked. "You devotion is admirable, Thomas. You and Cridwyn, both, have contributed so much. I can see that. I don't know where I'd be in the worship service without your help."

He ignored her and continued. "Up to now I've been able to cope with the organ because I had to. There wasn't enough money to keep up the organ."

"I know. I don't see how we can pay our bills within a month's time." Again she interrupted, wanting him to know she was on top of things.

"You have to understand that in a farming community the money doesn't come in until the harvest does. That's the way it works. And the people to whom we owe bills know we're good for it as long as the crop pays off. They'll wait."

"I understand that. That's why we need to manage the money better so we can lay aside enough to cover our regular bills until it comes in. People should not have to wait to be paid for their services."

He smirked. She had just proved what he knew was the problem with having an immature female minister. "What I'm saying is that if the crop is plentiful, that can work. But when you have a year of drought it doesn't."

"You can't run a church on luck. You have to plan ahead to cover the time of poor harvests." Megan was getting impatient with his kind of thinking. "What we need is for everyone in the church to tithe. How hard can that be?"

"Hell, if we did that we'd have enough to pay all our bills and Zion's too, but that just won't happen in this church."

Cridwyn bit her lip.

Megan snapped back, "You mean to tell me that there are more important things than the church?" Now she had him, she thought.

"That's exactly what I'm saying. Especially, they're not about to put up good money for a new organ. $15,000 is only about one third of what you'll need to buy a new organ. On top of that you will end up having to redecorate the whole sanctuary." He leaned forward looking fire into her eyes. "I'm telling you that people do not have the money, nor will they spend what they do have for that kind of thing. They will buy a new tractor, not an organ. They don't care about the church anymore." He leaned back.

Megan ached to battle with this man, but something stopped her. He was hurting. She softened her tone. "That, sir, is a very discouraging picture."

"I tell it like it is." He was satisfied.

"No, Thomas, I think you tell it like you want to see it." She paused for it to sink in and then went on. "I see it as an exciting challenge that can be met. And not just met, but met in time for the 125th anniversary. We have a full year to get it done."

"So that's your dream, is it? Young lady, you need —"

"Excuse me," Megan stopped him short. "PLEASE don't call me young lady. Call me Megan, or Pastor Megan if you like, but don't belittle me with that accommodating 'young lady'." She felt herself taking the power Hattie had given her. Thomas and Cridwyn stared at her surprised but without comment or apology Thomas continued.

"Pastor Megan," he paused for effect. "What I'm trying to tell you is that this is a dying church. Our young men are off to a fruitless war. The rest of the folks are spending every bit of energy and money they have on holding their farms together. They don't have time, energy or the money for the church anymore." He slumped back into his chair.

Megan was not going to accept that kind of negative thinking. "Well, you may have bought into that image but I haven't. I've cast my vote with the people who have a freshened faith and new vigor. Those who believe we can do it. It would please me greatly, Thomas, if you were to show that you still had some of that spirit in you. You have too many years invested to give up now." She rested her case. He stood and left the room. "I've had my say. You two talk."

"Thomas has been real depressed," Cridwyn began. "I'm sorry. You gave it a good try."

"I'm sorry, I didn't mean to be impatient. But I'm not giving up that easily."

"I can't even help him. He sees everything he's worked for all these years going down the drain. He blames himself for everything and it's killing him."

"I can see that, Cridwyn. But you aren't like that. How do you feel about a new organ?"

"Me? I'd love a new organ. What organist wouldn't? I think whoever gave that money is very wise. It's just enough that people won't want to let it go, you know? I think they'll grab it and go for the rest."

"We may have to campaign for outside money and maybe even make a loan, but it can be done. I'm certain of that."

"You're smart. I like the way you think, Pastor. You're bringing new life to this community."

"Thank you, Cridwyn. I needed that."

Cridwyn scooted her chair up closer to Megan as if to talk secretively. "You'll pardon my mentioning this but there's been a crazy rumor going around about you. I thought it my duty to tell you."

"A rumor?"

"I don't believe any of it myself, but not believing doesn't stop it in this community."

"If it's about me I don't need any more trouble right now."

"I've heard it twice now, yesterday a little more was tacked on. They're saying that your ministry is just a cover up and that your real work is with the FBI. They say you skipped college one year and traveled the world for them. Now they think it has something to do with the Vietnam War."

"Wait a minute. What? FBI? I don't understand."

"I'm sure it's all a mistake."

"Doing what since college?"

"Spying, I guess."

"That's preposterous! How could something like that get started?"

"Oh, you know. Somebody usually starts some little joke and someone says something that sounds funny and he tells somebody else and the first thing it's gone wild. They don't mean any harm, but harm comes anyway." Cridwyn was trying to apologize.

"Who told you this?"

"I can't say but she told me she heard it at the Post Office."

"From Bryn?"

"I really can't say."

"This is ridiculous. I've never known of such a thing."

"We all get it sooner or later in a small town like this. Rumors just spring up overnight sometimes."

"Well, it's not happening to me. I'm stopping this right now." She stood up.

"You'd better know it all then," said Cridwyn.

"There's more?"

"Whoever it was that told it, said that you copied some information off a gravestone."

Megan couldn't believe what she was hearing. "And that's the reason they think I'm some kind of a spy? I went to the cemetery for a walk. No one was around."

"Did you write something down?"

"Well, as a matter of fact, yes. A short poem I liked."

"That seems harmless enough."

"But how did anyone know that? I swear I was alone."

"Apparently you weren't."

"That's spooky. I'm not too keen on being stalked. Well, I'll just have to track it down. We can't have the whole community playing this kind of game or we'll have the real FBI down on us."

Cridwyn laughed at Megan's humor and was relieved.

"Thank you, Cridwyn. I'll get to the bottom of it soon. I hope Thomas perks up a bit." She had learned two things from the visit: that Thomas was depressed and Cridwyn straight-forward. Working for the FBI? She couldn't wait to tell Richard that one.

CHAPTER ELEVEN - THE VOTE

As Escrow agents, Haydn and Paul were under pressure to tell who the donor was. Knowing Megan would not approve, they went to see Berlin Miller and told him Evie had agreed to tell and they just wanted to inform him. Berlin, who should have known better, let it slip through without investigating and gave his permission. When they told Megan that they had Berlin Miller's permission to tell, she was furious.

Megan knew Evie had the statement in the document for a reason and the decision to release that information should and would be hers only. She wasted no words in telling the two men that they had been dishonest. That day, Berlin Miller had an unexpected visitor.

Megan strode into his office, a woman on a mission. Wearing a smart looking suit with a flowing scarf that flagged the attention of his two assistants, she passed their desks. Two heads bobbed up and eyes turned to view the attractive woman marching toward Berlin Miller's desk. She caught their glances, nodding to each, and politely said, "Good Morning." Berlin stood quickly to reach out a hand in greeting.

She wasted no time on details but in a business like manner informed him of the mistake he had made. She further instructed him that he should make an order to the Escrow agents and swear them to secrecy until the donor herself gave release of her name.

Berlin fumbled for an explanation. "They told me Evie was ready to make that move," he began, but realizing he had not checked with Evie, apologized. "Not only was I misinformed, I didn't check on their word." He promised to wait for Evie's personal direction. Satisfied, Megan walked out while Berlin stood staring after her. The two assistants, in turn, nodded good-bye and noticed the look of amazement on Berlin's face.

"Cambria's new minister," he mumbled in a way of explanation to them.

By Sunday, there were three rumors making the rounds: one, that the church was negligent in paying their bills to Presbytery and they were going to lose their church; two, a gift of money had been given by an unknown donor; and three, there was a scuttlebutt that Megan was a spy for the FBI. Even though most suspected it was one of Aycee's stories, it was enough to fill the parking lot and assemble clusters of men along the fence in front of the church. They talked animatedly while sucking on their last smoke before the service.

Women and children had gone on in. Not that women didn't have their opinions. They did, and often influenced their spouses. Women could even vote in church now. But men still clung to the power of sharing their own perceptions on important issues.

David overheard a bit of one conversation as he walked past the groups into church.

"How can they close us down? It's not their church."

"If we're not paying our bills, they can."

Tadcu was ringing the bell when Megan caught David by the arm. Trying to speak over the sound of the bell, she told him about the Escrow agents and her visit to Berlin. David grinned in approval. A glance around the church indicated a good attendance, and no doubt, curiosity, a strong trait of the Welsh.

Hedged with convention, people filed inside. Routinely, those arriving from north of town parked on the north side of the parking lot and entered the north door. Those from the south, parked on the south side of the parking lot and entered the south door. It followed that they also sat on the same side of the church. Certain families were in the habit of sitting in the same pew all through their generations. If they found a newcomer sitting unknowingly in 'their' seat, they stared, not knowing immediately what to do. A great deal of shuffling and fussing ensued until the innocent victim caught on and moved herself to an unoccupied pew which then became hers in an unspoken but clearly understood way. If, however, she seated herself in a pew recently vacated by departure of its occupant from this earth, and with no apparent heirs, no one seemed to mind. Recently, there had been quite a few vacant pews. This morning, however, one would have thought from the crowd that the crown prince himself was visiting.

David surveyed the situation to see if his family pew was vacant. It was, so he ushered his parents into it. In most families the women led the way, but David preferred to honor his parents with the gesture. Also, from that place he could be readily available for any emergency. Thomas was in front of the choir near the organ. As chorister, he led the congregational singing as well as directed the choir.

Betsy and John slid across the wooden pew. Betsy reached for a hymnal, marked the opening hymn with her bulletin and handed it to John. He traded his bulletin. It was ritual.

Megan put forth her best efforts for the full congregation but their minds seemed to be elsewhere. She could see them looking around to see who else was there, nodding and smiling, constantly shifting and squirming in their pews, even winking and waving across the sanctuary. There were even strangers there. Edwin Williams with his shock of white hair sat stiffly in his usual spot. She anticipated he would fall asleep as usual during her sermon. Tadcu had said his brother was partially deaf, which accounted for his boredom, so it no longer concerned her as before.

As she finished her sermon she noticed Aycee standing at the back of the sanctuary. Like a fox on the trail of a rabbit, she thought. Intuitively, she wondered if he were the source of the rumors about her.

During the last hymn a high shriek pierced the air. Some women covered their ears while Cridwyn frantically tried to push the knobs to stop it. Megan and David exchanged glances. What timing. Thomas flew through the little door and

David motioned for the congregation to stand. Their strong voices covered the sound. Soon it stopped and Thomas returned to lead the last verse of the hymn. David returned to his pew.

"Lead Kindly Light, amid the encircling gloom," they sang. It was Sandon, chosen to prepare them for the task ahead. Megan hoped they would see the value of the gift and have the courage they needed. She knew God had a plan for them. She just had to trust it would happen.

The service over, Cridwyn slid off the organ bench to join Thomas in the pew. Children left through the side room and Tadcu moved closer to the front. David was now back to serving as clerk and carried his books to the front. When all was ready, Megan called the meeting to order.

She explained the reason for the meeting and David read the letter. Megan watched expressions. She knew a new proposition was often viewed with suspicion until thoroughly understood. David had warned about tempers and the lack of proper parliamentary procedure. She was on her guard.

Abruptly, Edwin Williams, who had seemed to be asleep, was on his feet. "Now let me get this straight," he spoke slowly. "A lot of us folks don't understand the words in legal papers. Especially when we can't read it for ourselves and just have to listen. So, just tell us in simple words what that letter says."

Megan thanked him and carefully explained.

Edwin, trying to understand and to be sure he had it right, repeated it back. "So whatcher sayin' is that someone, we don't know who, gave us $15,000?"

"No," corrected Haydn. "The person has not given it. It has been offered."

Edwin reiterated, "Not given — offered. So, if we accept the money, do we have to buy an organ with it?"

"That's the condition," answered Megan.

"Well, then, let me ask this. Just how much money are we talkin' about?"

Tadcu interrupted, irritated with his brother. "Edwin, if you'd just pay attention, they said it was fifteen- thousand dollars."

"I know that Willie. What I'm askin' is, is that enough to buy a new organ or do we have to raise more — and if so, how much more?" That was very clear and both brothers sat down.

At that, Thomas called out without consideration of proper procedure and without standing. "Now who says we need a new organ? No-one ever asked me. I think we oughta pay our bills first."

An overheard comment from Aycee in the back was, "Fer as I can tell that organ's still workin' mighty good."

"Glory be, Aycee, didn't you hear that screeching this morning?" barked an irate Bryn.

"Order please," Megan called. "If we are to make progress, we must have order in these proceedings. According to Robert's rules, we do not speak until we are recognized by the chair. That's me. If you want to speak, stand and be recognized by me. Only one at a time. Understand?" She hadn't missed the glances flitting about the room.

A deadly silence hung in the air as they tried to absorb her forwardness. To them it was like an invasion of privacy. They had been used to Rev. Davis just sitting back and letting them work through it themselves.

"Oh, Christ," said David under his breath.

Megan pinched her lips and leaned over to whisper, "And that means you, too. You are not to speak unless asked a question." David blushed, grateful that she had whispered it.

"I'm waiting for order." Things quieted down and she continued. "Anyone wishing to speak at this time may stand and address the chair." Everyone froze. They were afraid to move for fear of doing something wrong.

"We are ready to move on." She recapped and added, "I have heard that a new organ would cost more than the amount of the gift, depending on which organ we would purchase." She paused to look around at them to see if they were following her.

"What we need for you to decide today is whether or not you want to take that on. If not, the donor will not give us the money." They sat quietly thinking. "Does everyone understand? Do any of the women have anything to say?"

Haydn Gwyn stood. "Miss Moderator."

"You may have the floor, Haydn."

"Miss Moderator," he began again. Thomas sighed and Megan threw him a firm glance, then nodded for Haydn to proceed.

"We've just been offered a generous gift. It's a good start. As escrow agent, I happen to know the donor is a person who cares about the music of this church. We all should care that much. Yes, we'll have to raise more money, but I believe we can do it. Our forefathers believed when they built this church that their children would keep it up. They did and now it's our turn. I think we owe it to go ahead with this here project."

Good, thought Megan, one step at a time. Then she saw Thomas rise.

"Thank you Thomas, you may speak."

"Well," he sniffed, "If you folks will take it from me, I can assure you that this present organ has seen its day. It no longer holds its tune. Short of building a whole new organ, it cannot be fixed. It is frustrating for Cridwyn, and I can't guarantee how much longer I can trot back in the closet and fix it." They sat listening intently.

"Now, I do know that it will cost at least $30,000 for a replacement, and we still have a lot of unpaid bills. If you vote to raise the money for an organ, you'd better be prepared to raise enough to pay not only for an organ, but for re-decorating the sanctuary as well as paying all the bills. To raise the money for all that you'll have to make a lot of sacrifices. That's all I have to say."

"Thomas," she nodded. "Your remarks are well taken." Suddenly Squire stood and began to speak before being recognized. "What about the Gymanfa? We have to have an organ for that." Megan quickly called him on it.

"Squire, you are an elder and you know better. You are to address the chair and be recognized before speaking." She knew she had to get them in line right now or she would never have order.

"Yes, Ma'am!" He snapped an army salute at Megan. David snorted back suppressed laughter and Megan thought it ridiculous. Squire was like a little boy playing soldier. Megan simply stared at him and waited until he settled down.

"I agree with Thomas." Squire straightened his face and cleared his throat. "Sooner or later we're going to have to do something about this old organ. It could be pretty embarrassing if what happened today were to happen at a Gymanfa. I think we should accept this gift so we can begin to investigate and plan how to raise the money to have it in by the 125th Anniversary. If we have to raise money, we'll raise it. It's just like puttin' a new roof on the house. If we need it, we do it."

Someone called out from the back, "Don't we already have a fund for the organ?"

Megan quickly referred the question back to Squire who stated that the Music Committee realized the problem with the organ some time ago and had started a fund toward Organ Replacement. The voice came again. This time Megan recognized Saddler Morris, Jim Morris's father.

"Miss Moderator," he said now in a proper manner, "I'd like to ask how much money is in that fund. If we have to raise money, I'd like an idea of what we would be facing."

"I can answer that," Jim volunteered. Megan nodded approval and Jim turned toward his father as he spoke.

"We've had the fund for about three years and there is close to three thousand dollars in it.

"What!?" barked Thomas. "You mean to tell me that the Music Committee was sitting on all that money? We could have helped pay the bills."

"It was earmarked," said Jim.

"How come nobody ever told me about that money?"

"You were at the meetings," said Jim getting angry now.

"Besides, it belongs to the Music Committee, not you."

"Hell, I'm on the Music Committee!"

Megan stopped it. "Hold it! I want order right now."

"Order, hell!" snapped Thomas. Cridwyn cringed in shock. "The committee could have used that money to pay bills and saved again for the organ. God dammit! Nobody around here knows shit about handling money!" Immediately, a large clap of thunder cracked overhead and the lights dimmed startling everyone, most of all, Megan.

"Good Lord, what was that?" she asked. Stunned they all looked at Megan, then Thomas and then began chuckling and laughing which grew until they were into fits of hysteria. Megan was appalled. They coughed and cried until it spread to everyone and got to the point where they were gasping for breath and trying to explain to each other but couldn't. They had handkerchiefs out to wipe the tears and were out of control.

Through fits of laughter, David tried to explain to Megan who hadn't a clue. One moment they were at each other's throats and the next, crying with hysterical laughter. Finally, she caught the drift of what David was trying to say. It was the timing of the thunder right after Thomas had spoken profanely and her startled response that set them off, as if the Almighty had been listening and pounded a fist at them.

Eventually, they managed to settle down and Megan, still trying to get order, was grateful for the relief from tension. She regained her composure and with a few after-waves of laughter, they continued.

"I was about to call for order but I guess a greater power did it for me," she said. "Jim, I think you were about to say something."

"I was going to tell Thomas that the money was earmarked, and as treasurer, I had no right to offer it for anything else."

Paul Jenkins stood. Megan recognized him. "Jim is right about his position and privileges, but there are ways to get around such situations if need be. What we have to think about here, is which is most important to us, paying our bills or getting a new organ. I believe we could raise the money from the harvest to pay our bills but to ask us to add to the fifteen thousand plus the twenty-eight hundred, the music committee has, may be more than we can raise ourselves. Unless you can think of other ways to get the money."

People began talking among themselves but no one had yet made any motions. She heard rumblings of a bake sale or rummage sale. Megan leaned over to speak to David who, at the same moment saw Haydn rise slowly to be recognized. He nodded and Megan saw and recognized him.

"Thank you, Miss Moderator," he spoke deliberately. "Although Thomas has suggested that a new organ could cost as much as thirty thousand dollars, we don't really know at this point. That would have to be decided by an organ committee's study of the possibilities. No doubt it will be a very big challenge, but that's the idea, you see. The donor is testing our faith. If we are willing to take a risk and try, we will be rewarded with the gift. If not, we won't get anything. So I would hope we would be brave enough to accept the challenge and give it all we've got. Having seen this church pull through worse things I believe we can do it. If we don't, I truly believe the church will slowly die away." He sat. An audible moan swept over the congregation. The members were hearing aloud the very fears they had been feeling, and yet, Haydn was giving them the way out.

Then, Megan recognized Tadcu who had stood, bracing himself with his hands on the pew in front of him. He spoke eloquently.

"Pastor Brown, I move we accept the gift that has been offered to us, along with its conditions, and that an organ committee be formed immediately to research with intent to purchase, and to report its findings to the congregation." He broke into a sweat and fell back into the pew. Megan could feel her own heart pounding in her chest for him. She was impressed at how well he could speak when in a formal situation.

There was a long pause and then, "Second," was heard from Saddler. There was no further discussion and the vote went through weakly. David recorded the action and Megan stated:"According to the letter, if the gift is accepted the donor will choose the time to be revealed. Meanwhile, we are instructed to work peacefully and creatively together to fulfill the wish of the donor or the gift may still be withdrawn."

The second procedure was to form the make-up of the Organ Search Committee. By request of the donor, Haydn Gwyn and Paul Jenkins as Escrow agents of the gift would serve on the committee; Pastor Brown, by reason of position, without vote; the organist, Cridwyn Evans; Squire Lloyd as Chairman of the Music Committee; Jim Morris representing the Session; Buck Jones from the Trustees and two members-at-large, to be chosen by the congregation. With little trouble they selected Steven Owens from the Zion church and Ruth Hughes Lloyd, a widow. So the nine members of the committee were chosen.

An immediate rumble of voices followed the dismissal and cliques of people assembled about the sanctuary to rehash the whole thing. It was typical to reiterate performances of a dramatic nature with a critical analysis, or as Tadcu said, 'Meat always had to be chewed before swallowing.' Haydn slipped quietly out the back. If there were any controversy, it would be because Tadcu had made the motion so swiftly and accurately that they might feel he'd been coached. But Megan had given them opportunity for further discussion which they disregarded and called instead for the vote.

Megan mingled a bit, answering questions and easing their minds. Gradually they dispersed and she found David waiting by the back door to escort her through the rain.

"What do you think?" he asked eagerly.

"I think we're on the right track," she answered.

"Me too. Are you glad it's over?"

"I'll say. I thought I'd lost it a couple of times."

"You did," he said chuckling, "but you did better than I could have." She thought that generous of him.

"Well, we're on our way. I pray to God we make it through."

"Come on, I've got an umbrella." They ran through the gust of downpour and puddles, huddled under the umbrella. Lightening flashed again and in seconds another thunder boomed overhead. Megan cringed at the closeness of the sound and David held her protectively.

"That is so loud," she said, concerned that it might be more than just a thunderstorm.

"Is it the sound you're afraid of?"

"Yes, aren't you?"

"No."

"I've never heard it that close before."

"People from the city say it sounds a lot louder in the country where there's nothing to absorb it. Do you want me to stay until it's over?"

"Yes, would you? I'll make us a cup of hot chocolate. We'll calm down together."

"Be glad to," said David.

Tadcu watched them from the back door of the church. When they made it safely in, he smiled to himself and turned back to close up the church.

With the rain pouring down, Squire offered to take Aycee home. Squire was the only person who knew exactly where Aycee hung out and beside that, he wanted to see if Aycee had any new information to pass on.

"Sure 'preciate the ride," Aycee responded.

"No problem. Have you seen or heard anything new?"

"Meanin'?" He stared at the windshield wipers bouncing back and forth.

"Has Pastor Brown done anything weird lately?"

"Weird? No. She makes a lot of trips in that there convertible that I cain't foller, but when I see her go I hang 'round 'till she comes back. Seems a bit myster'us to me. I think she might have a partner out there somewhere's. If'n I had me a truck, maybe I could follow 'er."

"Un-huh," said Squire, thinking that if Aycee was trying to get his truck away from him, maybe the game had gone too far.

"Aycee, I don't think nobody has to follow her. She gets money for mileage and she'll have to report that."

Aycee sat brooding.

"Tell you what," Squire glanced over at him. "Maybe you should just ease up on her a bit. Word's been gettin' out and she just might o' heard something. Best to play it low key fer a while. All right?"

Aycee nodded, said good night and ran from Squire's truck through the rain into his school house without even a thank you.

Old fool, thought Squire, he's likely to get us all in trouble.

Chapter Eleven

PART TWO

Chapter Twelve

CHAPTER TWELVE - TRACKING THE GOSSIP

The first thing Monday morning, Megan marched to the post office to track down the source of the gossip.

"I imagine if there were any news you would hear it here first," she said outright. Bryn looked up from her books a bit surprised.

"Probably," she said hesitantly.

"So, may I ask if you've heard any strange news about me?" The question was so direct that Bryn was taken off guard. "I'm not sure what you mean?"

"I've been told that a rather strange and untrue rumor is circulating about me and I would like to find its source. If you have heard anything that would help me, I wish you would tell me."

Bryn pulled up straight and faced Megan squarely. "I have heard a rumor which I didn't believe, myself."

"Could you tell me what that was?"

"It was quite ridiculous, to be truthful."

"Tell me, please."

Bryn hesitated in discomfort. "As I recall, this person thought you might not really be a preacher, that you might be an FBI agent."

"That's the rumor." Megan knew she had come to the right place.

"My opinion is that it was just something someone imagined."

"Did you tell anyone that?"

"I told the person himself he was imagining things."

"Bryn, it would help if you'd tell me who the person is so I can nip it in the bud."

"Pastor, it's just like any other gossip. Once it's out you can't stop it. You just let it run dry."

"Perhaps, but if I could speak to the person I could let him know the damage it has done."

"I warned him this could happen.'

"You know who it is then."

Before Bryn could say more, the door opened and Aycee, totally unaware of the situation, said, "Mornin' Pastor Brown," just a little too sweet.

"Good Morning, Aycee," Megan said and stepped aside.

"Mornin' Bryn," Aycee nodded. Bryn stared at him tongue-tied and he suddenly felt uncomfortable. He turned and caught Megan's steady gaze. Before he could do or say anything her question was in the air.

"Aycee, would you know anyone who would start a vicious rumor about me?"

"I, ah, ah, no Ma'am." He backed away reaching for the door.

"That's not true, is it, Aycee? You do know. Wait just a minute. Someone did say that I was not a pastor, right? But I am a pastor. And that someone also said that I was an FBI agent? But I am not an FBI Agent. So the person was lying and now everyone in town is lying."

"Is that so?"

"You know it's so, don't you, Aycee?" Megan was really suspicious of Aycee now and he froze up like a caught toad. She looked at Bryn who was staring at them over her glasses with wide eyes and tight lips.

"Bryn? Is this the person?"

"Oh, Lordy, Pastor, don't make me say it."

"Could it be that the two of you are in this together?"

"She ain't the one. She ain't done nothin' wrong."

"Oh, Aycee!" Bryn had wanted to protect him but it was too late now.

"Well, apparently, I've hit the target," Megan said. "Now I don't know how all this started but I think we'd better sit right down and get it all straightened out. I don't like untruths spread about me."

Aycee backed into the corner. Bryn opened the door between the lobby and her work space. "Best you both come back here," she said, and they walked into the back room. "Now if anyone comes in, just sit tight. Chances are they won't see you, but if they do, we don't have to say a thing. Aycee, you'd better fess up right now."

"Fess up?" Aycee whined. "Bryn, you know I weren't the one that spread them rumors."

"No, you didn't spread them much. You just started them, Aycee, and it's time you take your medicine. I warned you this could happen."

Megan had her answer. "Why, Aycee? Do you realize the damage you've done? Here I am, a new pastor in town, trying to build trust among the people and before I can even get a start my reputation is damaged."

He crouched, looking at her like a whipped puppy. Megan continued. "Do you know what it's like to have people talking behind your back and not trusting you?"

"Yes, Ma'am, I do." The answer gave Megan pause.

"Then you should be more kind and thoughtful to others." He nodded and she continued. "Why? Do you have something against me?"

"Nothin' agin ye – no, Ma'am. You jes' didn't seem like no normal Pastor."

"And that bothered you enough to start rumors? Couldn't you have come to church and found out straight on?"

"I ain't never been to church."

"I saw you there Sunday."

"He knows what's goin' on in the church, too, let me tell you," inserted Bryn.

Aycee shot Bryn a glance of disdain.

"Ma'am, I love this here place. Folks have been good to me. Give me a place to stay and a job at the cemetery."

"Cemetery. Were you in the cemetery when I was?" Megan quickly put it together.

"Yessum, I takes care of the graves, and that night, jes' when I was a finishin' up, I seed you come walkin' in and I asked myself, 'Now what does she want in the cemetery? Ain't nobody died.' So I watched, and when you was lookin' over them names on the war monument I got a bit 'spicious. Next thing I know'd you was headin' out acrost the bridge to the new side. Then right after that you bent down and copied somethin' from a grave. So that's when I knowd you was a spy." He stopped and stared straight at her. Megan stared out the window in disbelief. Bryn and Aycee exchanged a glance and looked quickly back at Megan.

"I was copying a poem from Tadcu's wife's grave, that's all."

"That's what I thought," snapped Bryn.

"See," Aycee pulled himself up, "I was afraid they was somethin' else a goin' on that would hurt the church and I wanted folks to watch out. I told Squire, an' he told me to keep a watch." Megan was absorbing it all in disbelief.

"It's true, Megan," said Bryn. "He came in here the morning after, all upset, trying to warn me. Aycee's not too bright sometimes, but his heart's in the right place. I'm sure he meant no harm, to anyone."

"I did wish her back where she come from," he said to Bryn. "But, I'm sorry if I was wrong." He looked worried.

"I'm sorry too," said Megan more kindly. "Aycee, what you did was wrong. I'm trying to think how we can correct it. If you remember who you told these things to, you must go back and tell them it isn't true, especially Squire."

"But they's already told other folks."

"Then, they'll have to tell the people they told. I will speak to it in church Sunday and that should take care of it this time. It would be helpful to me if you could be present in church when I explain it. Do you think you can do that?"

Aycee looked at the floor, then at Bryn and at the floor again.

"I'll see he's there," said Bryn. "Wouldn't hurt him any to go to church once."

"Now, I want you to promise me," Megan spoke to Aycee, "that if you ever have a question about me, you'll come ask me before you start talking to others about it. Okay?"

"Yessum. Well, I have a question then."

"All right."

"What was it you was writin' down that night?"

Megan smiled. "It was a poem about singing that I liked. I'll give you a copy if you want and you can check it out with the grave stone."

"I know what's on that gravestone," he said and seemed satisfied. So was Megan. Bryn, much relieved, escorted them out the door.

85

Walking home Megan realized that the breadth of her ministry reached beyond the church doors. She wondered how many more misunderstood souls there were in this community. She felt proud of herself. She had found the guilty, preached a lesson and turned idle gossip around, or so she hoped. She also hoped Aycee would be in church Sunday. Either way she would follow through. They must learn how damaging gossip can be.

Looking down the street ahead of her, she spotted Mary Morris running toward her. Now what, she wondered.

"Thank goodness I found you, Pastor," Mary said grabbing Megan's arm and pulling her along as she spoke.

"Betsy Thomas called. There's a fire in Evie Evans's barn and they want you over there right away."

"A fire? Is anyone hurt?"

"No, but Betsy thought you ought to be there for Evie. It had a pretty good start. They called the Spencerville Fire Department and Tadcu will be ringing the bell for a volunteer unit."

"Thank you," she told Mary and ran straight to her car. She backed out, screeching her tires as she sped off to the south, the church bell clanging behind her.

CHAPTER THIRTEEN – FIRE

David spotted the smoke coming from Evie's barn and ran to the house to call Bronwyn to spread the word, then called the Spencerville Fire Department. It would take them ten minutes to get there. He asked Betsy to call Megan, then, yelling at John, leaped onto Duke's back.

"Go, boy," he shouted and dug in at his horse's flanks. He rode bareback. Holding the horse's mane and leaning forward into the wind, he urged Duke into a full run across the freshly harvested bean field. Smoke billowed from the barn contrasting the blue sky. A lump thickened in his throat and his heart pounded at the thought of what he might find. John followed in David's truck tearing up a dust cloud behind him. As David got within hearing distance of the house he shouted, "FIRE! FIRE!"

The shouting aroused Evie from a nap. Smelling smoke, she ran to the window to see. "Oh, my God," she cried and raced out of the house heading for the water tank.

David slid from Duke's back. "Evie! Take Duke to the other side of the house and get the hoses hooked up." Corgi ran circles around their feet barking wildly. Evie grabbed Duke's reins and calling Corgi took them around the house. John drove past them, parked the truck away from the buildings and hurried to the scene.

"I called the fire department and Bronwyn," David yelled at John while he ran toward the barn. "I'll get the horses."

"From that stench, it has to be the hay," John shouted. Evie tied Corgi and Duke out of sight of the barn and ran back. John was lining up hoses to stretch to the barn.

"Get some buckets," he shouted. "And we need more hose if you have any," he added.

"There's one out by the garden," Evie answered, grabbing two buckets from the tool shed. Just then, David ran toward her with the geldings. "Here," he said, handing her the reins.

"The sheep are in the back pasture so they're safe," she said. She dropped the buckets and went off with the braying geldings when she suddenly remembered – - "David, the tractor's in the barn!"

David gave a startled look of recognition and sprinted toward the barn. She led the geldings around by Duke and Corgi.

John was back with another stretch of hose and, seeing David running, yelled "Where are you going?"

"The tractor's in there."

"Oh, God. That thing could explode!" John dropped the hose and ran after him. He reached the barn as David unlatched the lock.

"Help me with this door," groaned David. They pulled together and as the big barn door rolled open, a blast of flames broke through the opening, rolling up the side and over the roof.

"Look out!" shouted John. They ducked back and looked up at the flames.

"It's the hay all right. Can we get in there?"

"Maybe the back door."

"That would make a draft," shouted David over the roar.

"Maybe if we close this one first -"They tugged the heavy door shut against the flames and contained them, but they had seen enough to know that it had too much of a start on them. At the west door they got in and quickly cleared their way to the tractor.

Evie picked up the two buckets and filled them from the water tank. Then she picked up the hose John had dropped and began attaching it to the others. She had seen the yellow blast of flames and smoke burst through the opened door. That crackling roar of flames and their own anxious voices shouting commands seemed magnified in her head in the otherwise calm afternoon.

Megan, spinning her tires around corners to get there, also saw the burst of flame a half-a-mile away and floored the accelerator. Screeching to a halt a safe distance from the house, she leaped out, slamming the car door behind her, and ran to Evie.

"How can I help?" she asked breathlessly.

"God, I'm glad to see you. We need that hose attached to this one and hooked up to the house spigot. I don't know if these buckets will help much," Evie said. Megan attached the final piece of hose and turned on the water.

"David and John are inside the barn," explained Evie.

"Can we help them?"

"Grab some rags from the garage. Wet them and bring them out to the barn. I'm going out." She grabbed the two full buckets and ran awkwardly toward the south side of the barn. Just as she got there, the men came out of the smoke, pushing the tractor ahead of them. They were coughing from the smoke, but were all right.

When Evie saw them she called out, "I brought some buckets and Megan's coming with some wet rags."

"Good. Pour that water over us," David commanded. As she did, she felt the wave of heat sweeping past her from the open door now aflame. Megan came with the wet rags, dragging the hose behind her. They wrapped the rags around their faces and heads and others around their hands.

"Can we save anything?" Evie looked to David.

"Maybe, if we hurry. Megan, shoot that hose above the east door until the fire truck comes." Megan turned immediately to do as she was told.

"Here comes the volunteer rig now," called Evie.

"Good, go see if they need anything," David directed. "We'll make another try." He hoped they still had time.

"It's too late for the trailer," John's muffled voice came from behind the wet rags. He pointed up to the loft area. David looked and saw the beam above the trailer burning dangerously thin and close to falling. The heat made their wet rags steam but kept the smoke from their lungs.

"Okay, let's get the sleigh." David consented and the two men ran as if programmed to each side of the sleigh. The smoke stung their eyes and their wrapped hands sputtered as they touched its sides.

"Let's go," David shouted. They hoisted it and with snorts of heavy breathing, made their way through the open door. They set the sleigh a safe distance away, cheering their own accomplishment. David, bolstered by his own strength and bravery, started to head back in when John grabbed his sleeve.

"Whoa, boy, that's enough."

"We can get the trailer, Tad, there's time." he argued.

"No, David. It's not worth it."

"But you built that trailer!" His voice cracked.

"Think, son! We can't lose you!" At that second the roof exploded with flames, and billows of black smoke poured upward against the blue sky. The large beam over the trailer had burned through and given away creating a whirling explosion of flames. No one could go back in now. The volunteers quickly strung a hose from the nearby creek and were pumping water.

"You'd better take your hose up to the house," called a volunteer to Megan. "We'll work the barn." Evie came to help Megan pull it back.

"Can we save any of it?" called out John to the volunteers.

"Can't say about the barn yet." Two other volunteers came dragging a much larger hose and aimed it at the heaviest flames.

"I never thought about the house," said Megan to Evie as they struggled to drag the cumbersome garden hose back. David then took it from them and sent them around to check on the horses. He wanted the women in a safer place. Megan went, but Evie turned back to watch.

By then, two Spencerville fire trucks, sirens sounding and lights flashing arrived and pulled into the middle of the yard between the house and barn. In no time, they had two large streams of water fanning the flaming barn. The village volunteers then changed their water direction to the side of the house and garage. Cars and trucks already were lining the road and people gathered in clusters to watch. One man, voluntarily drove the tractor away from the heat, dragging the sleigh behind it and parked it a safer distance away.

Suddenly, the whole roof caved in with a crash and the roaring fire shot upward. They felt the heat even at the distance where they stood. It would have scorched the whole side of the house easily had they not wetted it down. The clouds of smoke billowed skyward signaling neighbors and soon more cars jammed the road.

Within minutes, the whole east side of the barn that they were facing collapsed under the pressure of water on the outside and the burning walls inside.

"Look!" cried Evie, for now they could see through to the back side. Two volunteers shot more water on the side of the house. The already heated side steamed as the cold water struck it. Megan returned to report that the horses seemed a little jittery but no one heard her. She looked at the bedraggled figures; their clothes, soaked and soiled, their hair stringy and singed. She saw the despair in their faces, tense and smudged, and her heart went out to them.

Evie stared in a daze, watching the years melt away. It had been an old unpainted barn when they first moved to the farm. Through the years they had all bent arms and backs to the tasks of re-building it. They had torn off old siding and replaced it with new wood and painted it all. For a while they had raised hogs in it, then a few feeder cattle. It stood unused for the most part while she was away. David had stored hay in it and some equipment, but when she came home again she bought the horses. Now she had hay and sheep and two horses and the sleigh. She had completely rearranged the stalls inside, built oats bins and a new loft for hay. They kept the small tractor, manure spreader, the trailer and various tools in it.

Their most prized possession was the old sleigh. When she got the horses, Uncle Thomas had said to take the sleigh. They had had such great fun with it. David and she painted it a bright red and she made cushioned seat pads for it. They rode the country roads, laughing and singing in the still cold nights of winter. Thank goodness they were able to save the sleigh, and the animals.

"Where are the sheep?" John asked, not having heard the first time.

"I put them in the back pasture just this morning," answered Evie.

"And the horses?"

"A bit jittery but okay," Megan reported again. She put her arm around Evie.

"We can't save it," said Evie softly. "The harnesses, the old trailer John built. It's all going." They knew now that it was hopeless and a heavy ache filled them. Tears trailed down Evie's smoke-smeared cheeks. All the memories, gone up in flames; the childhood years of good times, the feeding of livestock, the morning and evening chores with her father, the hours of playing hide and seek and kick the can, sitting on the beams high up watching below, and always that wonderful scent of hay.

"There's nothing in the world to compare with your own private barn," sobbed Evie.

"We'll build a new one," said David, "a better one."

He moved to the other side of Evie and the three of them stood in silence, watching. The firefighters stayed with their efforts to protect the house and keep the sparks from spreading.

"It won't ever be the same," said Evie. "Why didn't I see it or smell it sooner? Maybe I could have stopped it."

"Come on," Megan said, trying to turn her toward the garden but just then two other sides poured in with an explosion of heat and flames. People stood helplessly watching the last efforts of the firemen. Betsy had driven over on the road and Thomas and Cridwyn, too.

· "Get those cars back. We need water from the creek," called out the fire chief. People moved to accommodate. David went to help. The volunteers had already pulled up their equipment and were getting ready to leave. Megan wrapped her arms around Evie to let her cry.

"They've saved the house, Evie."

"I know. It's just the finality of it." She breathed in a jerky sob. Gradually, the flames were squelched. The soaked and charred remains lay in a huge mound, steaming with a smoke stench. The west side was the only side that remained standing. The black, muggy mess lay in stark contrast to the beautiful late afternoon sunshine. David looked at his watch. It had taken only forty minutes from the moment he first saw the smoke. A half an hour after the fire trucks left, everyone was gone except David's family and Megan. Betsy had brought a freshly baked cake along. She took over in the kitchen as if it were her own, making tea and sandwiches. Having someone there to talk with helped and they stayed until chore time. David took the horses home with him. Megan asked Evie if she wanted her to stay over but Evie said she would rather be alone.

"Call me anytime, day or night," Megan told her. She drove home more slowly than she had come, re-enacting the whole scene in her mind, judging if her own actions had been adequate and appropriate. She had never watched a fire before. It was so quick, so final, and left such a miserable mess to dispose of. Megan's heart lay heavy for them through the night.

At daybreak the next morning, neighbors arrived with manure scoops, tractors, trucks and wagons. They cleaned up debris, hauled and burned and buried until sunset. Daily, they came until the task was done, working when they could and for as long as they could leave their own work, taking no compensation. They carried in food and drink at meal times, motivated by their instincts of benevolence and their close ties. Megan witnessed their presence. They witnessed hers.

"Much obliged," David said over and over again to the people who came.

"Chroesaw, Dahveed bach." (You're welcome, David boy) was softly spoken just as often. These testy grumbling people who only a week ago were bickering and spreading corrupt gossip, were now working side by side giving of themselves for someone from whom they had been estranged through the years, yet, one they still called their own.

"I don't know how to thank you," she heard Evie say over and over. Ironic, Megan thought, they don't even know what she's already done for them.

Megan watched as David and Evie worked side by side, reliving their pasts, building their future. She knew then, that some day they would marry. She knew, too, that they had to discover that love on their own.

CHAPTER FOURTEEN - AYCEE COMES TO CHURCH

When Aycee's mother, who had taken care of him all his life, died, he was alone with no work, no house, and little money. He took only the clothes he could carry and a jar of coins his mother had kept in the cupboard. He rode freight trains and walked until he came upon the village of Cambria and decided to stay.

He told no one about himself. Until the town offered him a job in the cemetery, his life had been pretty miserable. He had made do with whatever he could scrounge up from farmers' dump piles, behind the store, or in the woods. He carried things back to the abandoned schoolhouse east of the village and tried to make a comfortable place for himself. When it was too cold, he found a corner in the church kitchen where it was warm. From there he could hear someone enter, and it gave him time to leave without being seen. He entered late at night and departed early in the morning, being careful not to be caught. He used the water and paper towels in the lavatory to clean up with.

After he was hired to work in the cemetery, he had a small salary which enabled him to buy shoes and food. To protect himself, however, he knew he must be ever vigilant about everything that was happening. He had just begun to feel safe when Megan came down hard on him. Forced now, to attend church, he was petrified. He had no good clothes. He couldn't afford a barber. He had been accused of telling an untruth and he would have to appear before the whole congregation.

He could imagine it now; Jim would point his finger at him and Squire would laugh in his face. Megan would shout out accusations from the pulpit. No! He couldn't go. He wouldn't go. He'd run away again. He dreamed himself into a sweat lying on his hay bales.

Three days went by, and he was out of food. He would have to get some more soon. He couldn't hide forever. They might come get him and that would be worse. Saturday morning he summoned up his courage to go into town. He had to have food and if anyone asked where he'd been, he would just say he'd gone on a little vacation.

Bryn worried all week about Aycee. She knew he wouldn't go to church on his own. He'd already taken to hiding away somewhere. She hoped he would show his face soon so she and Bronwyn could complete their plan. Bronwyn had promised to help her when she was told what happened at the Post Office.

On Saturday morning, Bryn decided to go to the Post Office in case he showed up. Sure enough, she saw him sneaking into the store like a hungry mouse. Bryn wasted no time. She walked directly to the store and found Aycee looking at canned goods. Keeping both eyes on him, she planted herself squarely in front of him.

"Where have you been?" she asked firmly. Startled by her sudden appearance, he dropped the cans he had taken from the shelf. In trying to pick them up and answer her question at the same time, he was hopelessly clumsy and at a loss for words.

"Well, it doesn't matter," said Bryn in a softer tone. "Put those things back on the shelf and come with me." They walked out of the store together, the owner watching bug-eyed.

"I jus' took a little vacation, Bryn."

"Vacation, huh. You could have let me know, Aycee. You had me worried."

"Yeah?"

"Yes. Come on, I want you to walk me home. I've got something you ought to know." They walked together and Bryn told him about Evie's barn burning down. She knew he wouldn't have known about that since he disappeared about the same time. He was all ears and she kept the tale going, with him asking questions and her stringing him along, until they reached her house. Realizing where he was he stopped dead in his tracks.

"I cain't come in. I'm too dirty."

"Dirty or not you're comin' in. I bet you haven't had a decent cup of coffee in a week." Bryn's coffee sounded good so he meekly followed her inside.

"Bronwyn, we have company," she called and locked the door behind her. "Sit down, Aycee. I'll make that coffee."

Bronwyn came and sat down across from Aycee.

"Whooee! You smell like a dead rat," she exclaimed.

"Thanks, Bronwyn. You smell like lilacs."

"You're forgiven this time."

"You, too. Jus' what are you two up to?" They shot glances over his head and Bryn passed the ball to Bronwyn.

"Aycee, we like you," Bronwyn began. He looked up at her sideways. "Bryn told me about the pastor talking to you last Monday and we know you most likely wouldn't go to church on your own, so we want to help."

"I don't need no help and I ain't goin' to no church."

"Hush up, and just listen," interjected Bryn.

"Aycee," Bronwyn continued. "We have a plan. You will stay with us today and overnight, and go to church with us in the morning." Aycee was stunned and suspicious but kept quiet. "You will have two home-made meals, a nice sofa bed to sleep on tonight and you can have a warm bath and get all cleaned up. I'll even trim up your hair."

"I cain't sleep here." Aycee stood up. Bronwyn also stood up and Bryn stepped in front of him.

"Yes, you can, and you will," said Bryn firmly. By now she knew how to manage him. "Now, before we do anything else you're going straight to the bathroom and get clean. You must have been sleeping in a pig pen."

"But I don't have no clean clothes," he protested as she pushed him through the hall with Bronwyn trailing along.

"You think we didn't think of that? You'll find everything you need right in there - soap, towels, shampoo, shaving stuff, even clean clothes." She shoved him into the bathroom and closed the door. "And wash your hair good because Bronwyn is going to give you a haircut." They stood by the door to be sure he stayed.

"Awhhh," moaned Aycee. However, he made no effort to escape and they could hear him mumbling indiscernibly. Grinning, the sisters shook hands and took turns waiting by the door.

The transformation was amazing. Aycee secretly enjoyed the attention he was receiving so that, even though he grumbled, he succumbed to their every wish. They fed him, clothed him, entertained him, trimmed his hair and beard, and fussed over him in every way. He slept like a kitten curled up in the mushy mattress of the sofa bed under a warm, moth-ball smelling quilt. In the morning he had another luscious meal of corn bread muffins, bacon and eggs (made just as he liked them) a big glass of orange juice and Bryn's good coffee. He was so full of their good cooking that he couldn't have run away had he tried.

Finally the hour arrived. He wore a nice pair of brown slacks, white shirt and a gold tie. He looked very nice and the twins stood beaming at their accomplishment.

"I cain't see why I have to be so fussed up jus' to be told I done somethin' bad'" he grumbled.

"Never you mind, Aycee. Cleanliness is next to Godliness and that's where you're headed this morning. So let's go."

Bryn and Bronwyn, side by side, didn't look a bit like twins. Bronwyn was tall, Bryn short. Bronwyn had light hair, Bryn, dark. Their faces matched, both had blue eyes, but their temperaments were different. Bryn was meticulous and studious. Bronwyn was sociable. Bryn was abrupt, Bronwyn more tactful. But they lived well together.

The three of them walked the short distance to church attracting some interest. Squire, standing at the door, was so dumbfounded he forgot to hand them a bulletin. The two sisters marched Aycee right down to a front pew where Megan could see him from her place behind the pulpit. She smiled broadly and stepped down during the prelude to shake his hand and welcome him to the church.

"Looks like Aycee's found himself a family," whispered Jim to Margaret. Aycee was as tame as a scolded puppy sitting between the twins but inside he was frozen with fear.

Megan was so touched by his presence that the harsh lesson she had planned was melting away. Still she must let people know she would not tolerate harmful gossip. When the planned moment arrived, she graciously thanked Aycee for being in church to verify that what she was about to tell them was true.

"When I am confronted with an untruth, I try to unravel it. That is why I asked Aycee to be here this morning." It caught their attention. "Aycee mistakenly thought I was an FBI agent." An uncomfortable snicker spread through the congregation. "He was suspicious of me because he had never seen a woman pastor before. So, in his curiosity, he followed me walking in the cemetery where, at one point, I copied something from a gravestone. Afraid to speak to me, he tried to figure it out in his own mind and came up with the wrong idea, which was very real to him." She pulled a slip of paper from a pocket and handed it to Aycee. "You said you knew what the words were that I had copied. Are these the words?"

The room was silent as Aycee held the paper up and read the words. He nodded. "Speak up, Aycee, are these the words you saw me copy from the gravestone?"

"Yes, Ma'am, they is." He handed it back to her.

"I was touched by the inscription on Tadcu's wife's grave. Let me share it with you." All faces were solemn.

Although called to the home where her soul belongs
We'll always remember her heavenly songs.

There was a stillness in the room. "We all are suspicious at times about things we don't understand, and in our fears we tend to imagine unreal things. That's understandable. What is wrong, is when we propagate those fears by exaggerating without searching for the truth. Apparently, those who were told Aycee's fear that I was an FBI agent, were all too willing to add to it and spread it for the fun of it. The result was that I, a new and innocent person in town, trying to build trust, became a subject of suspicion and ridicule. Is this the way to welcome a new pastor into your midst?" She paused for effect and their faces froze with guilt.

"But the greater harm you have done has been to Aycee. Some of you urged him to continue his surveillance of me, which sent him off in the wrong direction." Squire's face turned red. "As Christians, we carry a strong responsibility for each other, especially in a small community. You showed me that you know how to accept responsibility, by coming to help at Evie's fire." Now the silence lay heavy. "You know if you are guilty. I suggest you ask for forgiveness, and the next time you are tempted to spread too much manure on, think about what it will do to the crop." Megan was relieved. She looked at Bryn and Bronwyn. *God, thank you. Once again it took women to get the job done.* Aycee, too, was relieved. He had felt like a convict going to trial with Pastor

Brown as judge, but she had exonerated him. He hoped she would let him come to church again.

Megan's installation service was the following Sunday. Professor Jarvis arrived at the Dayton airport where Megan met and drove him to his motel in Lima.

He was not surprised at the enormity of tasks Megan had undertaken, nor their results. He was amazed at her home visitations and advised her to slow down. He also inserted some personal wisdom on handling situations like those of Aycee, which might help in the future, and he warned her about taking on too much in the beginning months. "Although, I certainly do understand that the circumstances of the organ and the fire both have forced you into immediate action," he added.

Changing the subject Megan asked, "Is there anyone you want to see while you're here?"

"There is one person, if it isn't too much trouble. I'd like very much to see how Evie has grown up."

Megan offered to drive him there.

"Her family always supported me. She was just a young girl at the time but I never fully expressed my sadness at the loss of her parents – and now with the fire - -"

Evie was pleased and available so Megan dropped him off with plans to pick him up in an hour. She was curious about their connection but did not prod.

"What a pleasure to see you again, Reverend Jarvis."

"And you, Evie. Somehow I knew you would grow up to be a lovely woman."

"You always were a charmer. I think my mother was secretly in love with you."

"And I with her, but she was a very wise woman. She kept me honest, Evie. Your father, too, was always gracious to me, but your mother was my mentor, one in whom I confided."

"Thank you. I remember you were always at our Sunday noon meal."

"Yes. It was always a special afternoon. I was deeply grieved at their deaths. I came mainly to express my great sorrow at the loss of both your parents. I lost track of what became of the three of you and wished many times that I could have spoken to you about it. Now, to learn that you and Megan have become friends has warmed my heart."

"Yes, she's become a very good friend."

Evie changed the subject. "I hear from Megan that you were her favorite professor at Princeton."

"That's nice to hear. I guess it's safe to say now that she was my favorite student. She's grown immensely in the past few years."

"I knew when I met her that we would be best of friends."

"She will challenge this community. But she too, will be challenged. From my own experiences, I know how much I learned here."

"The hardest part will be for the church to accept and enjoy a young woman for their pastor," said Evie.

The hour passed quickly and Megan arrived for pick up. She drove him back to his Lima motel and explained that Betsy Thomas would drive him to the Dayton airport following the service because she would have to be at Zion and then meet with the organ committee. She then invited him to have breakfast with her before the service.

Sunday morning Richard waited in the lobby with a package he presented to her when she arrived. It was a beautiful white stole with gold symbols.

"What a perfectly lovely gift, Richard. I didn't expect you to bring me anything."

"It's symbolic of the day and I hope you will enjoy wearing it."

"I'll wear it today, thank you very much." She spontaneously kissed him on the cheek. He blushed in pleasure and they walked into the coffee shop together both talking at once.

Both churches joined for the service which was well attended. Megan wasn't sure if it was out of respect for Richard or for her. Either way, she was happy they came.

Richard flavored the service with his confidence of Megan that reassured her. He was becoming a dear and faithful friend.

That evening she made an entry into her journal.

I have become immersed in the saga of these people, their lives, their concerns and struggles. I believe I have been called to help heal their broken spirits and help them rediscover the joy that is inherently theirs. But I will need your guidance daily, God, to lead them home again. Thank you for Richard's caring. I will have his thoughtful gift to remind me of this day and of his support.

October dwindled to an end. Megan decided to take a bike ride to enjoy the last splashes of color up close. At 55 degrees, the air was invigorating and crisp. Her strong legs pedaled with energy. Maples that lined the street gave up their green, yellow, and scarlet leaves that sashayed flamboyantly in a swirling game around her feet. She rode out past Evie's and around by David's, enjoying nature. A flash of orange bittersweet caught her eye along the fence row at the edge of the road. It reminded her of her mother. She missed her. She knew that part of her own rebelliousness was because she saw her mother give in to her father in everything. Wanting to keep the peace, her mother would hide things from her father who would most certainly disapprove; like writing letters to the editor about social justice causes for the local paper under a pen name. Early on she had sworn to herself that she would not let her father have that kind of control over her. She still felt his disapproval, even though he had given her the car at graduation. Even then she rebelled by choosing a convertible and a red one at that. She guessed she still had some things to prove before she could face him. She had not heard from them since she had arrived in Cambria. She would try to phone her mother when she got home, and hope her father wouldn't answer. He always monopolized the conversation and never let her speak to her mother alone.

A couple of cars passed her. Then an old gray pick-up truck pulled up and cruised beside her.

"You're pretty far from home," came a man's voice through the open window. She looked twice to identify Tadcu. He had grown a stub of a beard by now and it made his face appear thicker.

"Not so far," she answered pleasantly and kept pedaling.

"Be glad to give you a lift," he offered.

"No thanks. I'm loving this."

"Okay, then."

She could see it would be hard to be alone very long in this community. He pulled ahead and soon was out of sight and sound. At Route 709 she decided to take the long way around and began thinking about the church. The bills bothered her, Cridwyn was dragging her feet with getting the youth choir started, the organ committee was needing some professional help. The troubles are too many, she thought. How could she begin to change them? They were so cocooned into Welshness. After all, it's their church more than mine.

When she arrived home, Tadcu was raking leaves and talking to Aycee who was standing in the driveway. She parked her bike, greeted them both and went on in, a lot on her mind.

"She don't talk much," Aycee commented. "I don't think she likes me too well."

"She's probably just tired from her bike ride," Tadcu replied, continuing to rake.

Aycee stood with his hands in his pockets watching. "I seen her take off early this mornin'. Where'd she go?"

"How should I know? I just passed her over by John's was all."

"That's a long ways on a bike, and not the same direction she come home from neither."

"Un-huh. Aycee, you gonna stand there askin' questions all day or are you gonna help with these here leaves?"

"I'd be on my way then, nice talkin' to ye." He turned abruptly and wandered back toward the Post Office.

"You got them leaves cleaned up in the cemetery yet?" Tadcu called after him. Aycee pretended not to hear.

At noon, Megan called Tadcu in for lunch.

"You don't have to feed me," he said.

"It's the least I can do. You've done so much for me. Come on now, you can clean up on the back porch." The small lavatory came in handy for such a time as this. Megan had made soup and they sat down together to eat and visit.

"Tadcu, I think I've gotten off to a bad start."

"Why is that, Megan?"

"I can't get anyone to do anything. When I ask, they just squirm and walk away. They won't even discuss things."

"Oh, my, my," Tadcu slid his chair around the table. "It must feel like a terrible burden on you." His sympathy almost made her feel guilty. "But the Lord doesn't expect you to do it all alone. Onct the men get the harvest in they'll be comin' around. You'll see."

"What's the problem with the women?"

"Well now, you gotta remember. They've got freezin' and cannin' to do. It takes a long time fer things to happen in a church and you haven't been here two months yet."

"It seems longer."

"When you live in a farmin' community, you learn to wait. You plant yer seeds here and there. Let 'em set in the soil fer awhile. Then go back and water 'em. They'll grow. Soil's good here. They'll come around, you'll see." He leaned toward her looking through his slipped glasses into her face.

She looked back. "You are so kind," she said. "The other thing is that I don't know what to do about Thomas. He frightens me."

"Thomas?" Tadcu dropped his hands and sat back. "Thomas is an old fart!" he blurted out. Megan blushed and then burst into laughter. They laughed together and Megan felt better.

Tadcu went back to his work, piled the leaves up in the street and set a match to them. Soon the pungent odor came wafting into Megan's study window, giving her a sense of home and comfort. Thinking of home, she placed a call. Her mother answered and they made plans for a visit.

CHAPTER FIFTEEN - ORGAN PRELUDES

November came with cold damp days. Most of the corn was harvested and the fields plowed for winter wheat. Days had been spent rebuilding Evie's barn. The men spoke of the war and their strong, young sons and wished they could be there to help. It was hard work for these men and Megan began to understand that their livelihood came first. She, herself, had spent many hours helping Evie work her way through her losses.

Now it was drawing near the holiday season and Megan needed to check on Christmas decorations. She slipped over to the church and unexpectedly came upon Thomas sorting music.

"Oh, Thomas, I'm glad to find you here. I've been meaning to ask what music you're planning to use for the Christmas season."

"I assumed you had that all taken care of," he responded without looking up.

"Why would I do that?"

"You seem to have done everyone else's jobs."

"What's that supposed to mean, Thomas?"

He didn't answer but kept looking through the choral music. Megan tried again.

"Thomas, have I done something to offend you?"

"You know what you've done."

"No, I don't. I wish you'd tell me so we could get it straightened out."

"I don't want to talk about it." He shoved the music back in the cupboard and put his jacket on as if to leave.

"Thomas, this is upsetting. I wish you would talk to me about it."

He refused to speak. Pinching his lips tighter together, he turned away.

"What is it? What's the trouble?" She waited. He turned back to face her.

"I'm the Music Director here, right?"

"Absolutely!"

"Well, it doesn't feel like it anymore. Just think about that." He turned away and left.

Megan was stymied. She had believed everything was going along smoothly. They had had no real arguments. Megan couldn't understand his turn of mood or his remarks. She remembered what Richard had said in one of her classes. 'If you don't know what's festering it's like a boil. You just let it be until it comes to a head. Then you can fix it.' So, Megan brushed it off, figuring if it was serious it would come to a head.

The Organ Committee's first task was to get appraisals of the organ which would prove it was beyond repair at any cost. The next step was to study several different organ companies. They listened to sales talks, looked at pictures, compared prices and brought the choices down to three which they decided to go see; Moller, Shantz and a small local company which had been servicing their current organ.

To save time they split into three groups. Megan, Haydn and Squire had already gone together to see the Shantz Organ Company, taken a tour through it and listened to a sampling in an acoustically perfect sound room. Later they visited a similar sized church with a Shantz organ and heard it played.

Jim Morris set up Saturday the 13th of November for his group to see the Moller organ. He was glad both Cridwyn and Paul were on his team because of Cridwyn's knowledge about organs and Paul's about finances. Paul, who had inherited his father's turkey farm, didn't like turkeys; so he became a banker and was able to hire a man who did like turkeys to run the turkey farm for him. He was also one of the Escrow agents because he was Evie's banker. Both he and Cridwyn were pleasant company and Jim anticipated an enjoyable trip.

Upon arriving at the Indiana church, a congenial young man who served as organist, met them. He enjoyed giving them the tour, after which, Jim asked the young man to play the instrument for them. He did and then invited Cridwyn to try it. She had never played any other organ than the one in Cambria and was excited to try.

"I like the sound of this organ," said Paul.

"It reminds me a lot of the one we have," said Jim.

"Yes, it has that same mellow sound. Some organs have a sort of harsh brassy tone. This doesn't."

"I know what you mean," said the young organist. "It's called a baroque sound and a lot of fine organists like it."

"For Bach, maybe," said Paul, "not for Welsh singing."

"I think it's important we choose an organ with a similar sound to what we have," said Jim, "especially for the Welsh hymn singing."

"It's so easy to play," said Cridwyn already excited with what she could do with it.

"I notice you have carpeting in this church," said Jim. "Can you tell me what difference there would be in a sanctuary without carpeting?"

"Considerable. Our church added carpeting after the installation of the organ and it deadened the sound a lot. Be sure to tell the builders ahead of time if you are going to have carpet and how much and where. They can help that."

It was late when they reached Cambria but all three were excited with what they had heard and agreed that the Moller organ was to be desired. The cost would be between $28,000 and $30,000.

The same day, Ruth, Steven and Buck made a similar but shorter jaunt to the local organ company. The proprietor had been servicing the Cambria organ for some time and had been telling Thomas that there wasn't anything more he could do. So it came as a surprise when he told them almost immediately, that a new replacement was not necessary. He said he could rebuild the console, and put in three additional ranks of pipes, making it a sixteen rank organ, for a price of $16,250. Furthermore, he could add a twenty-five note chime set for another $895.

Buck was ecstatic. "This is great news!" he proclaimed. "There is no need to purchase a whole new organ. We found the solution for a lot less money."

Ruth and Steven were concerned. Why had this man suddenly contradicted himself? They noticed both the condition of the premises and the lack of supplies in stock. Steven was a cautious man, had known the history of this organ repairman, and suspected there was more to this offer than met the eye, though he could not quite put his finger on it. Ruth's instincts were that the offer was too good and came too quickly. She reminded Buck that the three of them were only one third of the committee.

"Well, my mind's made up. It doesn't matter what the others say, I feel we owe this man the business."

"We don't owe him anything," Steven corrected him. "We paid that man for every bit of work he did and to my mind he hasn't help it much."

Buck snapped back, "Well, mark my word, this will be the best offer we'll get. It's a far cry from thirty or forty thousand dollars." Bullishly, he kept the chatter going all the way home. Steven felt the offer was too good and suspected foul play.

Buck was a faithful member and a good singer. He was set in his ways, master of his household and cautious about change. A self-taught man, he wanted little to do with any university-educated or government-hired extension agent who came peddling new methods at his door. It took him years longer than most to give up his horses and purchase a tractor; and when the majority of farmers changed from livestock to grain farming, Buck clung tenaciously to his hogs and fences. He was not one to fool with. He dealt with issues head on and with a degree of temper that made others back off. Ruth and Steven backed off and settled into silence the rest of the way home.

On November 16th the three groups met for reports. Buck could not wait. He spoke excitedly of his discovery and kept repeating himself against all of their reminders that the rest of the committees should be heard. Finally, Megan, who was sitting next to him, simply put her hand on his arm. It stopped him cold.

"We would like to hear the other reports, Buck. Squire, do you want to speak about our trip?" Squire immediately began. Buck looked intensely at Megan. She returned the gaze with a gentle smile and slowly removed her hand.

Squire said the Shantz Company was reliable and their financial report showed them to be solvent. Steven and Ruth glanced at each other. They had not checked into the financial condition of the small company. That was the missing link. Squire continued, "The Shantz organ is similar to the size we would need and would cost $25,000."

"How about the sound?" asked Jim.

"There was something different about the sound," Haydn replied.

"A little more harsh," spoke up Megan, "but something exciting about it. Hard to describe."

"Baroque, I'll bet," said Paul, demonstrating his new knowledge. "I prefer the more mellow tones of the Moller, myself. It's close to our old one."

Buck saw an opening and jumped on it. "You know, everyone loves this old organ and we're used to the sound. It makes no sense to change it. If we simply rebuild it, we can save a lot of expense. It would be just like it was when it was new and at only one-third of the cost of the others."

Megan asked the other two members of Buck's committee how they felt. Both agreed more study was needed, and Ruth added, "We failed to obtain a financial report from this man. His building is in ill repair and there were no other workers around. I'd like to do a little more investigating." Steven agreed. Megan ignored Buck's muttering something about having known the person for years.

"I would like to hear another Moller," said Paul, "just to see if the tone is as good as the one we heard."

"And what's the cost of that Moller?" persisted Buck.

"Between $28,000 and $30,000," answered Jim. "But we're not considering the amount of money at this point."

"That's the craziest thing you've ever said," began Buck.

"Just a minute," said Squire, seeing an argument coming, "As far as money's concerned, it's been trickling in. We should have a report soon. Meanwhile, I suggest we do the rest of our investigating and meet again."

"We have to be ready to report in December," Jim reminded them.

They closed up the church and headed out. Haydn and Steven walked together.

"Looks like we're getting a little premature pressure put on here," said Haydn.

"He wasn't named Buck for nothing. That guy's got a one track mind," Steven spoke with frustration.

"I think I might ask Paul if he can find out about that guy."

"Good idea."

Two days later Haydn stopped by at the bank in town and asked Paul if he could look into the company's financial status.

"I thought of that while Buck was talking the other night. I've already sent in a request for information," said Paul. "I'll let you know when I hear something."

The next day, Haydn responded to a phone call from Paul and drove in to Van Wert to meet him.

"We have a problem?" he asked, standing at Paul's desk at the bank. Paul quickly stood and shook hands with him.

"Yes. Let's go talk over lunch." They walked to a diner across the street and found a private table. Paul began.

"I found out Buck has been campaigning."

"I heard it too," said Haydn.

"I think we'd better put a stop to it before it gets out of hand. The other thing is that I got that report back and you were right. The business operated at a loss last year and it has been on a downward trend for years. Extent of his current debt is not known but it looks shaky." He handed the sheet to Haydn adding, "This is strictly confidential. As fine a man as he is, if he can't handle the financial end of his business, I feel we'd be risking too much of our own resources to go with him at this time."

"I agree."

"So, we've got to slow Buck down somehow. I worry that Buck would make just enough fuss that it could get us all into trouble."

They sat sulllenly eating. Suddenly Haydn said, "I wonder –"

"What?" Paul looked up, chewing a mouthful of meat.

"Could we send him on a special trip to another company?"

"We could," said Paul, his eyes brightened at the thought. "I have one on the list that no one has seen. If we'd send him there it might give him something else to think about."

"What if he refuses?"

"We've got to make it sound as if this company might be the one we could settle on and lay it all in his lap. He'll be curious enough he won't turn us down."

"I hate to maneuver old Buck this way. The guy means well, it's just that he's so dad burned stubborn."

"Not only that, he makes mistakes that could get us into serious trouble."

"If this doesn't work we may just have to talk straight to him."

"Maybe we won't have to. Do you want to talk to him?"

"Hell, no. Your idea, you talk to him. But don't let Pastor Megan know or we'll get into hot water again."

"All right then."

The Saturday before Thanksgiving, Evie and Megan went to Lima to shop and see the movie "Love Story" with Ryan O'Neal and Ali McGraw. Evie cried all the way through. While driving home, she admitted to Megan how much she loved David. "I've loved him ever since I was a little girl. There's never been anyone else for me but I'm afraid he's looking for a more glamorous wife."

"Oh, Evie, he doesn't know what's right there in his own back yard."

"I'm more of a sister to him than a lover. I don't think he'll ever fall in love with me and that's too bad because I think we'd make a good team."

"You're already a good team."

"Megan, have you ever been in love?"

105

"Once," Megan replied. The question was unexpected and she had to do some quick thinking. "I fell in love with Charles in college."

"Charles?"

"Yes, he was a music student. He's now a concert organist. You should hear him play."

"Tell me."

"I used to listen to him practice. We talked about a lot of things. We spent two years in Africa in the Peace Corps together and then came back to school. We talked about getting married once but decided we both had such strong career decisions that marriage would interfere so we gave it up. My father was worried sick that we'd elope. You see, Charles is African American."

"Really? You have trouble with your father don't you?"

"Not so much anymore. He was great when I was little but as soon as I began to think for myself, he didn't know how to handle me. He was always barking commands at me and I thought he didn't love me. My mom still cowers around him. I could always stand up to him. I think that's what he didn't like. He didn't have control over me. I still am not sure if he loves me."

"Didn't you tell me he gave you the car for graduation?"

"Yes, but I think that was just a peace offering."

"I think it was more than that, Megan. I think he was trying to tell you he was sorry for making you have to work so hard to get through school, but his pride got in the way. He loves you, I'd bet on it. He just can't say it."

"Maybe. I know someday I'll have to settle that, but I have to prove myself first." Megan knew in her heart that what Evie said was true. Maybe she would make a trip home during the holidays.

"Evie, there's something else that has been troubling me that I'd like to ask about. I met Thomas one day in the church and he acted strangely."

"How?"

"He said I had done something wrong and that I knew what it was, but I didn't know. Apparently, it was something that offended him because he was very abrupt and wouldn't talk about it. He said, 'I'm the Music Director here, right?' and I said of course he was, but that was it. Do you have any idea what might be bothering him?"

"Did you talk with him first before asking Cridwyn to lead the Youth Choir?"

"No, I didn't. Do you think that's it?"

"Could be. He might be jealous."

"Because she's good at it?"

"Yes." They looked at each other in understanding, both feeling bad.

CHAPTER SIXTEEN - THE SINS OF THE PEOPLE

Megan decided she had to clear the air in two places: her relationship with her father and the misunderstandings with Thomas, ironically both with men. She went alone into the sanctuary early Monday morning when no one was around. The sun shone through the window of the Shepherd. Sitting in the stillness for an hour, she meditated and prayed. Then she left the sanctuary, called David from the manse and asked him to get a substitute for the following Sunday.

"There's a family matter I must attend to at home," she explained simply to David.

She made the trip easily arriving for lunch. Both parents were overjoyed to see her and threw questions at her faster than she could answer. They seemed much easier to talk to and she thanked God for that. Perhaps it was her own confidence that made a difference.

Her father immediately asked how she liked her car. She had the courage to admit that her choice of a convertible was not the best type for the area in which she was living.

"Maybe we could make a trade while you're here," he suggested. Surprised and pleased that he didn't say 'I told you so,' she agreed to think about it overnight.

The next day she had her answer. She was ready for a practical and substantial car that would go through the snow safely and have a good heater. Her father knew right where to go. The two of them spent the day looking at cars and talking. It came down to a Jeep and they made a good trade. Her father gave no arguments and made no demands. It was easy then, to move into apologies for mistakes made in the past and to agree on a new beginning. Megan owned up that she had taken her father's help for granted and had gone out on her own without explaining her dreams to him.

He appreciated hearing it from her and was able to stumble through his own awkward apology, admitting his pride had gotten in his way. His peace offering of a car hadn't even seemed to work the way he had hoped.

When they arrived home to show off the new Jeep, they drew her mother into the conversation. There were a few tears, some laughter at themselves and a good batch of healing. A small and wonderful miracle happened between them and a mood of happiness and love permeated the air for the rest of her visit. Megan felt a surge of happiness and security, that was missing for three years, fill her again.

On Saturday, David called.

"Megan, I'm sorry to have to call you but Hattie Jenkins died this morning and the family is trying to locate you. Hattie wanted you to do her service."

"Oh, I'm so sorry. I really liked her."

"I know. Will you be able to come for the service?"

· "Of course, David. My business here is finished and I can come today if that will help."

"I'd really appreciate it. The family needs a little more guidance than I can provide. When can I tell them they can meet with you?"

"I can be home this evening if you like." Megan felt a new warmth and respect in David's voice.

"Thank you, Megan. I'll call them then and I'll look for you tonight. By the way, it's snowing here so the sooner the better for your driving through."

"Not to worry, David. I now have a new Jeep!"

"Really? You traded in your convertible?" David was both surprised and pleased at her sensible choice.

"Yes, I think it will go through anything."

"Well, good for you. That's wonderful. You should have no trouble then. Give me a call when you get in."

"I will."

She hung up and looked at her parents who had heard her side of the conversation.

"You have to leave," they guessed together.

"Yes, a very dear old lady just died and I have to attend to the funeral arrangements."

"Duty calls," said her father with a strange touch of pride. "Thank you for coming," he added. "It means a lot to us both." She knew he meant it.

The Jeep purred. It was warm and comfortable and Megan felt that now she could keep up with the best of those pick-ups. She made good time and called David as soon as she arrived. He had arranged a meeting for her that evening with the family and Aycee was getting the grave site ready.

Deaths in Cambria set everything into a well-choreographed dance. As smooth as a greased engine, everything moved into place; telephoning, flowers, service, burial, vehicles, death certificate, obituary, coffin, preacher, musicians, casseroles, cakes, and singing all to help the soul upon its journey home. The casket in the back of the sanctuary for viewing, to the front of the sanctuary for the service and then to the grave site.

An amazing number of people came. Hattie had always cultivated friends younger than herself. Funerals, Megan discovered, are experienced and honored with two strong emotions in the Welsh tradition: grieving and joy. First, there were eulogies and tributes, then a singing of quiet hymns that released the tears and grief. Second, following the graveside service, they gathered in the family home to eat and laugh over stories of the loved one's life, then sing the joyful songs of celebration.

It was traditional and it was healing, a straight-forward way of acknowledging that life goes on. Megan took her part in it, listened and consoled when needed, grateful for the life that had touched hers only briefly but forcefully.

When she arrived home there was a light on in her back porch. Calling "Hello," she opened the door and as she stepped in saw Cridwyn sitting on the floor.

"Cridwyn! Are you all right?" She helped her up off the floor thinking there should be a chair there."

"I'm sorry to bother you."

"What happened?"

"Thomas and I had an argument. I just want to talk it out. I hope you don't mind."

"How did you get here?"

"I stayed after the service."

"You've been sitting here all this time? Cridwyn, does Thomas know where you are?"

"I don't think he cares."

"What do you mean? Of course he cares. Let me call him."

"Wait. Please don't call him yet. I'd like to talk a little."

"We will talk, Cridwyn. You can even stay here all night if you like. I just think it better if I call and let him know you're here so he doesn't call the police to find you."

"Oh, I never thought about him calling the police. All right, you can call him, but could I stay here until I get things cleared up in my mind?"

"Absolutely." She put the call through and Thomas answered abruptly.

"Hullo."

"Thomas, this is Pastor Megan. I just wanted to let you know Cridwyn is here at the manse."

"At the manse? Why didn't she call me? I was worried sick."

"I just got home from Hattie's wake and she was waiting for me. I think we have to talk and I've asked her to stay the night. I'll bring her home in the morning if that's all right with you."

"I think I know what this is about."

"She hasn't said yet. I just wanted to let you know where she is."

"All right, then." He said and hung up abruptly.

Megan sat down beside Cridwyn on the davenport.

"Was he upset?" she asked.

"Just worried."

"Was he okay with my staying here?"

"He said it was all right. Do you want to tell me what this is about?"

"We had a fight."

"What kind of fight? Did he abuse you?"

"Just a word fight but it hurt, Megan." Megan waited.

"I really was pleased that you asked me to lead the Youth Choir. I knew deep down that Thomas would be jealous but I didn't care, you know? I really wanted to do it. I knew I could do a good job. I like kids.

A couple of weeks ago we were eating dinner. I was babbling on about how wonderful the kids were in the choir. He got more and more quiet and before I knew what was happening, he stood straight up and turned the whole table right over on me. I landed on the floor with the table, food and dishes falling right on top of me."

"Oh, Cridwyn."

"He shouted something about he didn't want me leading that choir, that I didn't know enough to do it. Here I was stuck under that mess and him mad at me. I said 'Thomas help me up,' and he said, 'you made your bed. Lie in it.' and he walked out."

"Were you hurt?"

"Only my feelings, but I could have been and he wouldn't have cared a bit. There I was left with all that mess to clean up and not a word of apology from him. I was getting pretty mad, myself."

"I'm sure. You said that was a couple of weeks ago. What happened today?"

"He hardly spoke for days after that. He'd go off for hours and I never knew where he was. At home he gave me the silent treatment. He just sulked until I figured it out that he's jealous of my leading the youth choir. He thinks he's the only one who can do it and he thinks by giving me the silent treatment I'll just give in, like I always do, and then he'll take it over. So today I decided I was going to get him to talk about it."

"Right. How did that go? Obviously, not too well." She choked up and tears filled her eyes. Megan suggested a cup of tea and put the water on for it. Then she built a fire in the fireplace and gave Cridwyn an afghan, giving her time to settle her emotions.

"A good fire and a cup of tea should warm us both up," Megan said as she sat down beside her.

"He says the whole church has turned on him and it's all because they're being suckered in by you. I said it wasn't true and that if the church people were turning against him he'd brought it on to himself."

"That was pretty brave. What did he say to that?"

"He lost his temper. He said something like, 'Woman, now you listen to me. I'm the head of this household and if you want to keep your happy home you do what I say. Now just so you don't forget, I'm the head of the music at Cambria church, not you. You are the organist and that's all you are. I direct the choirs. I've always directed the choirs. All of the choirs.' By this time I was really mad at him and I yelled back, 'Not this one' and that did it. He raised his hand and I thought he was going to hit me but I guess he thought better of that and he dropped his hand and he said, 'Cridwyn, I'm only saying this one more time. If you want to keep your happy home, you will not direct that choir' and that scared me." Cridwyn began to sob, "Megan, for the first time in my life, I'm afraid of my own husband. He's become angry and mean and I think I'm to blame for this but I don't know what to do. I've never cowered before but he frightens me. I don't know what I'd do if he left me."

"He won't leave you, Cridwyn and you are not to blame. He's using that tactic to frighten you into doing what he wants you to do.

I ran into him at the church a while ago and he was angry at something then, but wouldn't tell me outright, just gave me phrases like 'I'm the director of music here, right?' and left me to guess what the problem was. Well, now we know. I suspected he was jealous but I never thought he would take it out on you. The thing that worries me is that it could get worse if we don't do something about it right away. Are you willing to have the three of us talk about it?"

"I'm willing to try if he is. We certainly need help. He won't listen to me."

"Tomorrow, I will go home with you and we'll try to get him to hear you. He should be easier to handle with two of us. For now, I think you need some rest. Then in the morning we'll work out our approach and get this settled once and for all. I promise."

"Thank you, Megan. I knew you'd understand."

"Now come on upstairs. I'll run a nice warm bath for you."

In the morning both of them felt better and they had had time to think. Megan coached Cridwyn on not backing down but on speaking the truth as gently as she could until he heard it.

When they arrived, Thomas came out of the hog pen and walked toward them a little confused that Megan was along. He apologized for his clothes and Cridwyn said "Megan's come to talk, Thomas. Let's go into the kitchen."

"Don't believe I will," he said and started to turn away.

"The Pastor has come to call, Thomas. I suggest you be polite and come in."

"All right, then," he said sulkily and followed them in.

"Sit down, Megan, Thomas," Cridwyn directed, pulling the chairs out from the kitchen table. Thomas pulled the chair further back and sat on its edge across from Megan and Cridwyn. Clearly he was tense. "What's all this about?" he asked.

"Thomas, I'm sorry that all of this trouble is happening to you. I want to help you both if you'll let me."

"What trouble? We're not having any trouble."

"Cridwyn feels that you are. She's upset about it."

"Why didn't you come to me? Why did you have to go to the Pastor about this? This is a private thing, Cridwyn."

"It's not private anymore, Thomas. It involves her and it's tearing us apart."

"What did she tell you?" Thomas asked Megan.

"That you had an argument. That you threatened to leave her if she kept on directing the youth choir."

"Oh, Cridwyn. I didn't mean that. You know I wouldn't leave you. What made you think such a thing?"

"You said if I wanted to keep my happy home I should do as you say and quit the youth choir. You said it Thomas and you weren't nice about it either."

"Sure, but that was just to get you to listen to me. You were going off half-cocked like you knew all about directing a youth choir and you don't."

"I do! And I wasn't going off half-cocked, as you say." Megan saw trouble and intervened.

"As I look at this from another angle I have to admit I am to blame for some of the trouble here."

"You're dad right!" spit out Thomas.

"Let her finish, Thomas." Cridwyn held her ground.

"I didn't talk to you first, Thomas, when I decided to start a Youth Choir. Probably because I understood from you that you already had too much on your mind. I made the assumption that you would be delighted to have Cridwyn carry that load alongside you because you gave me the impression that the two of you work very well together. I see now that you were hurt by my actions and not able to tell me to my face. I want to apologize for making that assumption."

Thomas softened and glanced up at Cridwyn. Megan continued.

"I wish that you could have come to me with your feelings and not taken them out in anger at your wife, because you have hurt her deeply. It will take some time for her to trust you again." Megan paused to let the words sink in, then added, "I think she would like to tell you in her own words how she felt when you spoke to her as you did."

Thomas squirmed uncomfortably and looked from Megan to Cridwyn.

"Thomas?" Cridwyn asked permission with the tone of her voice.

"Go ahead." He stared at her with hurt in his eyes.

"I really was happy when Megan asked me to start the Youth Choir because I've always wanted the chance to do that."

"But Cridwyn, you've not had the training. You don't know –"

"I do know, Thomas. Do you think I've not observed what and how you do things all these years of working with you? Do you think I haven't learned what works and doesn't in directing a choir? Don't tell me you didn't know you've been teaching me all these years." She had looked directly at him and kept her voice steady.

"I get along well with young people. I know the kind of music they like and we're having fun. You, yourself said how well they did the first time they sang. I love every minute of it. Please don't take that joy away from me. We've worked too well together through the years for it to fall apart now. When you said that about having to quit the choir to keep my happy home you frightened me,

Thomas. I don't want our marriage to fall apart over this, but neither will I be a slave to your every command. One of us has to change and this time I have to say, it isn't going to be me."

"Humpft. What am I to do?" Thomas held up his hands. "The two of you have ganged up on me. You went ahead and did just what you wanted to do with no thought of me. I knew there'd be trouble with a woman trying to be pastor."

"Just one minute." Megan held up her hand. "I resent that, Thomas. This has nothing to do about my being a woman or the pastor. You are an unhappy man but you are a good man. Maybe you thought I didn't respect you when I asked Cridwyn to lead the youth, but that's not true. I do respect you. You've given much to the church. But until you work out your problems and begin feeling good about yourself, things can only get worse. If you don't want to alienate your friends or hurt your marriage you'd better start thinking right now about what you can do to make things better."

"You don't know what people are saying about you."

"Stop right there, Thomas. Don't say anything you'll be sorry for later. If I'm a part of your problem then talk to me about it and we'll get it out into the open where we can deal with it and that will be for the sake of everyone, not only us. You know, having someone else contribute to the music doesn't in any way take away from the wonderful ministry the two of you share." He settled down and Megan had more to say.

"Now, while I'm here, let me make one more thing clear. I was brought to this church by a majority vote to pastor the people of this church. Right or wrong, that's a fact. There's a lot at stake here, Thomas, and right now you have a lot more to lose than Cridwyn or I." There was a long pause. They waited. "Let's bow our heads in prayer," said Megan. "Lord, we come to you humbling ourselves and wrought with fears. Touch us with your care, help us find ways to unburden ourselves, and fill us with hope that we may find the joy that is rightfully ours. We need your help, Lord. Amen."

"Well, maybe I was wrong. Let me think this over."

Megan knew he needed time. She stood to go and said, "Perhaps now you can understand that there are more sides to this than just yours. I'll be going now. If either of you want to talk, I'm available."

"Thank you, Megan." Cridwyn got up to walk her to the door. Thomas sat brooding. Megan left, heaving a large sigh as she walked to her car. *"Oh, Lord. I wanted people to come to me for help and now I feel so inadequate. Am I really cut out for this kind of work? It's so much more than preaching. They're good people but they have such problems. Help me find ways to help them. Amen."*

Meanwhile, Paul had stopped to see Buck and gave him the assignment to make a short trip to see another organ by himself. On Wednesday the group met and began exchanging their information. Paul had not spoken to Buck since his return from the assigned trip so hoped for the best.

Megan held back, listening and trying to get the general consensus in mind. She knew nothing of the secret plan Haydn and Paul had concocted. Paul asked for a report on Buck's trip.

"How come he went alone?" asked Squire right away.

Paul was ready. "It came up at the last minute and we didn't have time to get a team together. I brought it up to Buck and he was glad to do it." The answer seemed to satisfy. They had all been busy anyway.

Buck's report was brief. A good company, probably more modest than the others but nothing stood out for him. Haydn and Paul exchanged glances knowing they still had a problem.

"Let's vote," Haydn said right away. Everyone nodded in agreement.

The first result was 3 votes for the Moller, 3 for the Shantz and one for the local with two abstentions. "Time for discussion," said Paul.

Buck immediately began on his rampage. "This committee has been against me from the beginning. You're all money happy and if you go with the Moller you won't raise the money, if you go with the Shantz they won't like the sound I say we let the congregation decide."

Haydn and Paul knew Buck had been campaigning. They needed something solid to present to the congregation or there would be trouble and trouble meant the gift would be retracted.

Ignoring the comment Paul asked Steven, "Why didn't you vote?"

"I prefer the Moller but I think it's more money than we can raise."

"How much money has come in?" asked Cridwyn.

"We've had good response," said Jim. "I'd say we have a very good chance to raise twenty-five thousand."

Immediately there were three different responses: the Moller people believed they could raise the money; the Shantz people felt their goal was feasible; and Buck was so surprised that he switched his tactics and said now they could even do the redecorating. The redecorating plan was not new, although it had not yet been considered officially. Following an extended discussion, Paul asked for a final vote which went unanimously for the Moller except for Buck.

"Can't we make this unanimous, Buck? Vote with the rest of us."

"No, sir," he said adamantly. So they would present it, as voted, to the congregation. Meanwhile they had to get a final contract price from the Moller Company, present it to the Music Committee, Session and Trustees for approval and then prepare their presentation to the congregation for their final vote. Megan whispered a small prayer of gratitude that they were moving ahead, and turned her thoughts toward Advent.

CHAPTER SEVENTEEN - LOST SHEEP

The first Saturday in December, the women gathered at the church to fill stockings for the annual Christmas party. They also packed boxes of canned goods for the poor and assembled hand-sewn bibs, knitted slippers and mittens for the orphanage in Van Wert. In the afternoon, Tadcu, Haydn, Squire and Jim volunteered to hang greens in the sanctuary, and set up the Christmas tree cut from Robert's woods.

When they finished with the ladders they carried them back to the basement storage room. It was then they noticed Tadcu talking strangely.

"I'm not a superstitious man," he said, "but a strange thing happened to me."

They turned to listen to him.

"I dreamed I heard the owl call my name a few nights back."

"Dreamin' don't count, Tadcu. You have to see and hear it," explained Squire.

"Yeah, well, I did see and hear it. I just didn't want to scare you all."

"You're kidding," said Jim.

"Nope. There's been an owl up in my barn for several days. I seen him sittin' there, quiet like. But this mornin' he blinked at me and hooted." They were all attentive. "It struck me as a bit funny so I laughed at him and said *whoo-mee?* back at him and he hooted again and I'd swear he said my name. So I walked away feelin' kinda strange. Only heard it onct so couldn't be sure ya know. Anyways, it kept haunting me. So, I got all my papers put together in my right hand desk drawer, if anybody needs to know." They stared at him, trying to absorb the story.

"Just wanted to let somebody know." He flipped on his cap and walked out muttering something about getting his Santa Claus suit cleaned.

It gave them an eerie feeling. Tadcu believed the Native American legend that if you hear the owl call your name, you will soon die. Jim squinted his eyes shut and quoted, "From witches and wizards and long tailed buzzards and all them things that get through other men's hedges, Good Lord deliver us!"

"Right. Time to get home," added Squire.

There had been ample signs of an earlier-than-usual arrival of winter. Farmers kept a constant vigil on the weather. The radio warned of a winter storm heading this direction. True, the woolly worms were thicker this year, and news was of more rain than usual rolling up from Texas and the Gulf. With a cold front moving down from Canada, if these two frontal systems met, there would be blizzardous conditions for all of the mid-west. At the very least they would have snow for Christmas.

Following the choir rehearsal Wednesday night, Thomas dropped by to talk.

"Pastor Megan, I think a true confession would be good for my soul. Do you have time?"

"I'll take time for you, Thomas. Can I get you some tea?"

"That would be nice." He sat quietly waiting until she came in with the tea and joined him.

"When I was young, my voice was magical. I could sing and read music well. It came naturally – and harmonize? - why, I could jump from one part to another without a hitch. I knew all the parts by heart. We grew up with that sound, you know, and it gets into one's blood early."

"How did you start leading choral groups?"

"Not until I'd sung in them and knew a lot of music. Then one day I put up a sign at church and in three days I had enough men signed up to start a male chorus. We had so much fun and got so good that we decided to enter contests, and we'd win."

"It must have been very rewarding for you."

"It was. People followed us and cheered us on. Those were wonderful days. Today, I can't seem to get those harmonies anymore. We've lost the quality. I miss it."

"Not having heard it, I can't imagine what it is you miss, or what makes you sad."

"Part of it is growing older. The whole world is there for you when you're young. You can make things happen. When you grow older, you lose the quality and richness in your voice. Not only in your voice, but also in your life."

"What do you mean by that?"

"You get to remembering and you realize how bad the mistakes you made were. But you can't go back and fix 'em, you can't change things and you weep for that. Then you live in the constant fear that someone is going to tell you you're no longer needed and that would be the end of it."

"What would you change if you could, Thomas?" she asked, not letting him feed on his fear but trying to challenge him.

"I don't want to talk about that."

"It would help if you could."

"How? How could it help? It's over with and there's nothing that can be done about those things now."

Megan knew he wanted to tell her something. "What things?"

"It was a long time ago."

"But it still bothers you. Let it out, Thomas. Get rid of it and get on with living today. Let me help, Thomas."

"You really think you can help?"

"I want to try – but you have to trust me."

He looked into her eyes. "I really believe you do."

She reached across and touched his hand. Immediately tears welled up. "Oh, my," he sighed and groped for his handkerchief. "Oh, God. It's been so hard." She waited as he cried and then dried his eyes.

"I made a very bad decision when I was in the prime of my life. We were all such a happy family, my brother's and mine together. Then he was killed. Gone. Just like that. I guess you know Evie was one of his children."

"Yes."

"At the time there was no one to take care of the three children." His face filled with pain. "I should have taken them in." He shook his head back and forth. "But I thought, then, that I couldn't do it. I told everyone I had my hands full. I was grieving, had a large family of my own, land to farm and the music to lead at church. To take on three more children was beyond comprehension to me. It would have meant getting another job and giving up the church music. I was scared and I wouldn't do it. So I let the authorities take those children. It was wrong, so very wrong."

"No one could blame you for that. You did the best you could at the time."

"It's good to hear that, but I know I was selfish. Inside I knew I could have done it. Cridwyn was willing to help. If I would have raised them they'd all be sitting in church today. Two of them never came back, and look at Evie. She won't even step inside the church. I've lived with that guilt for years. Now here she is, right across the field like I'd always dreamed of, and I can't bring myself to face her. All of this has tortured me and spoiled the very music I sacrificed everything for."

"Evie isn't too far off base, Thomas. I wouldn't give up on her yet. She has a deep faith. In some ways I think she could teach all of us some things."

"She lives in the past, in her memories of how the church was when she was a child. Why else would she not be in church?"

"But she also sees a future for it. Have you ever told her any of this?"

"We don't talk. She stays to herself."

"And so do you."

"She'd never forgive me."

"You have to forgive yourself first, Thomas."

"I know, but that's a very hard thing to do."

"I think you've made a step forward. I know it's difficult, but I also know how rewarding it can be. I'm glad you're trying."

"Thank you. You understand better than I thought you would."

"Thomas, you have a God-given talent for choosing music for worship and presenting it in such a way that touches people's hearts. That's your ministry. Not just having prize winning choruses. You're the one who makes the worship meaningful. Remember that."

"Hmmm. I never thought of it that way."

"Our worship would not be as effective without it."

"Thank you. You know, young lady — oh, whoops —I'm sorry. Megan, yes, Megan, — I've underestimated you. You are more mature than I thought." He stood to leave. They smiled at each other and he added, "Maybe there's some hope for this old buck after all."

"That's up to you," she said gently. "Give Cridwyn my love."

On Sunday a congregational meeting was held after worship for the Organ Committee to make its recommendation to the church. Paul Jenkins gave a quick recap of the formation and progress of the Organ Committee.

"The committee's choice has already been approved by the Music Committee, Session and Trustees, and authorization for contract has been approved. All that remains is for the approval of the congregation.

We agree that the Moller Company presents the most suitable organ for this church's needs for the amount of money. It is a highly reputable company. According to their contract, the Moller Company would remove the present organ right after Easter and have the new instrument installed in July in plenty of time for the 125th celebration on Labor-Day week-end. We have until March to change any terms of contract depending on the financial position of the church.

As to the financial status, when we began soliciting funds we had $18,000. With earnings and increasing value of the stock gift, plus the additional gifts and pledges, we now have $25,099, two thirds of the way toward our goal of $35,500. And as you all know, we have not yet solicited from our own members.

Therefore, Miss Moderator, with great confidence, I recommend that this congregation purchase a new two manual organ, with fourteen to fifteen ranks of pipes, from the Moller Company at the contract price of $35,500. I hope you will unanimously vote to purchase the recommended Moller Organ."

"Thank you, Paul. That was an excellent report." Megan stood to take questions. Robert raised a question.

"I'd like to know how many of the committee voted for the Moller."

"All but one," answered Paul.

"That was me," shouted Buck getting up and walking to the front. "Before you vote I think you should know why I voted against it. For one thing, it was too expensive."

"You're out of order, Buck," reminded Megan trying to avoid trouble. But someone shouted from the back, "Let him speak." Others echoed the command so Megan called order and told Buck to proceed.

Buck told the story quoting the man as having said that the organ did not need to be replaced.

"Not true," interrupted Thomas.

"I have witnesses," said Buck, "that he told us he could build a new console, add three ranks of pipes making it 16 ranks for a little over $16,000." An audible gasp swept the congregation. Then he added, "And with the amount of money we've already raised we could also redecorate the sanctuary without raising more money." Megan looked at Paul for response.

"I'm sorry this happened, because it forces me to disclose information that should be kept confidential, but I also have to protect this church." He spelled out the financial standing of the company and the risks involved. "Further, we would have no guarantee that one year from now that the older parts of the organ, which incidentally can no longer be obtained, would not need repair. Or, for that matter, that the man would still be in business at all." A mumble rose in the congregation and Buck fearfully spoke, "That's a risk you take with any business."

"No Buck, it isn't." Paul was calm and direct. "In my business we don't dare take risks such as this, and I highly recommend that the church doesn't either. Let it go, Buck. Yours was only one vote against eight." Buck walked back to his seat.

Suddenly Thomas rose to his feet. Megan called on him.

"I am impressed with the financial support that has already come in for this project. Even a month ago, I wouldn't have believed it. And all of it from outside sources. It says to me that we have a lot of friends who have put their trust in us. They want us to continue to be here with a good organ and a good music program so they can come back each year and sing their praises to God. Even if we have to take a loan out to do it, I think we should show the same kind of faith in ourselves. I move we approve the Organ Committee's recommendation and go ahead full force."

"Well said, Thomas!" Megan was thrilled at his turn-around.

Ruth Hughes Lloyd shot to her feet. "I second the motion." *"Joy!"* thought Megan, *"at last a woman."*

"Questions?"

Buck shouted from his seat, "If you vote for this you're making a big mistake and I'll have nothing to do with it."

"Question!" demanded Squire calling for the vote.

"We are voting FOR - by standing," called Megan.

Seeing the number of people rise, Buck grabbed his wife by the arm and marched her out of the church.

Jim Morris was so dumbfounded he got half way up for the vote and sat down staring after Buck. Some later would say that he voted against the motion, some that he didn't vote at all.

"The tellers agree that a majority vote has been cast in favor. The motion carries," stated Megan to a rousing applause.

"Miss Moderator," called Edwin, rising to his feet. "We've witnessed some temperamental Welsh stubbornness here today. I think it has been disrespectful and potentially harmful. None of us knows what's behind all this but when temper flares, as it did today, it is sure to hurt others. In that respect I would judge this manner of behavior as undisciplined and challenge our session to disciplinary action before it spreads poison throughout the congregation."

Now Megan had seen everything, one man spewing forth temper, another reaching for the whip to punish. She moved quickly and spoke the command of the Holy Spirit within. "Let us pray. Dear Lord, have mercy on us. Understand our desires and our human weaknesses, and grant us strength to overcome them. Help us too, to ponder in our hearts what we have learned here tonight, and to separate the harmful from the good. Forgive us and temper our spirits that we may act kindly toward one another and work together in the task you have now laid before us. Be with us, protect us and guide us in your holy name, Amen."

"Margaret, did I vote or not?" asked Jim of his wife.

"Do you think Buck walked out for good?" Megan asked David.

David hoped he had gotten it all on paper correctly.

Haydn thought about the wording of the contract if there were trouble.

Paul was praying he hadn't said anything illegal, and Megan were wondering how she would follow up on Edwin's call for disciplinary action. She would first check the Presbyterian Law book.

Driving home in the car, Cridwyn said, "Thomas, that was a very good thing you did for the church tonight. You'll see." He reached out and patted her knee.

Addendum:

"The Session is charged with maintaining the spiritual government of the congregation for which purpose it has power to inquire into the knowledge and Christian conduct of the members of the church; to call before it offenders and witnesses to admonish, to rebuke, to suspend or exclude from the Sacraments those deserving censure." Book of Order: Presbyterian Church USA

CHAPTER EIGHTEEN - GAUDY WELSH TEAPOT

The next morning, Megan drove to Buck's house. His wife answered the door and began to apologize.

"You are not responsible for his actions," said Megan. She caught a glimpse of Buck through the window. "Tell Buck we don't want you to leave church and we hope things can be cleared up."

"I hear you." Buck stepped around his wife in the doorway. "They don't need to think I'll be comin' back, because I won't."

Megan began to speak but he held up his hand. "I said I'm not comin' back."

"I'm not here to argue, Buck."

"I spent my whole life trying to help that church and still they don't give a whit about me or my wife. All they want is their big reputation and fancy organ. What about a kid needing schooling, or a homeless person needing a house? It's them pure bloods that get to me. Some day they're gonna learn not everybody's a pure blood. Sure, I'm proud of my roots, but so are people who are not Welsh."

"That's a good point, Buck. I've been hoping that when the organ project is finished, the church will look into a mission project of some kind." Buck's face relaxed a little and Megan continued. "Right after you left, a request was made to the Session that I think you should know about."

"Don't need to know anything more." He turned to go back in the house.

"The Session might have to discipline you."

"What's that supposed to mean?" He turned back to face her and stepped outside.

"It's Presbyterian law. They can restrict you from the sacraments."

"Christ!" he half laughed. "They can't keep me away from anything. I'm keeping myself away."

"Buck, I hoped you and I could find a peaceful way to settle this, both for you and the church. You'd have to accept the majority vote on the organ but certainly the church could apologize for the way they treated you. I'd be glad to intervene for you."

"I'm done fightin' with them. What's the use? It's over and I'm not comin' back. Not now, not ever." Buck's wife, who had been standing at the door listening, turned away and went into the house.

"I'm sorry," said Megan seriously, "not only for the church but for you and your wife."

"She'll get over it."

"And you?"

He shrugged his shoulders and sauntered off toward the barn.

"If you change your mind please come talk to me," Megan called after him.

She stopped by David's on her way home to tell him what had happened.

"He's sure a queer duck," said David. "I suppose he means well, but he just irritates the heck out of people. I think this is the worst I've ever seen him."

"What about the disciplinary action Edwin called for? It seems ridiculous at this point. Do you think I could change Edwin's mind?"

"Anything to keep him from bringing it up at session."

Megan went straight to Edwin's and talked at length with him until he finally agreed to drop it. As Clerk, David wrote the letter to Buck, explaining that there had been no intentional quarrel with him, that he would have to concede to the majority vote on the organ but that they hoped he would prayerfully consider returning to church. He would be welcomed back with no grudges. The rest was up to him. They appointed Saddler to serve in his place as Trustee and Thomas to sit in with the Organ Committee. Megan sighed with relief, as did David.

Saturday afternoon, the week before Christmas, Tadcu pulled into Megan's drive. His white beard flecked with snowflakes and his cheeks rosy red. He stepped inside the enclosed porch and stomped his wet black boots on her throw rug. His glasses immediately steamed up. He set a large bag on the floor and took off his heavy overcoat, shaking snow onto the floor. She laughed, overjoyed, because he was wearing his red velvet Santa suit. From the top of his bag he took out a Santa hat and put it on beaming at her. She saw immediately that he loved doing it.

"You're him! You're absolutely Santa Claus," she said grinning broadly. He reached into the bag again, and this time pulled out a package for her.

"For me?"

"For you, from Santy Claus." They sat at the kitchen table as she opened it to find a lovely old teapot.

"It was my mam's," he explained. "I thought you might like it for tea." He knew she had no teapot because she always made tea with a bag in a cup. "Tea's better in a pot," he added.

"I absolutely love it! Thank you, Tadcu."

She held it up turning it all around to look at the details.

"It's called Gaudy Welsh and some think it is gaudy, but this here one was brought straight from Wales, packed in my mam's trunk. I don't use it no more since Mary died. The only time I drink tea is with you so -"He stopped.

Megan set the pot on the table carefully and wrapped both arms around him for a hug. "It's the loveliest gift I've ever received. I promise we'll use it often."

He took his handkerchief out to wipe his eyes and glasses. "There's a story about it that my mam told me onct if I kin remember it. It had to do with vessels that held hot bodily nourishment of different kinds, so that they become known as symbols of inspiration and rebirth. Later they called it the Holy Grail because it gave out healing and spiritual wisdom. The Holy Grail was, supposedly, carried to Wales, you know. Wales played an important part in moving the Christian faith forward. You probably know those old stories about King Arthur.

Actually, Edwin says – you know Edwin was a history teacher – well, Edwin says, there were two King Arthurs in Wales and the legends of each grew into one. You can see some of them symbols on the pot." Megan was intrigued and immediately wanted to know more. "If Mary was alive she could tell you. But right now I'd better git on over to the church. Them little ones will be wondrin' what happened to Santy Claus." Megan tagged along to watch, thinking about the two King Arthurs. I should go talk with Edwin and learn more about Welsh history, she thought.

The youth choir had met with Cridwyn and learned some songs for the Christmas pageant. That afternoon, they were decorating the tree and supervising the party for the children.

Twenty-one children were happily playing games and eating cookies while waiting for Santa. Santa knew every one of these children, and what each one wanted; so he had his bag filled with something special for each one. They squealed and danced around him in excitement when he arrived. When he finally sat down, they gathered around him, waiting expectantly. He placed each youngster on his knee and gave each gift separately. The youngest children always believed him to be the real Santa. Megan watched him with growing admiration. Such a good man, she thought.

The Sunday worship went well, but Megan was disappointed in the attendance. She must assume that some were down with the flu or too tired with the business of the season. Only five showed up at Zion. But the Christmas Eve service was yet to come.

On Wednesday, after hearing more warnings of bad weather, Megan drove her new Jeep into Van Wert to get supplies. She was not alone. The stores were crowded with shoppers. By the time she got home she could see an ominous swath of dark clouds moving in from the northwest. A misty rain had begun and by one o'clock, was freezing on tree branches and power lines. Schools closed early. By four, there was a good covering of ice mixed with snow.

Megan carried a supply of firewood inside, grateful that Haydn and David had neatly stacked a generous pile beneath her back porch. She checked her extra water supply and batteries. Schools would remain closed for the rest of the holidays. Through the night, Megan heard snow plows scraping past her house and on through town.

The day before Christmas dawned with a six inch blanket of snow and temperatures hovering at zero. The snow had stopped. A cold sun peeked in and out of ominous gray clouds just long enough to brush a brilliance on the shimmering ice and snow.

Trucks and snow plows scraped through the village all day long and by evening the parking lot was cleared and the Christmas Eve pageant and service were well attended.

The pageant went exceptionally well. People said it was the best in a long time. The story of the nativity was enacted with men, women and youth taking part in costume and a reader telling the story. Carols were sung interspersed with the enactment and they even had angels in the balcony waving sparkling wands. At the end, everyone held a lit candle and sang "Silent Night," which brought tears to the eyes of many, and made Megan feel that they had truly celebrated the birth of the baby Jesus.

Christmas day dawned white, gray, cold and quiet. Megan and Evie were invited to come to the Thomas Family for the noon meal. David was to pick up both of them around noon. Mid-morning Megan was just planning to call her parents when the telephone rang. It was Richard calling to wish her a Merry Christmas and to ask about the weather and her services. They had a good long visit with no interruptions. Afterwards she talked with her parents.

"Good thing we got you the Jeep," her dad said immediately. "Weather report doesn't look so good out there."

"I know. It got me right through on my trip to Van Wert Wednesday. I really am glad we did it." Suddenly, her mother's voice came on the line, too.

"My goodness! How did you do that? Mother, do you have a new phone?"

"Yes. It's my Christmas present from your dad so we can all be on together."

"When are you going to get some real phones out there in the country?" asked her dad.

"Believe it or not, they're saying next year. I heard it just a few days ago at the post office. Bryn knew because her twin sister is the operator here." They chatted happily for an hour and then called an end to it so Megan could get ready to go to the Thomases.

David arrived in his truck with the snow plow mounted on front. He had taken down his gun and replaced it with a wreath in his back window and had picked Evie up first. They squeezed in together all bundled and laughing.

Betsy's meal lived up to her reputation and they ate more than usual. Afterwards, they shared stories of past Christmases while large white flakes drifted down past the windows. At dusk David drove them both home.

"Looks like I'll be on the road again tonight," said David. His radio warned of severe winter storm conditions. A westerly wind picked up in strong gusts that began building drifts across the north/south roads.

Snow continued through that night, and the next day and night. Megan laid a flashlight beside her bed and got out extra covers and a candle.

David and others plowed steadily, keeping farm lanes open until it got ahead of them. Then, they concentrated on the roads. At times the snow fell so heavily that they could hardly see the edge of the road in front of them.

County snow plows worked in shifts, barely keeping ahead of the drifts covering the highways. Monday morning Megan donned her snow pants, boots, jacket and mittens and plodded her way through two and three foot drifts to the Post Office.

"There's no mail today," said Bryn. "I was about to shut down and help Aycee get a batch of wood inside."

"Good idea," agreed Megan. "Are there people who don't have wood stoves?"

"Quite a few. In bad storms like this, we and the store always put in enough to hold us through, so anyone needing to be where it's warm can stay until it's over. Especially, we need to have the stove going if the electricity goes out. Aycee's got a wood pile in back but it's getting covered up."

"I have plenty of wood at the manse and if you run out of space some could stay there."

"Thanks, Pastor Megan, that could happen. Some of them have generators but we never know until they show up."

"Have you seen David this morning? I know he was plowing roads last night."

"He hasn't been by yet. You have plenty of food?"

"I'm all set. Let me know if you need me for anything." As she walked home, the sky turned an eerie yellow and a howling wind blew icy snow in her face. The ice-laden tree limbs clicked in the wind. Just as Megan started between the parking lot and the church, a sharp crack caused her to look up, barely in time to see the lines on both light poles of the parking lot break and go down. She lurched to her right to avoid being hit. Ice and wires fell, sparking in all directions and splattering the snow. She hurried to the house to report the break by phone. Luckily, she reached Bryn whose lights had gone out and told her what had happened, then laid a fire. Before she had a chance to light it, David arrived.

"Hi," she said sympathetically as she greeted him at the door. "I heard you were up all night. Are you hungry?"

"Yeah, but isn't your electricity out? I saw the lines down on the parking lot."

"It just happened as I came back from the Post Office."

"How close?"

"Close enough," she said and David shook his head.

"David, I think we'd better be checking on stranded people."

"I agree. I've been doing roads all night. It's time to get to the people now."

"Have you seen Evie?"

"She's fine. Plenty of food, and that old cook stove. She has a generator too, so she'll stay pretty warm in that kitchen."

"Speaking of kitchen, have you had anything to eat? I was about to light the fire and make a sandwich."

"I'd appreciate that." Megan took his coat and laid it over the register which was still giving out a little heat from the furnace. Then she lit the fire and went about fixing them a sandwich. He stretched out on the floor and fell sound asleep until she woke him to eat.

CHAPTER NINETEEN – BLIZZARD

At the Morris farm, Jim came into the house from the barn after checking the livestock and stacking hay against the doors to keep them from blowing open.

"Margaret, I think we'd better go to town and get that generator for the barn. It's ready and it looks like we might be needing it. With this storm we could get caught without power and them cows'll need water."

"I want to go," begged Kevin.

"You stay here with the twins, Kevin. If we don't get back in time, you'll have to do the chores."

"I want to go with you and Mom," coaxed Kevin again.

"Let him go," said Cathy. "Carol and I can do chores."

"Okay, Squirt, get your duds on," Margaret smiled. They piled into the pick-up and the three of them headed toward Van Wert.

"We didn't start any too soon," said Jim. "This storm's moving in fast." He could feel the slickness of the road which he knew would slow him down and decided to take the angling road to town. It was usually better in a storm. It was already 1:30pm.

The visibility got worse. Jim leaned forward into the steering wheel to glare through the windshield wipers, trying to stay at the right edge of the road.

"Do you think we'd better turn back?" asked Margaret.

"No, we're on our way now. We'll make it." Jim tried to reassure her but was wishing he'd come alone. Kevin sat on his mother's lap. Suddenly, out of the screen of white, the dark shape of another truck loomed at them. Margaret yelled, "Watch out!" and Jim pulled to the right but too late and too sharp. An horrendous explosion of sound and a jolting impact of both trucks meeting head on, knocked their bodies forcefully against metal and glass. The right door flew open. Darkness numbed and stunned them and as Jim's senses returned he saw Margaret sliding out the door on her side.

"Are you all right?" he asked.

"Kevin flew out the door, Jim. I've got to find him." She was unaware of the cut on her own forehead. She moved with the instinct that comes midst shock. Kevin lay still in the snow in the ditch. One look told her he was hurt. Jim climbed painstakingly out of his side and met the other driver.

"I couldn't see," he said, visibly shaken. "You just came out of nowhere."

"I know. I think it was a white out. Are you all right?"

"I think so. Is that your wife?"

"Yes, and my son." Jim tried to walk around the truck. His knee felt like the cap was cracked and pain shot through as he tried to move.

"Jim!" Margaret screamed.

"Coming," he answered and tried to walk faster but his foot slipped and pain shot through again. The other driver moved ahead to help.

"Oh, my Lord," he exclaimed upon seeing Kevin. "He's just a little lad."

Jim took one look at his limp son in Margaret's arms. "Oh, my God, Margaret. Is he alive?"

"He's unconscious. I think his leg is broken. Are you okay?"

"Something's wrong with my knee. I don't think I can drive but we've got to get him to a hospital."

"We can't leave these trucks here either," warned the other driver, "or we're likely to have a worse pile up."

The snow let up briefly and Jim saw a familiar farm house. "I think we're at Bob Jones's. If we can get Kevin in there we can call an ambulance."

"We'll have to," said Margaret. She was still not aware of the growing welt and gash on her own forehead. She carried the limp child with a strength that comes in emergencies.

"Be careful," warned Jim. "We'll get the trucks moved."

Jim's truck wouldn't budge so they left it and the other man drove Jim to the house.

Margaret had just about reached it when Bob Jones, who had been watching at the window and thought he'd heard a crash, saw them. He went out to help them into the house and tried to call an ambulance. In the warmth, Kevin's eyes opened in a daze, unresponsive.

"You're going to be all right, sweetheart. Mom and Dad are right here." Margaret spoke gently to him. She wasn't sure he heard.

"I can't get through. The line just rings busy," said Bob.

At the bank in Van Wert, reports were coming in that traffic was blocked on routes 127 and 116. That was enough to close early and Paul walked precariously on slippery streets two blocks to his car. It took him several minutes to get the snow off of the windshield so he could see. He looked at his watch. It was 2:00pm.

By 1:30, David had rested, warmed up and eaten so was ready to get on the road again. He began pulling on his clothes and Megan ran to get her snow pants and boots.

"Where do you think you're going?"

"I'm going with you."

"No. It's no place for a woman out there."

"David. I'm also the Pastor and there could be someone who needs encouragement, including you."

"I said no!" They stared at each other both with jaws jutted and then Megan took a big breath. David let his go and backed off just a bit.

"I really need to go. I can't just sit here in his house like a protected princess of some kind. I need to be doing something useful." He seemed to understand that approach so he agreed. They left the house unlocked and climbed into David's big truck.

"I can see why you feel safe in this," she said. They broke through drifts causing snow to fly over their heads. At the Post Office, Aycee was shoveling a path to the store across the road. The grocer had sent food and two families had already come and marked out their places in the room. They had plenty of wood in and a rope to the out-house.

"I think the two of you could check on Ruth and Henry Rees," said Bryn. "They might not be able to get out. The snow looked pretty deep when I walked by this morning. See if you can get them over here."

"I was wondering about Tadcu, too," said Megan.

"Yes. We'll check both places." They drove down the street and stopped across from the Rees's. The county plow had made a pile along the street and the wind had whipped a circular stroke about the house piling snow and totally blocking the doorway with a six foot high drift. Between the house and street the snow spread out at four foot deep. Megan wondered how they would ever get through.

"Sure glad I have this plow," David said and began shoving his way through the drifts, banking snow on either side."

"I have to admit," said Megan, "when you bought this big truck I thought it was an ego trip but now I understand why." David was too intent on his work to let her comment bother him.

"When we get to the porch we may have to hand shovel. Shovels are under the tarp in back." It took fifteen minutes and when they were finished they had a tunnel four feet wide and eight feet high.

"I wonder if they're in here," said Megan. "I haven't seen anyone at the windows."

"Where else could they be?"

"Maybe somebody else got them out last night."

"Well, we have to check, anyway."

They pounded on the door and called their names.

"They are a little deaf," said David.

"Can we just go in?"

David tried the door and found it unlocked but frozen shut. They chipped at the ice to break it free and entered cautiously and concerned. Megan took the kitchen and David headed toward the bedroom.

"In here," she heard him call and went back to the bedroom.

"Are they all right?"

"I think asleep. We've got to wake 'em up."

"They look so sweet, all snuggled up."

"Probably was the only way they could keep warm. Still they can't stay here. Henry." David touched his feet. "Henry, wake up. We gotta move you over to the Post Office."

"What? Oh, David?"

"Henry, we gotta move you. Can you get up and get dressed?"

"Am dressed," he said and sat up. "Ruth, wake up." Ruth opened her eyes.

"Oh, my gracious. Who's here?"

"They come just like I said they would." Then he explained to David and Megan, "We had no other way to keep warm and we couldn't get our door open so we just went to bed and prayed somebody'd come. Howdja get in?"

"We'll tell you about it later. Where are your coats and boots? We have to check on some other people too. You had a mountain of snow out there. Another day of that and you'd been buried alive." Ruth had packed things ready to go and they quickly got themselves out and into the truck. Megan walked the short distance back to the Post Office so they could ride. Once they got settled in and began to tell their story, Megan and David slipped out and headed toward Tadcu's farm.

Paul crept along the drifted road at twenty miles an hour listening to his radio. *We interrupt this program for a special weather bulletin. There is a severe winter storm warning out for all portions of the Midwest. Ohio has blizzard conditions between Dayton and Toledo moving eastward with gusts at forty miles-an-hour. Roads at this time are extremely hazardous. The highway patrol advises all motorists to get shelter immediately. The National Weather Bureau is estimating up to 8 inches of snow for the area with winds increasing and temperatures plummeting to minus 15 degrees over-night. North/south highways are already impassable in many places.* It took every bit of concentration Paul could muster to drive. Visibility was so low that he didn't see Jim's smashed truck by the ditch until he was passing it.

Realizing it was Jim's, he backed up to look. When he saw no one in it he drove up Bob's lane and saw another truck parked in front of the house. He plodded awkwardly to the house through the deep snow. When Bob opened the door, Paul was struck with the scene inside.

"Paul, how did you get here?" asked Jim.

"I was on my way home and saw your truck. Are you all right?" They all began talking at once and the problems became obvious.

"Let me drive you to the hospital. If we're careful, I think we can still make it."

"You're a life saver," said Margaret and Jim added, "We've got to get Kevin there soon."

"You all need to be there," answered Paul. "Bob, will you help Margaret? I'll carry Kevin. Can you walk, Jim?"

"I'll make it."

"I think you'll be fine now," said the other driver. "You've got my name and number if you need anything."

"Yes, thank you, Ralph. You've been a help."

"I hope the boy'll be all right."

"Come on we're running out of time," urged Paul. He was praying he still had time to get them there safely. "Bob, stay on that phone and see if you can get through to the hospital. Tell them I'll go straight to emergency. Then try to call my wife and let her know where I am and what's happened. I may have to stay in town tonight."

"Call the twins, too." Margaret called back. "They're home alone."

"I'll get on it," Bob promised. "Be careful."

It took every ounce of concentration for Paul to drive through the accumulating and blinding drifts. Jim sat beside him in both mental and physical agony. Kevin stretched out on the back seat, his head in Margaret's lap. He looked up at his mother. She never realized how horrible her face must look to him. Bob had cleaned up the blood but the cut and welt were swelling and it was beginning to throb. Paul tried his CB. No answer. Other calls and static drowned them out.

"Try Channel 9," suggested Jim. Paul tried the emergency channel, "Breaker Channel 9."

"Go ahead Breaker." The immediate answer brought smiles of relief to all.

"This is KPE 1660 mobile. I've got three accident victims. I'm on the angling road from the south and want to cut over Hospital Drive."

"10-4. How far out are you?"

"About a half a mile from Hospital Drive right now."

"10-4 mobile. We have a unit in that area. We'll have him meet you and take you in."

"Roger - much obliged."

"What's the condition of those victims?"

"A four year-old with a broken leg and bruised parents, shaken up a bit."

"Roger, I think I see your unit now." The flashing yellow light of the parked unit bit through the snow a good 100 yards ahead and Paul slowed to a stop behind it. He blinked his lights to signal. An officer came back to check on them. Paul rolled down his window letting snow in. The officer took a quick look and directed, "Follow us and go easy."

"You can count on it. Thanks." Paul was relieved. At 3:25 they pulled up to the emergency entrance of the hospital. Hospital crews were ready and waiting.

East of the village, David and Megan crept their way toward Tadcu's farm. From a short distance they could see what looked like his truck pulled into a large drift at the start of his driveway.

"Looks like he had to walk in last night. His tracks are covered over."

"Maybe he's in the truck," said Megan.

David pulled up behind it and parked. Snow had piled up on the back window so they couldn't tell. "Be careful," he said to Megan as they stepped down out of the truck. The wind blew snow about them and stung their faces.

They approached the truck on both sides and tried the doors. "This door's frozen shut," Megan shouted over the wind and began brushing the accumulated snow off the window to look in.

"This one is too. Can you see in?" He pulled a hand scraper from his pocket and began scraping. Megan tromped her way around to his side.

"Oh, my God, Megan. He's in there. Tadcu! Tadcu, can you hear us?" He was sitting upright behind the wheel as if asleep.

"Is he all right?" Megan leaned up against the window to peer in.

"I can't get the door open." David pounded the packed door. "I'll go get a crowbar," he said. David came back and began stripping the ice around the door. Several times he used it as leverage and tried to force the door, but couldn't budge it. Megan could stand it no longer.

"Just break the window!" she shouted. "We have to get him out of there!"

"I know," he said, "but I can't do it on this side. I might hit him. Let's go around." They scrambled through the snow and with one blow David shattered the window. They could now see Tadcu sitting stiff and straight.

"God help us," said David breaking away the rest of the glass so they could pull the door. Both of them grabbed and pulled until it gave away. David crawled up on the seat.

"Is he breathing? David, can you tell if he's breathing?"

"He's frozen, Megan. But I think he's still alive."

"We've got to get him to the hospital."

"I'll drag him out. Go get the tarp out of my truck."

David tugged on the cold body and dragged him across the seat. Together they pulled him out of the truck onto the tarp, then dragged him across the snow to David's truck. Struggling together they lifted him up and into the truck propping him upright on the seat between them.

Megan patted his cheeks trying to arouse him. His eyes opened a small slit and closed again. David turned the heater on high and headed back to Route 116.

"No one ever told me how hard it is to live in the country. Do you think we can make it in time," Megan asked.

"We have to make it. I just wonder how long he's been sitting there. There wasn't a track around his truck anywhere."

"Do you suppose he got home and couldn't get in his lane, and just sat there waiting for help?"

"Yeah," David nodded. "Probably had the engine running until the gas gave out. Why didn't the son of a bitch walk somewhere?" he asked angrily.

His words hurt Megan. "David, he's ninety years old. How could he?"

"I know, Megan. I just don't understand this. I'm just so dammed mad. It should never have happened." Megan saw tears come to his eyes.

"You think he's dead, don't you."

"Yes, I think he's dead. Oh, God." David stopped the truck and began sobbing on the steering wheel.

Megan reached across Tadcu and put her hand on his shoulder. "No, David. He's not dead. He's not. And you and I have to get him to the hospital. Right now, David." Her voice was firm. David pulled himself together and started to drive again.

"Is there anyone we can call on the CB?"

"Christ, why didn't I think of that?" He took the microphone off its hook and began trying.

"Breaker Channel 9. Breaker Channel 9. Breaker anyone."

There was static and then a lull. David tried again.

"Breaker Channel 9."

"Go ahead breaker," came an answer.

Holding the mike to his mouth, David smiled at Megan who gave a sigh of relief.

"This is Rover 1220. I've got a man appears to be frozen up. Found him in his truck. Can't tell if he's still alive or not."

"Where you at?"

"Route 116 north of Cambria."

"Where you headed?"

"Van Wert Hospital."

"Roger Rover. The best way is to stay on 116 and take Hospital Drive into the back emergency. Do not go on 127. Road is impassable. In fact, at this point I can't even guarantee 116 is open."

"10-4. I have a plow"

"10-4. That's good. Anyone with you?"

"Ah, one other passenger."

"10-4 Rover. We'll check with you in ten minutes. Be careful."

"10-4. This is Rover 1220, over and out."

"All right. We can make it." David was back in control but he kept talking to Tadcu all the way in. "Come on old man, you gotta make it. Don't you go to sleep on us now. We still need you. Hang in there." David talked and Megan silently prayed while keeping her eyes on the road. There were drifts every fifty feet or so. It was 4:00pm and already dark. He flipped on his lights and emergency blinkers that sent colors across the white. The scenery was a strange world of unfamiliar shapes and hills, lit by an eerie yellow glow that kept the night visible and vile. Periodically lightning flashed. The ride seemed endless. Tadcu's beard began to thaw. Megan put her hand on his chest. He seemed to be breathing ever so slowly. The heater in the truck was making the cab warmer. Neither of them spoke now, running low on adrenaline. The windshield wipers padded back and forth piling snow around the edges of the windshield.

Suddenly the CB blared. "Calling Rover 1220, This is Levi here. Can you hear me?"

David answered. "This is Rover, Go ahead Levi."

"Where you at, old buddy?"

"116 about 2 miles from Hospital Road."

"You okay? I heard you call channel 9."

"I will be as soon as I get Tadcu into the hospital. He's frozen up pretty bad, Levi."

"Awww. You take care of him, you hear?"

"Roger, Levi."

"Rover?"

"Yeah?"

"You got the preacher with you?"

"Roger."

"You take care of her, too." David and Megan smiled at each other again.

"Who's gonna take care of me?" David asked grinning.

"Figure that one out yourself, old buddy. Stay in touch." They signed off.

"Was that Squire?"

"Yup."

"I thought I recognized his voice." Just then Channel 9 broke in again saying emergency was ready to receive. They crunched to a stop and got out of the truck as aids pulled Tadcu out onto a stretcher and into the hospital. Paul met them at the door.

"What are you doing here?" they both asked at once.

"I'll explain later. I was watching emergency activity and heard you were on your way in. You're not going back, are you?"

"No!" they both said together.

There were no extra rooms for them to stay in. They would have to use the waiting rooms. The cafeteria was staying open and they could give them a blanket and pillow.

They had gotten in just in time for now radio stations were announcing every ten minutes for people to stay off the roads and take shelter. Even the road crews had stopped keeping the roads cleared and were putting all efforts into rescuing stranded motorists instead.

CHAPTER TWENTY – WAITING

Carol and Cathy did chores early because the power had gone off and they had to milk by hand. They began to worry about their parents. The phones were out. They had a CB in the basement but neither of them had ever used it. When it got late enough they decided to try it.

"Anybody out there? This is Carol and Cathy."

"Hey, there. This is Levi 4321. It's Squire, kiddos, in case you don't know my call name. I bet you want to know about your tad and mam."

"They haven't come home yet."

"I know. They had a little accident on their way into town and they're in the Van Wert Hospital. They got banged up a little but they're OK, and Kevin has a broken leg. They have to stay there because no one can be on the roads now, so I'm glad you got on the CB. You okay?"

"Yes."

"Can you make it by yourselves for a day or two?"

"I guess so."

"Do you have food?"

"Yes."

"How about electricity? Do you have heat and lights?"

"No. We milked by hand but we have candles and flashlights."

"Tell me this. Can you build a fire in the fireplace?"

"Yes."

"You could do that but be careful and be sure your draft is open. If that doesn't work or you get cold, put on warm clothes or snuggle up in bed together with lots of covers, okay?"

"It's not cold yet."

"Good. The phones won't get fixed right away so if you need anything call for me on the CB and I'll try to help. As soon as I can get out I'll be there on my snowmobile to check on you, and when the phones are on again your mam and tad will call you, okay?"

"Okay." They signed off. Squire gave a sigh of relief and put a call in to Robert who made a call to a Van Wert CB who in turn called the hospital by phone to leave a message for Jim and Margaret.

Kevin and Jim were in the beds and Margaret was stretched out on a cot the nurses had brought in. Because of Kevin's age and the rapid growth stage of his bones, the break could not be set in a plaster cast. Instead, they drilled holes through both heels, inserted steel rods, then attached these rods to pulley ropes on a traction unit above his bed. It positioned him flat on his back, hips slightly elevated with the legs extended straight up at a 90 degree angle. It kept him immobile. He would have to lie this way for six weeks. Jim and Margaret watched the procedure with heavy hearts. Jim's knee was packed in ice and

Margaret had a bandaged head and swollen black eyes. They were glad to hear the twins had talked with Squire. Megan kept prayers going for all of them.

David suddenly felt fatigued. Except for the 15 minutes at Megan's he had had no sleep for 48 hours. Paul showed him the waiting room where he stretched out under a blanket and quickly fell sound asleep.

"That's the best thing for him now," said Megan. "When he wakes up he'll be starved." She and Paul went to the cafeteria together to eat and exchange stories. Afterwards Megan checked on Tadcu and Paul returned to Jim's room.

Snow plows, rescue operations, traffic had all halted but the snow kept coming down. The barometer reading was the lowest in history at 27.9. Predictions were that the blizzard could last another two days. It was a lonely and anxious night for many. Megan prayed for the people.

In the hospital lights were dimmed to low for night hours and to save electricity. Megan stood beside the bed where Tadcu lay. His face, expressionless and white. He had been cleaned up and she watched his chest move in weak, shallow breaths. His eyes were closed. There was only a slim chance he could live.

She sat beside him, holding his hand in hers, watching him breathe. In the short time she had known him, he had been like a grandfather to her. She didn't know if he would come through this but, for the community's sake, she prayed he would. His hands began to warm in hers and she thought he squeezed just the tiniest bit. It brought tears to her eyes. Leaning closer, she spoke softly: "The Lord is our shepherd, we shall not want. We are made to lie down in green pastures, we are led beside still waters, our souls are restored. We are led in the path of righteousness for the Lord's sake. Even though we walk through the valley of the shadow of death we fear no evil for the Lord is with us, comforting us like a shepherd. A table is prepared before us in the presence of our enemies, and our heads are anointed with oil, our cups run over. Surely, goodness and mercy will follow us all the days of our lives and we will dwell in the house of the Lord, forever. Amen."

She listened to his faint breathing for awhile then stood and, turning her back to him, placed his life in the hands of God. Through the obscure window she watched the endlessly falling snow and relentless winds piling the snow into sculptured drifts, burying cars, snow plows, even emergency vehicles parked in the hospital parking lot. The nearest light pole looked faint and distant blinking through the gusts of snow. The snow piled half way up the window-sill. She imagined Cambria, where the wind raced full force across open fields, would be drifted in. She questioned if she would have been better able to help more people had she stayed home. Probably not. There were more there to help each other. She was with the neediest.

Her mind played tricks asking why these good people were hurt and why did she believe she had to fix everything herself? Had they all forgotten the greatest power of all? Was all of this to make them stop and take notice of the gifts they have and to say, 'Wait a minute. This is Christmas. There is a birthday to celebrate. Pay attention to the important things.' Was that what this was all about?

A flash of light momentarily blinded her. Turning, she saw a nurse standing by Tadcu's bed.

"He's gone," the nurse said softly. The grief of finality gripped Megan's heart and turned to a weight in her stomach.

"He was a remarkable human being," she said to the nurse who nodded.

"Stay as long as you like," she responded kindly, and left the room.

Megan sat beside him studying the now sweet expression on his face. It seemed to her the look of a heavenly creature she had once dreamed of who, she had believed, was watching over her. In her heart she thanked Tadcu for watching over her in her first ministry.

"You were so kind to me," she said softly. Then bent over and kissed his forehead.

"That's for everyone who loved you. Peace."

Paul sat in the hall between David's cot and Jim's room. She told him Tadcu was gone and he pulled up a chair for her. Together they sat in heavy silence through the long night.

Tuesday morning came early in the hospital with nurses tending many patients. Megan walked from window to window trying to see through the crusted, packed glass. David finally awoke and she told him about Tadcu. The three of them went together to tell the Morrises.

Jim had not slept much. Margaret's eyes were bloodshot and the skin around them was deep purple. She sat by Kevin.

"Hey, big man. That's some contraption you're in," said David.

Megan touched his shoulder, "You're a real trooper, Kevin."

"How's the knee, Jim?" asked David.

"Pretty painful," he tried to muster up a smile. Then Megan broke the news. None of them said a word but grief was visible on all their faces.

"They're holding his body here until he can be transferred," explained Megan. "We haven't been able to contact Edwin yet."

Jim began to talk for the first time since they had been in the hospital. He felt guilty for taking Margaret and Kevin along, he worried about the twins alone and he was deeply grieved about Tadcu. Memories tumbled forth as they all worked through their grief together. Gradually Jim spelled out his main concern which was how he could handle the work load of the farm with bad knees. If he could get his younger brother home from Vietnam it would help a lot.

Megan remembered that Cambrian Hall was going to be auctioned off in January and wondered if that could be made over into a house.

"No. It's too old, but if I could buy it reasonably enough I could tear it down and rebuild on the land."

"Then rent out the farm for income," suggested Megan. She was learning how things were done in the country.

"Yes. I hate to think of quitting farming just yet but you've given me an option to think about if needed, Megan. Thank you."

David always had the impression that Jim wasn't a strong man. But now he saw him pull all his forces together to hold himself up under extreme difficulty. The Jim David was seeing today was a stronger man than he had known. He admired what he was seeing. David was learning that to know the heart of a person, you have to listen. He had never really listened to this man before. The two of them spent a good part of the day visiting and becoming closer friends.

Back in Cambria at the Post Office, eleven people were camped-in with cots and blankets, boxes of canned soup, crackers, peanut butter, cookies and drinking water. To pass the time they told stories, played games, worked puzzles, listened to the weather reports and slept.

They had a good warm stove and plenty of wood. The men took turns shoveling the snow away from the doors, tunneling out to a clear spot that allowed them to cross the street to the grocery. The only disadvantage was that the one toilet inside couldn't keep up with the demand so the men volunteered to use the tee-bach behind the building. The rope Aycee had tied between the two places would guide them.

Betsy and John had to milk the cows by hand and in the cold, they had a few problems but dealt with them. They worried about their neighbors, Thomas and Cridwyn, and by Tuesday afternoon the wind had died down a bit although the snow was still falling. John was restless. He decided to try David's brand new snowmobile. He bundled up with a ski mask over his face and pulled on the big mitts.

"John, I hate to see you go out until the roads are cleared, but I'll feel better to know about Evie and the Evanses," said Betsy.

"Don't worry, Betsy. I've been wanting an excuse to ride this thing and this is it. I can just go across the fields in it and around the drifts. I'll be back before dark."

Betsy watched him through the window taking off toward Evie's. Stick with that old man, God. Bring him home safe, she prayed.

Evie was fine but her back door was frozen shut. She was thinking about how to get it open when she heard the snowmobile and spotted the dark figure scoot around a drift, disappear and reappear at her door. Maybe David, she thought, then hearing the voice knew it was John.

"You all right?"

"I'm frozen in."

"I'll go get something to pry it loose," he yelled.

When he got it open he came in to warm up. John caught her up on the news he'd heard from Squire on the CB. She cried about Tadcu and Jim's family but was relieved to hear David and Megan were all right.

John warned her about letting Corgi out in the fresh snow. "He can lose his scent and wander away from you and get lost. I've known many an animal to die in this kind of blizzard," he told her. He strung a rope to the barn, watered the animals and headed out. He later described it as the most beautiful sight in his lifetime. The white on white rose and fell in gracefully sculptured drifts varying from four to twelve feet high and stretching out in some places for fifty to one hundred feet. John must have been the first one to see the village from a mile away. Even from there he could tell it was pretty well buried.

His next stop was Thomas and Cridwyn's. They had kept their doors open but John found Thomas chipping away at his garage door where the ice had frozen it shut. They had had a pipe burst but, aside from that, they were doing all right.

From there, he drove on to the village guided by the tops of the power poles. As he approached it he slowed to a stop and stared. A monstrous wall of snow blocked the road into town. The size of it was unbelievable. It slanted from the roof of the house beyond the livery barn across the road to the porch roof of another house. It was too high to ride over. He would have to go around to the fields behind the houses. Gripping the handlebars, he felt his chest tighten with anxiety at what he might find beyond the drift. He wondered if he had pressed his luck too far. The cold air bit at his nostrils and an eerie void of life sent a chill down his spine.

Carefully now he made his way over the roller-coaster drifts behind the houses. He reached the parking lot which was the only open area. Looking back, he saw two huge drifts: the one he had seen from the other side, and another in front of it which covered the front porch of the manse. The village was freakishly still, yet, excitingly beautiful. Driving the snowmobile around Cambrian Hall he coasted down a long low drift to the front of the Post Office and parked in the middle of the street. He dismounted and walked through the shoveled-out tunnel to the Post Office door. A heavy silence rested on the snow and all he could hear were his own footsteps crunching and his own breath. When he opened the door cheers went up and applause. They gathered around him for news. They had not ventured out so his description of the large drifts made them eager to bundle up and see for themselves. Standing in both wonder and concern, they guessed it would take days for equipment to reach them, much less clear all that snow away. Tomorrow, if the weather held, they would try to return to their homes knowing many would have to dig their way in. The daylight was fading so John left, anxious, now, to reach home before dark.

Following his own tracks and guessing where they were drifted over, was exhilarating to him. It was wonderful to be useful, just like old times. A heady

139

confidence and a strong sense of power caused him to accelerate his speed and sailing along he began to sing at the top of his lungs:

God of snow and God of wonder
How you've covered all the earth
With this gift of white and splendor
What a present for Christ's birth!
"Songs of praises – songs of praises
I will ever sing to theeeeehahhyowhhhhh!"

He was suddenly air-born heading downward in flight.

Before he could think what to do the machine dove into the steep side of a large drift and died. Whooof! The snowmobile was half buried and when he opened his eyes he was confronted with a wall of white.

The jolt had stalled the engine. He wasn't hurt, just very, very humbled. Then it struck him funny and he laughed and laughed at himself relieving all the tension. Even the sound of his laughter fell muffled into the silencing snow. Slowly he pulled himself off and jostled and jerked the 250 pound machine until he pulled it free. It started easily and he took off again at a safer speed and paying closer attention. He flicked the headlight on, so if Betsy were watching she would see him coming, and whispered a few words to his great companion. "Thank you, Sir, for getting me out of that one. I know it's about time I give up trying to be young again, but sometimes I just have to be reminded. Now I'd appreciate it if you and I just keep this one a secret for the time-being, if you don't mind."

Following supper at the hospital cafeteria, David and Megan found a private area to sit in and talked for several hours: starting with the weather and Tadcu's life, then of Vietnam and the struggles it caused their community; of the changes that would be happening when the new organ was installed, and ended up sharing some of their personal lives. Both were struck with the reality that life can be taken at any minute and how important it is to live each moment in the best way one can. For David, that brought up the subject of Evie.

"Evie should be my wife," he spoke honestly. "She's the one I love. I've always believed that some day we would be married but it never seemed to be the right time to talk about it. I realize, now, that I've never courted her or actually told her I love her. I really haven't been fair to her. Oh, God, Megan. I have so much changing to do."

Megan touched his hand. "Evie is forgiving, David."

"I've done some pretty immature things, you know. I've chased a lot of girls. I even thought about dating you once." Megan pretended shock but let him continue. "I never was serious about any of them, because I knew Evie was there for me whenever I was ready to settle down. Now I worry that she might not want me anymore. We do everything so easily together, we're more like brother and sister."

"I've seen the boy in you, David. But I've also seen the man. I'm very proud to call you my friend. Let me pray for both of us." She took his hand. "Dear Lord, thank you for showing us our lessons in life, and for loved ones who care for us as we learn. Give David the strength to face his issues and please continue to guide us both in our journeys of faith that we may be better servants in your grace. Amen."

There were tears in his eyes as she looked up.

"You're a dear friend, David."

"And you're a damn good pastor." He choked up and reached for his handkerchief. "I want Evie to be my wife, I know that now," he said directly. "I love her so much. I've always loved her. God, I hope she'll have me."

"All you have to do is let her know how you feel."

"How?"

"Buy her flowers. Take her out for dinner or a movie. Put your arm around her. Kiss her." Megan half smiled as she spoke, as if to ask 'why do I have to tell you this'.

"Do you think she'd go for that? From me, I mean?"

"Just be honest, let her know how much you love her. Tell her what you told me. She'll go for it. Trust me."

"How do you know all this? You really are good. I mean it. You say what you think and you say it with compassion. Beyond that you always seem to show up right where you're needed most."

"Well, let's just say I'm trying."

By Wednesday the snow had stopped. The sun was out and as soon as they got the truck uncovered and a path cleared on the parking lot, David and Megan left to drive home.

All the familiar landmarks were gone. It disoriented them, somewhat. At crossroads piled and drifted snow stood ten to fifteen feet above them. They drove slowly, taking it all in, thrilled at the wonder of it, in awe of the power that created it.

At one point they met a tow truck dragging a car coming toward them. It stopped and waited while David maneuvered back and forth widening the path enough for them to squeeze by each other. When they reached the cemetery curve they were blocked by a pay-loader bucketing out a ten-foot drift across the road. Working together they widened the curve enough for two cars or one large truck to pass through and crept on into Cambria.

They stopped at the Post Office, amazed by the huge drift that confronted them. A few people were milling about. Two highway trucks were pulling in behind them getting ready to work. Megan, anxious to get home, headed out walking around the drifts. David cleared a route down the alley behind the Post

Office and made his way along the edge of the ball park toward the church parking lot. Several Snowmobilers were parked around the open space and the men began yelling for him to get out of the way. He rolled down his window and yelled at Squire. "What's going on?"

"There's a Red Cross chopper comin' down right where you're sittin' in about two minutes flat. That's him up there."

"Here?" asked David looking up to where Squire was pointing.

"Right there. Move it."

David moved back just in time as the loud descending chopper with blades whirling blinding snow landed. David watched the pilots hand out supplies of food and medicine to the farmers who came to the machine. They took the boxes and drove off over drifted fields, disappearing in all directions. Squire called up to them, "What do we owe you?"

"No charge. It's from Red Cross," the pilot yelled back closing his door. Squire scooted the safe distance away to watch the big machine lift off in a whirl making a sharp swing toward Van Wert, then walked over to David.

"Magnificent machine! Absolutely magnificent! They didn't charge us a nickel and to think it takes ninety gallons of gas an hour to keep that bird flying."

"Lot more expensive than a tractor, I guess," responded David.

"Whatever it costs it's worth it." He explained what had just happened.

"I can't believe how well you all banded together."

"Folks are good, David, and we've got some of the best right here in Cambria." He teared up and his face reddened in the raw cold air. "I tell ya, the CB was our life saver. If we hadn't had that we'd have been a sorry lot, David. I've been on that wave day and night. Ain't had no sleep for four days."

"I'll bet. Sometime I'd like to hear about it."

"Sorry about Tadcu. Where'd you find him?"

"End of his lane," said David, not able to say more.

Squire nodded and tightened his lips. "We got word to Edwin. I'll miss him," he choked up and it was all he could say. They parted and David headed over to wait at Megan's until he could get through.

He watched from her window as the pay loader and trucks broke open and scooped away the huge drifts. The phone lines had been temporarily fixed. Workers had said that new poles, wires and dial phones would soon be replacing the old system.

As soon as the road was open David called upstairs to Megan. "It's open. I'm heading home."

"Go see Evie soon, David," she called back.

"I will."

By 9:00 at night the lights and heat came back on. Furnaces kicked on and people cheered to themselves, happy to be back in their own homes. There remained pipes to thaw, melted food in freezers, and full refrigerators to clean.

Megan made herself some tea in the gaudy teapot, remembering Tadcu in his Santa suit giving such special gifts to the children, and curled up in her chair to write in her journal. *I don't know why people find pleasure in making fun of others, or why some suffer the blows of others, or even why some feel they know so much more than others and leave the church in anger. I don't know why good people get hurt and others die but with all of that, in the past few days I have witnessed amazing acts of kindness and bravery for the sake of their love for others. Like snow on snow on snow, you pour down your grace upon us, loving us still. I am amazed at the love that has moved into the hearts of these people for one another and even more amazed at, and grateful for, the great love I am feeling in my heart for all of them right now.*

She set her empty tea cup down and gazed out the window at white nothingness feeling, suddenly, alone. She went to the phone and first called her parents who were greatly relieved to hear from her, and then tried Richard's number. There was no answer, so she went to bed. Glad to be back in her own bed, she snuggled under her big down quilt and breathed in the crisp cold air from her open window. Then, quickly sank into a long, sound sleep through yet another white night.

The next morning, before she was fully awake, her telephone rang. Leaping out of bed and grabbing a robe she ran down the stairs to answer it.

"Good morning," Richard said and her heart skipped a beat.

"Where were you last night?" she asked right off.

"Where were you all week?" he asked in response.

"I wanted to talk to you."

"I wanted to know if you were all right." They talked for an hour. He was saddened about Tadcu and the concern he expressed for Jim's family made her appreciate him even more.

"I wish you were here," she said.

"I know."

It took a full week to get all roads and lanes opened. Edwin made arrangements for Tadcu's burial. Aycee asked for and was granted the custodian position at the church. The Organ Committee set a time to meet. Notices went up about the telephone system being updated as soon as the poles could be replaced. A community meeting was held to vote to auction off the Cambrian Hall building. Megan attended the meeting with Mary Morris who was able to tell her the names of the villagers who were there who didn't attend church. Megan made note and promised herself to visit each of their homes. A date was set in January for the auction of Cambrian Hall.

Megan helped Edwin arrange Tadcu's burial and visited a few of the people who had been stranded, listening to their stories. The spirit of Christmas became more meaningful than at any other year in their history, for good will and peace on earth had come into all their lives, and they would tell the story in many different ways for years to come.

So at the Watch Night Service held at the church on New Year's Eve for anyone who could get there, carols were sung because the Christmas service had been missed. Afterwards, Megan helped Aycee close up the church. Walking to the manse she stopped to look up at the full moon just rising over the church belfry, casting a mellow glow on the white landscape. The air was crisp and still. Across the moon-lit space, twinkling barnyard lights guarded distant farm homes. It was the beginning of the new year, one that was filled with dreams and plans. So immersed in the scene, she imagined she heard angels singing and turned an ear to listen closer. Down the street she spotted a dark shadow coming toward her and recognized the voices singing "Jingle Bells." It was David and Evie bundled in blankets in their horse-drawn sleigh, with a lantern dangling from each side lighting up their faces.

"Happy New Year!" they called out. "Get some warm clothes on and we'll take you for a ride."

"Perfect!" she exclaimed excitedly. "I'll only be a minute," and ran to do as they said.

She returned and climbed in, snuggling under the robe, her feet finding the warm bricks on the floor of the sleigh. David tapped the reins lightly on Duke's back and off they went around the back of the church and out the drive on the other side onto the firmly packed snow of the roadway. Like a young girl again, Megan laughed and squealed in delight as they scooted through town and out toward the cemetery by the light of the moon. They sang to the rhythm of the muffled clopping of Duke's hooves on the hard-packed snow, circling the cemetery and heading back toward Tadcu's farm. Duke trotted steadily, head up and puffing steam out of his wide nostrils. Their chins and cheeks stiffened with the cold but their body heat beneath the robe kept them cozy. The thin blades of the sleigh sliced tracks up Tadcu's lane where they circled in front of his house, stopping to let Duke rest a little as they reminisced. Then they headed back to the manse.

"Please come in. I'll make hot chocolate," coaxed Megan. Ready for warmth, Evie climbed down with her. David tied Duke to a tree and followed. He built a fire while the women made hot chocolate and they all sprawled out on the floor talking until the logs burned down to glowing coals. Then Evie looked at David.

"Now?" she asked. David nodded smiling.

"What?" asked Megan.

"Pastor Brown, will you marry us?" Evie grinned broadly.

"Did I hear what I think I heard?" asked Megan.

"She asked you to marry us. Will you?" They both watched Megan eagerly for her response.

"Is this true? Are you really going to do it?" Megan beamed.

"Yes!" they said together.

Megan squealed un-pastor-like, "Oh, I will, of course I will. When? Now? Let's do it now!"

"No, not now," they laughed together, "but soon." They fell into a threesome hug, the two of them talking at once trying to tell Megan how it happened.

"I was so glad to see him after being shut up so long and not knowing anything about anyone. I think I would have said yes to anything he asked for," laughed Evie

"She flew into my arms, practically crushing me."

"Yes, and I just looked at him through my tears and asked him, 'David, do you have any idea of how much I love you?'"

"Yeah, and that made it so easy. I just told her right there that I'd always loved her more than anyone and that I'd always figured she'd be my wife and before I knew it I'd asked her to marry me ―"

"And, of course, I said yes, immediately! No more chances of him slipping away. 'This is it, mister' I said."

"I couldn't believe it would be that easy."

"I always thought I'd like Reverend Jarvis to marry us until I became friends with you and when David asked who did I want to marry us, I told him you, and he said he never thought it could be anyone else. So we both want you. You are our dearest friend as well as our pastor and we know you'll do it right."

"What a gift. I can't tell you how happy you've made me," replied Megan to their enthusiasm.

And so it was set for the end of March. It was 3:00A.M. when they left with sleigh bells jingling. Calling back, "Happy New Year!" they disappeared from sight.

Megan dashed into the house and put a call through for Richard. She was high with excitement. She wanted to tell him about David and Evie and her emotions spilled over. "Oh, Richard, you have been so good to me. I can't tell you how much I owe you for leading me to this wonderful place. David and Evie are so great together." She went on telling him how it all happened. There was no way he could get a word in, himself. "I'm just so totally happy, I wanted you to know it. You must come for the wedding, Richard." She stopped abruptly, shocked at herself. *Lord, what have I done? It isn't my place to invite him to the wedding. What was I thinking that he's just part of the family?*

Before she could attempt an explanation, he responded.

"I will be happy to come, Megan. But let's talk about it later. I really need to get my sleep."

"Oh, Richard. Of course. How stupid of me."

"Don't apologize. I'm thrilled that you wanted to share it with me. We must talk about it soon."

They hung up: Richard cautiously ecstatic, Megan embarrassed. What ever got into me, she asked herself. *What must he think of me?*

PART THREE

Chapter Twenty One

CHAPTER TWENTY ONE - UNEXPECTED CHANGES

Megan wondered if Jim had thought any more about Cambrian Hall, since their conversation in the hospital. Notice about the auction had been posted so Megan walked over with Mary to watch.

"It served as the church in the village before the present one was built," Mary told her. "Then it became the center of all the music competitions called Eisteddfas,"

"That must have been what Thomas was talking about."

"Probably. He directed a male chorus that sang in competition. That all disappeared in the fifties. Just too much work and costly."

As they approached the scene, Megan noticed a lot of unfamiliar faces. "Do all of these people live here in town?" she asked Mary.

"I reckon most of them do. Could be some from neighboring communities."

A large crowd had assembled. Mary saw someone she knew so Megan began working the crowd, talking to as many new people as she could, inviting them to Sunday worship and telling them about the youth program. One young woman invited her to come call. Megan was taking it all in when she felt a nudge on her arm and there was David.

"Hi, where's Evie?"

"She isn't too interested in auctions."

Megan nodded, "It's a good crowd."

"Mostly curiosity seekers. They want to know who's buying, why, how much they're willing to pay. It'll be topic of conversation for weeks."

The auctioneer stepped into position, made a brief explanation and then went into a language Megan never heard before and could barely understand.

"What is he saying? I can hardly understand him," baited David.

"Me either," she said, then saw his grin. "Tease," she said and punched him.

He then explained what was happening and Megan learned how to follow the bids. Suddenly, she spotted Jim. He was standing with crutches but he was bidding. Gradually it dropped down to only a few and they couldn't spot who was bidding against him. They watched closely until, finally, David saw who it was.

"It's the Dutchman," he said. "Jim's bidding against the Dutchman. He's either bidding him up to get the best money for the town or he wants it, himself. Let's see how Jim hangs in there."

"What do you mean, Dutchman?" asked Megan. She'd heard the term before.

"He's a Catholic from east of here. He's been buying up everything he can get his hands on. I heard the church loans their people money cheap." Megan said nothing but frowned at the thought.

The auctioneer was having a hard time moving the bid higher. Slowing it down, he banged his mallet and shouted strongly, "SOLD, for $15,000 to the gentleman in the green jacket." It was Jim.

"He got it!" exclaimed Megan.

"He sure did. Maybe he decided to follow up on your idea, Megan."

The crowd broke up fast and David walked her back to the manse. Aycee caught up with them going to the church.

"Whatdya think of that? Jim bought that there buildin'. Now what would he want that old thing fer?"

"I guess we'll have to wait and see, Aycee," said David. Then he noticed Aycee carrying a book and asked. "What's that you're reading?"

"Nothin' much."

"Looks like a bird book." Megan tried to read the title.

"It ain't about birds. It's about houses," said Aycee.

"Bird houses?" asked Megan.

"Yup."

"How to make bird houses," guessed David.

"Yup."

"So how long have you been doing that?"

"Not long. Edwin seen me readin' it at the Post Office an' asked me if I understood how to build 'em. I said I was learnin'. Then he asked me if I had tools an' I answered him 'no.' So then he says, Tadcu had some tools he'd give to me if'n I wanted to try my hand. I said I did an' he said 'Okay then' and the next day he took me out and showed me. Said I could take what I wanted. So, now I have me some tools and I started one already."

"That's wonderful, Aycee," they said together.

"Not only that. Now I got tools when I need 'em to fix things at the church." He listened as they praised his efforts and called back at them as he went into the church, "Bryn, she was the one that got me the book."

They walked on to the manse and Megan asked David to come in if he had time. She wanted to talk to him about Zion church.

"David, when I came here, one of the big things on my agenda was to bring Zion and Cambria together. I thought it would be easy, but it isn't. In fact, it's as if they're saying 'Hands off.' Still, I know they're struggling. Two of their young people belong to the youth group here, the few middle aged members aren't interested in anything, and the few older ones try to keep it going. I end up preaching to about eight people each Sunday and it's hardly worth it for either them or myself. Beside that, they really can't afford that building. They need to join Cambria but I don't know how to make it happen."

David was pleased that she'd asked, but he had no easy answer. "That's been a problem for a long time," he began. "There were some hurt feelings years ago and some of those feelings have been passed on down through the generations;

although now, I think it's more a fear of not being accepted at Cambria. I don't know how to change that.

Personally, Megan, I don't think anything we say or do can make them take the chance. I think it has to be an act of God before they'll come."

"They were so warm and excited when I moved in. I feel I've failed them somehow."

"They must feel pretty bad that Cambria is raising so much money for an organ and there they sit in a run down building with not enough to keep it going."

"I know."

"Just a day or so ago I talked to - -"The phone interrupted and Megan went to answer. David could hear the tone of her voice and it sounded serious. He waited until she came back to the kitchen.

"Talk about acts of God."

"What happened?"

"That was Haydn."

"I was just going to tell you I'd talked to him the other day."

"Well, the boiler burst at Zion."

David's face dropped. He waited and Megan went on.

"Haydn had stopped by to check on things when he heard it making strange noises. He bent down to look at it when it burst. He got soaked with hot water. And it flooded the floor but no pieces of metal hit him. His feet got pretty hot when he was trying to get the water and gas shut off. He said it was the fastest he's ever moved."

"Is he all right?"

"Yes, but there's a mess to clean up."

"How bad a break?"

"He doesn't think it can be repaired. He called for someone to come look at it tomorrow but he thinks they will need a new boiler and they don't have the money for it."

"Does he need help? I can go over and help. I think I will anyway. Poor guy seems to be carrying the whole load over there, and they've been giving him a hard time because he's working with the Organ Committee here at Cambria."

"That would be good, David. I'll go with you." She put the rest of the coffee into a thermos. "Maybe we should stop and get some dry clothes for him at his house," Megan suggested, then added, "I'll drive."

"Let me get my boots then," he said and ran to get them from his truck. He hadn't ridden in her new Jeep and was pleased she suggested it. It had begun to rain. They made their stop for clothes at Haydn's and told his wife what had happened. When they arrived at Zion they found Haydn and Gomer Davies, who lived close by, in the basement wading knee deep in black water. They were setting up a sump-pump to draw out the water. A smell of sulfur soured their nostrils as they started down the steep steps.

"Oh, Lordy, Pastor, don't you come down here," called up Haydn.

"We brought you some dry clothes," she said.

"Just keep 'em up there somewhere. I'll get to that later. Right now we have to get this pump working." Megan did as she was told. David waded right in with his boots already on.

"How hot is that water?" asked Megan.

"It was hot enough to burn when it burst out. Luckily, I ducked but the steam was terrible and the water on the floor was pretty hot for a bit. I turned the cold water tap on until I could stand in it and then shut everything off. That's when I called you."

"You're lucky you didn't get burned," she said.

"What a mess," said David.

"'Tain't very pretty," added Gomer.

"Where'd you get the pump?" asked David.

"Gomer, here. I knew he had one. I was wet anyway so I just walked over in the rain to borrow it. He brought it over in his truck."

"Lucky I was ta home," added Gomer feeling a little glory in his rescue operation.

Haydn finished setting the sump-pump up. "There now, let's see if it'll work. We've got to get the suction goin' so we can pump it out o' that window. The drain is plugged. It just don't want to take it all." He had strung hose from the pump in the deepest part of the room up through a small basement window to the outside. He gave the cord a good yank. The motor roared and the water started to swirl. They all cheered above the roar and watched it a few minutes until they were sure it was working, then went upstairs to wait. Megan hopped up off the stair step.

"I'll get you some coffee and maybe now you should change your clothes, Haydn."

He was shivering and agreed that would feel good. They sat around a table in the all-purpose room at the back of the sanctuary. David, having taken a good look at the boiler, judged it definitely beyond repair. "You were very lucky you didn't get burned or a piece of steel cut into you," he added.

"I know. I don't know what we're gonna do."

"I knowd it was gonna go," said Gomer. "It's been actin' up fer a long time."

"You can't have church here this Sunday. You'd better plan on coming over to Cambria," suggested Megan tactfully. There was a pause and a long sigh from Haydn. Megan said no more.

David leaned closer to Haydn and said, "I know how hard this is, Haydn. We all know it's probably going to have to be replaced, and we all know the church doesn't have enough money to do it. Even so, they might not want to spend that much on it. From what you told me the other day, folks are giving up anyway."

"Maybe there's a reason for this happening," added Megan.

"I hate to admit it, but you're both right. It's just, I can't be the one to tell them. They have to make up their minds together, ya know? It has to be their decision."

"I understand," said Megan. "Would you like me to call the meeting for you?"

"I suppose. Word'll get out soon enough anyway."

"Have to face it sooner or later and I always say the sooner the better," Gomer injected.

"Gomer, why don'tcha go down and check the water. See if it's goin' down any," suggested Haydn.

"All righty," he said and David went with him.

Megan sat quietly with Haydn, giving him time to absorb what he had to face, then asked quietly, "How can I help?"

"You could say a prayer for us."

"You've got it."

"Thanks for coming, Pastor. The dry clothes and coffee helped."

"It's a goin' down!" yelled up Gomer.

"Good." Haydn hopped up and stepped outside to adjust the direction of the flow. It had stopped raining.

"That's a good pump, Gomer," said David. "Lucky for Zion."

"Yup," he said. "'Bout ready to mop?"

The three men began mopping and carrying buckets of the dirty water up the stairs and outside while Megan looked around at the building thinking. *I can't say anything now, but this could be a great community place for the migrant workers when they come — a good project for our youth..*

It happened more smoothly than Megan believed it would. Megan called the Zion members to an emergency meeting at the church where they could directly see the damage. Haydn had estimates of the cost to replace the boiler, and the immediate consensus was that they give it up and join Cambria. In their hearts they were ready. They had only needed a good excuse. Under these circumstances the Cambrians would sympathize with them and it would be easier. When someone asked what would become of the building, Megan suggested it might become a mission project for the youth to make it available for community needs. Their hearts seemed relieved then and they began showing excitement about making the move. So it happened without Megan having to twist arms, politic, beg or hassle. *Praise God!*

Kevin's six weeks were up and he was put into a body cast and brought home. The family never knew they had so many friends. Phone calls poured in. Friends stopped by. The topper, though, was the day they took Kevin to church to sing with the youth choir. They carried him, in his cast, up the front steps, then put him on his wagon to pull him down the aisle. Propped against the front railing, his happy face glowed as he sang with his friends. That day, every heart was touched by the appearance of the little red wagon and the brave little boy who had led them back to caring. Not only was Kevin healing, everyone was healing. Everyone but Edwin.

"Ever since Willie died," he told Megan, "I haven't felt right somehow. It's as if I didn't do right by him."

"You mean, we didn't give him a proper funeral, Edwin?"

"Yes. I missed being with friends who shared the grief. We just buried him and that was it. I missed hearing the music, all of that, and I don't know how to fix it." He sat holding his hands, looking at the floor and a deep line wrinkled his brow.

"Edwin, you're right. We can arrange a memorial service where all that can happen whenever you like."

"Could you?"

"Of course."

"When?"

"Whenever you like." So a memorial service was held the following week. In an informal way Megan lit candles on the communion table, had a picture of Tadcu placed between them with flowers in a vase behind. Against background music that Cridwyn played softly, Megan talked. They sang his favorite hymns and it was the last verse of *Sandon* that washed away the grief for Edwin.

So long Thy power hath blest me, sure it still
will lead me on
O'er moor and fen, o'er crag and torrent, 'till
the night is gone;
And with the morn those angel faces smile
Which I have loved long since, and lost awhile.
John H. Newman

A few days later, Edwin stopped by at the manse and handed Megan a sealed letter.

"It's for you. I found it in Willie's desk drawer. He wrote it the day before he died."

She opened it while he waited. A check fell out to the floor. When Megan reached to pick it up she could see it was made out to the church and was a very generous amount.

"I wondered if there was a check in it," he said. "Not long before he died he told me that since I was pretty well taken care of, he thought he'd give some money to the church for the redecorating. That must be it. May I ask the amount?"

"$4,000. Can that be right? That's a very generous gift."

"Yes, that's right. I had intended to match his gift so I'm glad to know. I'll have another check for you in the same amount very soon." He turned to leave without waiting for her response.

"Wait, Edwin," she called out. He turned on the steps looking up at her. He had always thought her a beautiful woman. "Are you sure you can do that? This is very generous and yours added to it will put us very close to goal." She was afraid he was just trying to keep up with Tadcu.

"I have no one but the church now," he explained, smiling up at her, "plus, I'll be getting money from his farm as well as my own. I'm happy to do it. The church has been a real church since you've come. If it's more than you need, use it wherever you see a need." She watched him walk out to his car and drive away without looking back.

Overjoyed at the check, and the promise of an additional matching one, Megan called David immediately. He was overwhelmed. "Megan, do you know what that means? We can do everything we've been planning for without borrowing. What generous men they are. This is making me cry."

"I know. I had only figured them for a thousand at the most."

"I have to give you credit, Megan. You pulled it off."

"It's not my doing, David, and let me remind you, it isn't over yet."

"But, we're definitely running toward home base."

"Yes, we are. Ever since the blizzard they've been like different people. It's like God stepped in to help me see what good people they are."

"Here, now. That's not quite the way I see it."

"Well, anyway, this is the Blessed Assurance."

She hung up and the phone rang. Richard was checking in.

"You always seem to catch me on a high," she apologized and immediately explained the two gifts.

"Marvelous, Megan," he responded and moved on immediately. "Ever since your last call I've felt the need to talk with you. I'll be in Dayton next Tuesday and Wednesday. Would you be able to drive down for any part of that?"

"I'll make the time. What's on your mind, Richard?"

"Many things. I just need to have a good talk with you. I'll get us rooms at the Holiday Inn. Okay?

"Richard, you sound worried."

"Not worried. I just need to talk. Thank-you, Megan."

"All right. I'll be there." They hung up.

She stood wondering what he wanted. Had she done something wrong? She had called him in the middle of the night. Maybe he was disturbed by that, or was there more to their relationship than she knew? She felt mixed emotions, both fearful and excited. But she knew he was right about one thing. They had to talk.

She finished her report for the annual meeting and outlined her plan for the year. The first thing on her list was the name Charles Houck. Somehow she had to convince the 125th Celebration Committee that he should be the guest organist for the organ dedication recital. In her excitement, the list grew.

At the annual meeting her report stated only two deaths in the year and one lost member over disagreement, twelve new members from the village and twenty-five from Zion. Megan had been able to influence the nominating committee to nominate Ruth Hughes Lloyd as Session member along with Saddler Evans. Ruth won the vote and became the church's first woman session member ever.

She was also happy to announce they had gone over the top in their financial campaign which would enable them to buy the organ, pay for the installation, do all the new construction and decorating needed and still have money left for either an endowment or mission project. David stepped up to complete the story.

"How did that happen you ask? I am proud to say that Tadcu and Edwin Williams gave us gifts of $4,000 each." People turned around to look at Edwin in the back of the room. He stood halfway up and nodded as they applauded.

This evening, I have another surprise for you. It is my honor to introduce to you a person who has not been back to church in a long while, yet a person you all know and remember well. Evelyn Davies Evans, would you please come up here with me?"

Everyone watched Evie walk to the front. They had seen her there but hadn't thought about why she was there. The general assumption was that she had finally decided to come back to church. Evie stood by David and he continued. "About six months ago this church received a gift of $15,000 from an anonymous giver." Immediately, people began looking around at each other and at Evie. David continued.

"I see you're catching on. Well, you're right. Evie is the anonymous donor of the original $15,000 gift and challenge for us to raise more money to buy a new organ." Applause and excitement rippled through the room. Some stood immediately until the rest caught on. Quickly then, everyone was standing and applauding. Evie beamed back and waited for them to be seated.

"I've been a long time away from you. Partly out of fear, because I wasn't sure I could handle your sympathy." The people became still and attentive. "Also, because I preferred to do my own thing. I think word has gotten around that I'm some kind of weirdo." They chuckled. "Not entirely true. I've always been interested in the church. I knew when the choir was growing smaller and when there was trouble with the organ. Like my Uncle Thomas, I feared that if the music were lost, the church would die. That's why I scraped up my savings and gave it. But because it was all I had, I wanted to be sure that it would be used successfully. That's why I also gave the challenge. For awhile I wasn't sure you were going to make it." An anxious silence hung in the air. "But then you began pulling together. Now, the goal is in sight. I know I have made a good investment and that's why I decided to let you know who you could blame." They applauded again and she sat down. Someone called out, "Are you coming back to church now?" and David stepped up to answer.

"I'd like to respond to that," he said and waited for their attention. "First, I'd like to officially thank Evie for her generous and thoughtful gift. I believe this church will always be grateful for her generosity and insight. We have realized again that what we have in this church is precious beyond measurement and that we must preserve it for the generations following after us. FOR THERE WILL BE GENERATIONS FOLLOWING!" They applauded and cheered and he continued. "I speak for all of us here at Cambria Church and that includes the wonderful people of Zion who have now become part of our family."

"Now, in response to the question, will Evie be coming back to church? She will. Because she has agreed to become my wife and you are all invited to our wedding." Now people leaped to their feet cheering and applauding as David took Evie's hand to stand together acknowledging the warm appreciation.

"It's about time," called out Squire and everyone laughed.

"With that happy note we adjourn this meeting," Megan said and they had already begun to swarm about their celebrities.

They lingered longer than usual, talking in clusters and getting bundled up to go outside. It was a good sign. Megan watched David and Evie receiving congratulations from members. It made her happy that they had come together in their love but now she would have to make adjustments in her own relationships with each, for it would be different. And there was a distracting element under-riding everything else in her life, that of Richard. Had she made a mistake in her exuberance? He wanted to talk. Had she led him to believe there was more than there was? And how much was there really? She knew she had to get things straight soon.

Jim and Margaret walked out with her.

"How's the knee doing, Jim?" she asked.

"Oh, coming along but I still have a lot of pain. Looks like I won't be farmin' this year. We're trying to get the Army to let my brother come home to help us farm."

"I didn't know you could do that."

"We're not sure about it either, but it's worth a try."

"Absolutely. How's Kevin?"

Jim looked at Margaret who answered the question, "Not well. He seems depressed and we don't really know how to handle that."

"I'd be glad to stop by and talk with him."

"Oh, would you? He talks about you and David."

"I'll ask David. Maybe he and Evie can go too. Jim, I saw the demolition crew pull in. Are you taking down the old building?"

"Yes, they start tomorrow. Your idea to build a house on the lot convinced me I should be getting ready for retirement. Then if or when I need it, it will be there." They talked some more and then called it a night.

Aycee had slipped easily into Tadcu's place as custodian. He turned the lights out, closed the doors after them and walked off down the empty street alone. Jim watched him as they turned out of the parking lot and wondered what kind of a place Aycee lived in.

CHAPTER TWENTY TWO - SHEPHERDING THE FLOCK

When David announced at the Annual Meeting that Evie was the anonymous giver of the challenge gift to the church, Thomas and Cridwyn were shocked. So much so that they left the scene early because they didn't know what to say to Evie.

She had wondered what happened to them for she had seen them earlier. So she was pleased when they came to call the next day. "I'm glad to see you both," she greeted them warmly.

They shed their coats and boots and sat in the living room. Evie offered tea and cake which they accepted and when they were all seated Cridwyn began the conversation.

"Evie, we want to tell you how pleased we both are for you and David. We've hoped for a long time that you two would get together as a couple."

"Thank you."

"It will be nice to have you back in church, Evie," Thomas added. "We've so hoped for that."

"Well, don't expect too much. I plan to start out slowly."

"We understand," said Cridwyn. "We also want you to know how very grateful we are for the generous challenge gift you gave the church. We had no idea you were the one. We are both of the mind now that it was a wise gift. I, especially, am happy about having a new organ to play."

Thomas nodded in agreement. Evie watched him because it was he she most wanted to hear from.

"Uncle Thomas?" she addressed him. He came to attention.

"Are you happy with the new organ plans?"

"I am, Evie. I think Pastor Megan has proven her worth. I never believed all of this could happen. As I look back at the way I acted at first, I'm ashamed, but they proved they could be the good music-loving people I always believed them to be."

"I understand, Uncle Thomas. I'm happy it all turned out so well."

"Thomas has something else he wants to tell you Evie, but he wanted me to be along when he talked to you."

"What's that?"

"I want to tell you why I never came to see you when you lived in Van Wert. It's been hard for me to talk to you since you moved back because I treated you very badly when you were a child."

"No you didn't. I remember wonderful times with you. Why do you say that?"

"I mean when your parents died. I always felt a deep regret and guilt that I didn't take the three of you in and raise you. Cridwyn wanted me to. She wanted to help and she would have."

"I would have," echoed Cridwyn.

"But I knew the only way I could have done that was to give up the church music and get another job and I wouldn't do that. I was selfish. I know now that that's what made me feel angry inside and it caused people to turn away and that's why we lost the good music program at church."

"But you were grieving too, for your brother. It wasn't that bad for us, really. What was hardest for me was that when I did return you hardly ever came over to see me. I didn't understand that."

"I know. I worried because you didn't come to church. Your brother and sister went off in other directions. It wouldn't have been that way, had we raised you. You'd all be sitting in church every Sunday."

"Perhaps. Perhaps not. You can't take on that burden. Besides, it's over now."

"I need to be forgiven, Evie. Can you ever do that?"

"Of course I forgive you, Uncle Thomas. I love you."

"He's been trying to get his courage up to say that for a long time," added Cridwyn. Thomas pulled out a big handkerchief from his pocket and gave a good blow into it.

"My family in town was a good one even though my life was different. In my heart I always knew I would come back. Rich and Marilyn got more accustomed to living the way their families did and had little interest in the farm. But I knew I'd come back. I knew David was in college and that he would someday farm for me. I knew, you were busy and that was all right." Thomas was listening intently and she continued. "I loved coming home. I got busy fixing things and picking up where I'd left off. I knew a lot had happened over the years and that you had changed. I noticed you weren't as happy as when we were young but I also knew a lot of things had happened to all of us and I just kept looking for what I could do that might bring back a little of that happiness for all of us, and I found it."

"Yes," they both nodded, "you did, you certainly did."

It was snowing again and they decided they'd better get on home. Evie hugged them both good-bye with an open invitation to come see her anytime and Thomas heaved a big sigh and said "The same to you, my dear. We would love having you stop by."

The next day the demolition crew took down the old Cambrian Hall. There were onlookers and scavengers milling about, carrying off odds and ends of old furnishings, and people just watching as it all came apart and down and out. But Megan missed all of it. She told David she had some personal business to take care of and would be gone for the day and possibly overnight.

Megan drove through a light snow to Dayton with mixed feelings. Richard had never made a request like this before. She knew her own fervor on the phone probably stirred things up, and waking him up in the middle of the night certainly didn't help. She was nervous.

At the motel the clerk handed her a note and key. She found her room and the note told her he would contact her after his meeting. They met for dinner.

"Thank you for coming," began Richard. "I have hardly been able to sleep since our last phone call."

"I knew from the tone of your voice that it was important to you."

"I hope it's important to you as well."

"What is it, Richard? What is so urgent?"

"Megan, remember when I called after the blizzard? It was as if we really connected with our feelings for the first time. You said 'I wish you were here.' Did you mean that?"

"I did. There was so much to tell you I couldn't do it over the phone."

"And on New Year's, you were so excited to tell me about David and Evie."

"I know. I was just so happy for them that I had to share it with you. I didn't even think about the time, Richard. I apologize for that, but it was such a perfect day."

"I felt terrible about cutting you off but I was so groggy I couldn't begin to match your enthusiasm."

"I'm really sorry. You always said I was too spontaneous."

"For some occasions, but it's also the very thing that attracts me to you, Megan. You must know by now."

"What?"

"You know – that I'm attracted to you."

"Richard?"

"What?"

"Are you serious?"

"Well, yes. I wouldn't be saying it if I weren't." He looked a little surprised. "Are you?"

"Am I what?"

"Are you attracted to me?"

Megan beamed at his embarrassment as he tapped his fingers nervously, but she caught a look in his eyes that locked in her heart. She knew that look. She had seen it in Charles's eyes when they were in Africa, when he told her he loved her. She had felt a passion she hadn't known before. This can't be happening again, she thought.

She asked, "Is that what all this is about?"

"You didn't answer my question." The look didn't change. She swore he was holding his breath.

"Richard, I don't know how to answer that. I've been so busy. I don't know how I feel about you. I just count on you. You're there for me. You're an important part of my life."

"You're hedging," he was ready to back off.

"No, wait! I practically worshipped you when you were my professor."

"I'm not God, Megan."

"I know that. Just let me think." He waited intensely watching her face. She continued. "I am deeply grateful that you had faith in me and found Cambria for me."

"You're very welcome."

"I admire you, Richard. I look up to you. So –"

"Go on."

"So, yes, of course, I'm very fond of you."

"Fond of me? Megan, what I'm asking is do I attract you in any way? You know," –– he motioned with his hands like magnets being drawn.

"Mmmm." She teased a bit. "It could be. I just never thought about it before."

"You're not teasing me, are you?"

"No, I truly have been occupied with other things. I'm sorry."

"It's all right. You did say it was possible. So, will you think about it?"

"Yes." Megan said immediately and smiled positively.

Richard shook his head grinning, "You are something else, Megan Brown. You really are."

"Is that it?"

"Yes, That's it."

"That's what I came all the way to Dayton for?"

"Unless you want more, but I don't think you're ready."

"True. I'm not. You realize this doesn't make sense, don't you? We live in two different worlds practically."

He pressed a finger to her lips. "Just think about it. That's all I ask for now."

They retired to their separate rooms for the night and Megan thought about it. In fact, all night long she thought about it. She knew she wasn't ready for this. She had pledged her full attention to the church; yet, she also recognized a longing inside of her that was hard to deny.

They met for breakfast and conversed about other things but an undercurrent of intrigue flowed between them, drawing them into the same stream. It's so hard not to be attracted to someone who is attracted to you, she thought, but how much dare I tell him? That look in his eyes is disarming.

They managed to talk all around it until it was time for her to leave.

"Thank you for coming," said Richard, politely trying to stay cool.

"I'm glad I did."

"Will it still be all right for me to attend David and Evie's wedding?"

"I'm certain they would want you there."

"I'll see you then," he said. "I guess this is good-bye for now." He stepped toward her and she lifted her face to his. They kissed then, a friendly, gentle kiss; then looked into each other's eyes and kissed again. But this time the moist softness of his lips sent a flame surging through the center of her body. With every bit of strength she had, she forced herself away from him. "Good bye, Richard. Thank you."

"I'll call you," he said closing her car door. She drove off with a pounding heart, a man waving in her rear-view mirror and a secret in her soul.

She arranged to pick up David and Evie to call on Kevin. When they arrived, he was taking a nap and Evie and David had a chance to ask Jim and Margaret to stand up for them at their wedding. They were pleased and consented.

Margaret told them that Kevin had begun therapy and was afraid to make the effort to walk. "The minute he tries, fear takes hold and he simply falls down crying, 'I can't'."

"If I could talk to him I'd like to," said David. "I think I might be able to help."

"I'll go get him," said Margaret leaving the room.

"What did you mean?" asked Evie.

"I had a broken leg when I was six and I remember how scared I was to walk again."

"David, what if we asked him to be ring bearer?"

"Good idea. But that leaves the twins out."

"You can always have two flower girls," suggested Megan.

"Why not? Let's try."

Margaret carried Kevin into the room. "Look who's come to see you." He was still a little sleepy but smiled shyly.

"Hi, big guy. I see you got your cast off. I bet that feels good," David said.

Kevin nodded.

"Do you feel lighter?"

"Yes. I think I could float up like a balloon."

"You know, Kevin, Evie and I have something to ask you. Would you sit on my knee?" He moved Kevin over onto his knee and sat him facing toward Evie.

"Did you know this leg you're sitting on was broken once?"

Kevin glanced up into his face and asked "Does it still hurt?"

"No, but it did when I was six years old. I didn't get to go to school when I was supposed to because of it."

"I'll go to Kindergarten this year. My mom will take me if I can't walk."

"You wouldn't want your mom in Kindergarten. The other guys would make fun of you. You'll have to learn to walk so you can go by yourself."

"You have big legs," Kevin pretended he hadn't heard.

"Kevin, Evie and I want you to do something for us."

"Why?"

"Because the two of us are going to be married – just like your mom and dad."

"You're going to get married?" he whispered it as if it were a secret.

"That's right," answered Evie, "and we want you to be the ring bearer in our wedding."

"Oh, Evie," said Margaret, pleased.

"What's a ring bear?" he asked.

"Ring bear-er," inserted Megan. "It's the person who carries the wedding rings down the church aisle and takes care of them until the pastor needs to give them to the bride and groom. We need you to do that for us."

"Mom, can I?"

"You'll have to learn to walk smoothly."

"I can walk real smooth."

"Good! We'll count on you. You have six weeks to practice, Kevin. If you can walk for the wedding, you'll be able to go to Kindergarten all by yourself," said David.

"I will?" His eyes were bright with sparkles. "I walk real smooth."

"I know you will, partner." David set him down on the floor. Kevin stiffened just a little saying, "I just have to stand a little first."

"Thank you," said Margaret and Jim together. "I think you've been just what we needed."

"Well, while we're asking, if it isn't too much maybe the twins would like to be flower girls," asked Evie and everyone laughed.

"A family affair," Jim looked at Margaret who replied, "I'm sure they would be very excited."

From that day on, Kevin tried. His desire to walk, run and play had gnawed at him, but to be a part of a wedding where he would have to walk in view of everyone was the motivation he needed. He did everything Margaret and Jim asked. The hardest part was getting his foot to turn straight. It turned outward causing a slight limp. There were times when the anger and frustration took hold and tears of discouragement overcame him, but someone always encouraged him, and little by little he improved.

"I going to be a ring bear, Mom. I going to do it. How many days?" They made a calendar so he could measure his progress. Kevin had a deadline and at last he was trying fervently to meet it.

A few days later a construction crew began building a modest new home on the other side of the church on the lot where the Cambrian Hall had stood. Aycee was a regular visitor, stopping on his way in and out of the church to watch the progress and ask questions. Jim noticed him and began taking time to talk with him.

David reminded Megan about the traditional annual St. David's Day Banquet which was fast approaching. She made it a point to ask Betsy, who was the community story-teller, about it and she gave Megan a written copy of the St. David story. *St. David was born of noble parents in the fifth century, ordained into priesthood, traveled to the Holy Land where he was consecrated bishop, and upon returning to Wales founded many churches in the southern part of Wales. His feast day is March 1. He founded a small village known as Menevia* and there were more stories but, armed with this much information, Megan was ready.

The banquet tables were spread with the traditional green and centered with yellow daffodils. Behind the speaker's table hung the Welsh green flag with its fiery red dragon. One hundred or so guests wore leek corsages and satisfied their appetites from many good casseroles and cakes such as bara brith and teisen lap. The singing of the Welsh National Anthem and American National Anthem was rousing and it was followed by a speaker, who, this year, was not a Welshman and not so rousing. Edwin fell asleep and nearly tipped off his chair. Jim's twins found a corner in which to play tic-tac-toe on the back of their father's program and the women retreated to the kitchen to wash dishes.

So it was not so much the banquet that positioned them for spring but rather, the return of the crows. One crow was considered a bad omen, but two or more had been sighted so word was out that a good year was in sight.

March, brown and barren, was the messiest month of the year to live through on the mid-western farms. The time for reading *The Ohio Farmer* was over. The air, teasingly flirted with spring warmth, yet hid the nip of winter in its sunshine; the ground showed signs of thawing but was still muddy underfoot; feed lots were seas of muck softened to a mushy depth of ten or so inches from the workings of sow's feet; even a sudden snow squall swirled into teasing little drifts. All were taken in stride.

Megan, trying to make her house calls, found people working in their barns or chicken houses, hauling out the winter manure, moving feeder pigs into lots away from farrowing sows, men mending fences or greasing machinery, and women spring house-cleaning. It was never a good time for her to come calling. In spite of the gloom, church activities progressed with a series of Lenten Prayer Breakfasts which several managed to attend, although some felt it was a nuisance to change clothes after chores. The Easter choirs sounded promising, Kevin was singing with the children's choir again.

Megan campaigned for Charles, her college friend who had gone on to become a world renown organist, to be invited as guest organist at the Organ dedication recital. She began by having a tea party for her friends of influence; Evie, because of the power of her gift of money; Cridwyn, an organist herself and also on the Organ Committee; and Betsy, because next to Evie she was the most open-minded and most influential over David. Women were more supportive of her, she felt, and she knew these three could persuade men. She begged God's forgiveness for her scheming. She admitted to the women that she had a favor to ask and told her story about being in college with Charles, how good a musician he was even then, how they spent two years together in Africa in the Peace Corps, and even about their participation in helping to register black voters in Mississippi together.

At one point Betsy wanted to verify that Charles was African American and Megan replied by telling even more. "Yes, we actually were romantically involved and even considered getting married; but we were wise enough to see that our choices of professions were so important to us that we would have had little time to nurture our marriage. We knew a mixed marriage would take a lot of nurturing and explaining and that we had to make wise decisions. Painful as it was, we both chose our separate careers. I have not seen him since our college graduation." She went on to explain that she was concerned about the kind of reception he might receive from the people of Cambria. She wanted him to be welcomed.

Evie knew it was the Charles Megan had told her about before and her eyes shown with excitement but she waited for the others to speak.

Cridwyn said, "Megan, I personally would take anyone you recommended without question. We haven't been exposed to people of color here and unless the people are prepared, it might be uncomfortable for him. I think they would be willing if they were prepared ahead to know what a fine musician he is."

Betsy agreed, saying, "If you convince the Session first and they agree the rest will go along."

They looked at Evie. "Let's do it. I get excited just thinking about having such a well known musician in our little church."

They tossed it around, thinking of ways they could help prepare the Session members, how Megan should approach it, and how it should be publicized. Megan felt supported. As they left Betsy said, "Sometime you'll have to tell us more about yourself. You never cease to amaze me."

A few days later David stopped by to ask about it. He felt Megan had some kind of crush on this man.

"Why do you feel so defensive about him?" he asked.

"He's my friend. He's a minority and I don't want him hurt. It's very hard being a minority."

David listened, trying to understand. "I have to say, I'm concerned. I think there are people in this church who are just not ready."

"In what way, David?"

"I think they're afraid. They don't have exposure to Negroes around here."

"They prefer to be called African Americans."

"See? Even I say the wrong thing. What else might I say to him that would set him off?"

"First of all, you wouldn't set him off, as you say. He's well educated, tolerant and understanding, to say nothing of his talent. I just want to be sure he will be welcomed, that's all. Like any guest we would have."

"Just how close were you?" he asked as he was leaving.

"Very close, David. We almost got married."

"Oh," he said and left with no more discussion. Megan knew it was a big piece for David to accept and she thought she had detected a tinge of possessiveness.

Thomas and Cridwyn had spent time assisting the organ specialists design the new organ, and from all reports were an immense help.

David was working overtime trying to get Evie's place ready for them both to live in, getting his machinery ready for spring planting and trying to work with the committees at church. He stopped by the manse as Paul was going over the financial picture with Megan. He heaved a big sigh and dropped into the ottoman, cap still on his head.

"David, you're working too hard," said Megan

"Tell me about it. It's like bendin' the paddle in a canoe as if an ocean liner were behind me."

"Well, there's some hold up on the construction of the front of the sanctuary. Thomas won't talk to me about it."

"I'm sure," said David. "Cridwyn has said very strongly where she wants the console and she knows you suggested something else."

"David," Paul interrupted. "I'd like to make a suggestion. You can't possibly do all this and get ready for your wedding too. I think we should appoint someone who understands carpentry and wiring to be available as a liaison between the contractors, organ people, trustees and our committee."

"That would be of great help to me right now," David agreed.

"I have someone in mind."

"Name him."

"Haydn Gywn. Now that Zion is closed he's free and I certainly would trust his judgment and knowledge."

"Good suggestion," added Megan.

"I'd agree to that."

Paul, thus avoiding a possible conflict, consented to talk with the trustees and Haydn became the "hit man," as he later called himself. He made himself available, spending hours in the church refinishing the pews and keeping an eye on all the activities. Between Haydn and Aycee nothing slipped by them and everything was reported.

The first Saturday in April arrived with a fresh spring breeze and sunshine for David and Evie's wedding and all went off according to plan. Even the organ didn't act up. Kevin was the star as he walked down the aisle straight and balanced, and smiling a smile so broad it made everyone smile. Margaret caught Jim biting his lip to keep from crying while her own tears of joy slipped down her cheeks. They had seen him suffer and struggle so long to reach this moment. David placed a gentle hand on his shoulder, winked and whispered, "Well done." Megan thought she had never seen David looking so handsome. The single ladies sighed as he turned, watching his face as they would an actor on stage. When his eyes brightened and a smile spread across his slender cheeks, they stood *en masse* to watch Evie, on the arm of Thomas, float down the aisle, beautiful and radiant. In that inviolable moment when her hand touched David's, they became one with each other, with God and with the church. Something very special happened in that hallowed gathering. Many spoke of it but it was Megan who felt the most privileged to be binding two of her dearest friends in wedlock.

Afterwards, Cridwyn and Megan walked downstairs together to the reception, telling each other how great they did.

"What is this, a mutual admiration society?" asked Megan.

"How could we live without it?" Cridwyn went to help in the kitchen and Megan looked for Richard who had come especially for the day. Haydn, who had new bi-focals and was feeling pretty chipper walked up to join Thomas. He jammed his elbow into Thomas's ribs, nearly making him spill his punch. "Look-it there. I believe the preacher lady's got herself a boyfriend." He looked at Thomas who nodded back as well as he could with his mouth full of wedding cake.

"Can't you say anything, Thomas?" asked Haydn teasingly.

"Good cake," he mumbled.

"Is that all?"

Thomas took time to swallow while Haydn stared at him through his new bifocals. Then nodding affirmatively Thomas said, "You see a lot more since you got those new glasses."

"Yeah," Haydn chuckled.

"Haydn," barked Thomas.

"What?"

"You got that Belling ready?"

"Oh, yeah. First night they get back." He raised his eyebrows and walked away to mingle.

CHAPTER TWENTY THREE – BELLING

The honeymoon over, Evie and David arrived home late in the day to relax by the fire and read accumulated mail. In another place in the community activity was buzzing. Men were hitching up wagons, women cooking food, young folks collecting cowbells, sleigh bells, automobile horns, anything that would make noise. Two youth were posted with a CB to watch for lights to go out at Evie and David's.

Inside the house the newly weds were ready for bed. They turned out the lights and standing by the burning coals kissed and caressed each other tenderly.

Outside, the two watchers saw the lights go out downstairs and waited for them to go on upstairs.

"Why aren't the upstairs lights going on?"

"Maybe they're sleeping downstairs."

"Naw, there's no place to sleep downstairs."

"How do you know that?"

"'cause I been there."

"Maybe they're still watchin' the fire."

"How do you know they have a fire?"

"Dummy – there's smoke comin' out of the chimney."

"Oh. Maybe they're sleeping by the fire."

"Oh my gosh. Now what?"

"We want to catch them in bed if we can."

"Then we better wait."

"What if they don't go to bed?"

"Every honeymooner goes to bed, dummy. I say wait."

Soon a light went on upstairs. "There we go. Make the call, buddy."

"Wake up. Wake-up call. This is QT."

"10-4 QT. We read you. Stand by while we get started and let us know when the light goes out."

Around fifty people started out in wagons and cars, headed to the honeymooners' home.

Inside, Evie slipped into her soft pale green negligee and lay in the four-poster bed that was her grandmother's. Her face glowed. She watched David undress, aching for his smooth, strong body. "I always dreamed of being in this bed with you," she said as he slid in beside her. They moved quickly into a passionate embrace.

Suddenly a glare of lights hit their windows and an horrendous noise shocked them into an upright position on the bed.

"What in God's name is that?" asked Evie.

"Oh, no!" exclaimed David. He knew the sound. "It's a God damn belling!" he shouted upset with himself for not remembering. He leaped out of bed and grabbed his pants.

Stunned at hearing him swear, she repeated, "Belling? What's a belling?"

"Where are my shoes? I gotta have my shoes."

Following his lead, Evie reached for her robe. David took a quick look out of the window but was blinded by the lights.

"There he is. I saw him in the window," someone shouted. Bells, horns, tin pans, every conceivable noise rose up around the house. Someone had brought an old army bugle and was blasting away on that.

"I'm sorry, love. I completely forgot about a belling. You'd best get some shoes on."

"But what is it?" she asked again. Somehow she had escaped ever being a part of one.

"There's no time to explain," he said turning on the light and leading her down the stairs. "Just go along with whatever they want. Be a good sport. You can handle it."

"What do they want from us?" She could hear them pounding on the door.

"It's just an old tradition for newly-weds. That's us." He kissed her and holding her hand, opened the door.

The crowd immediately raised up a cheer and before they could say anything, they were swept off, each to a separate wagon. David climbed up on one and Evie was quickly hoisted onto the other. Women and men went in separate wagons moving off in opposite directions. Down the back roads with lanterns swinging and voices singing, they covered a good distance and span of time. When Evie asked where they took David she only received teasing responses like "Don't worry, he's well taken care of," "Are you afraid you'll never see him again?" or "You've been with him two weeks, can't you be apart just a little while?" When she finally got over her anxieties and went along with the fun, she began to enjoy the ride. There was a clear sky with vivid stars and they snuggled under blankets to keep off the chill. The women told stories about their wedding nights, laughing or groaning as the story required. Eventually, both wagons arrived back at the house where Thomas and John had built a roaring bonfire and were roasting wieners. Cridwyn and Betsy had laid out more food on picnic tables. They were not yet allowed to go into the house, so ate their fill and enjoyed the greetings of their friends. When the people were ready to leave they allowed the couple back into their house where they found everything tidy and clean, fresh flowers in vases in each room, the breakfast table set, food in the refrigerator to last a week and the cupboards stocked full with homemade goodies. Little love notes were tied on everything.

In the bedroom sheets had been pulled up neatly and folded open at each side. On a pillow was a poem:

Please forgive us for this Belling
If it spoiled one night of sleep.
It's just a simple, old tradition,
one we think is nice to keep.
Your friends and neighbors welcome you
into this blissful life.
May all your days make memories
of a happy man and wife.
Congratulations - we love you both.
Cambria friends and neighbors.

The well initiated newly-weds fell into bed, happy, tired and very soon asleep in each other's arms.

While they had been honeymooning, the telephone company had moved into town hoisting new poles, stringing new wires, and exchanging the old wall crank phones with new on-the-wall dial phones; or cradle phones for an additional fee. Bronwyn would still have a switchboard in her home but would only have to answer if someone called the operator for information. It would make her job much easier and she could semi-retire. Bryn worried that she might not be as happy.

Easter Sunday was the first Sunday in April. Cridwyn played "The Lost Chord" for her last prelude on the old organ. The large congregation watched her tall frame reach and sway on the bench as she pulled out each burst of sound from its old pipes. She warned Thomas ahead of time that she was going to pull out all the stops, even if the old monster screamed at her or fell dead. She knew Monday morning workers would arrive to remove the old organ and she wanted it to have its *day in the sun,* as she put it. Thomas teased her about all the other "lost chords" she had already had with it. He thought it a most appropriate choice.

When the choir sang "He is Risen," she opened it up again. Megan beamed as they cut off the "Amen" and the domed ceiling echoed it back. She complimented them on such memorable music before she gave her sermon. Almost everyone thrilled to the sound, although afterwards there were a few whispering to each other that she had played too loud.

When it came time for the final hymn, there was no music to be heard. Megan looked over at Cridwyn who was fussing with the controls to no avail. She glanced toward the pulpit, then slid off the bench and said simply, "It just died." She looked as if she could cry, but with head up and the control of a professional, she walked across the chancel to the piano on the other side and played the final hymn. It affirmed the need for a new instrument more dramatically than any of their arguments, but some still complained that Cridwyn had played the old dear too hard.

"It's uncanny, the way things react to human thought," Megan said later to Cridwyn.

"That's the truth. You'd think that old organ just knew, from all of us talking about it, that now was its time."

"Right. It was not about to play any of this simple hymn stuff after having lifted the roof performing "The Lost Chord," for heaven's sake." They laughed together, both realizing God's unfathomable mysteries. Cridwyn was too excited about the new organ to be very sad about losing the old.

After the service, members moved the pulpit, communion table, chancel chairs and hymnals to the basement dining room, where they would be holding services until work in the sanctuary was finished.

As Megan and Cridwyn left the building, they spotted Aycee and Bryn scoot off around the side of the church.

"Where do you suppose they're going?" asked Megan.

"I'd say the cemetery," said Cridwyn.

"Are they a couple?"

"I think so," Cridwyn raised her eyebrows knowingly.

"Well, for goodness sake," was all Megan could say.

At eight sharp the next morning, David drove in from the south and a large truck with two men pulled in from the north and met in the parking lot. From her study window, Megan saw the men shake hands. They talked briefly and David led them into the church.

In two days the two men disassembled the entire organ. They were not alone, however, as they had a series of curious spectators mulling about and slipping into the back of the sanctuary to watch. Aycee's curiosity kept him on the scene constantly. Later, he would tell everything the men did and just how they went about it. His version became the authentic rendition of how the old organ was removed. Many asked for smaller pipes for souvenirs. There were both square wooden and round metal pipes in all lengths and sizes. Megan wished she had asked for one, but they had disappeared in a hurry. She knew those who got one cherished it too much for her to even think of asking for one.

Under Haydn's capable and careful guidance, construction work began the fifteenth of April. The new organ would replace the old one in the same area but it had to be cleaned out thoroughly and a new platform built across the whole front of the church. The new console, would not be built in. Rather, it would be a separate unit on wheels, attached electrically with a long cord so that it could be moved to any position on the chancel platform.

On one of Megan's daily trips to the Post Office, Bryn began telling her about Aycee taking her to see where he lived in the old school house.

"You wouldn't believe what that man made out of nothing," she told Megan. "He went through junk piles and old barns and found things that were discarded. He dragged them home and used them. I expected it to be a rat hole but it's really nice."

"Really?"

"He's been watching the contractors build Jim's house and asks questions and then goes and tries things himself. He picked up their extra scraps of lumber and built a table and stools, even put in a cabinet under the old sink he had."

"Amazing," Megan said, fascinated. "How good of you to watch out for him as you do."

Bryn blushed and said, "You know, I started out just helping him get to church, but one thing led to another and now I've grown quite fond of the man. He's a very caring person."

As Megan walked home she was thinking it was time for Aycee to join church.

When she arrived home she saw a car parked in her driveway and Betsy standing on the front porch. She had come to talk about her husband, her son and the farm. She and John were finally facing the big decision. They knew it was time for them to let David run the farm by himself but they were stuck on the best way to do it. It was already into the season.

"What plans do you have for yourselves when you turn it all over to David?" Megan asked.

"We want to travel," said Betsy with no hesitation.

"Then, I suggest you start making those plans right away. Decide where you want to go and when. Then you will know when to turn things over to David."

She knew all they needed was a date.

A week later Betsy rested against the white board fence and watched the sun turn a vivid orange. She remembered something Megan had said, that 'if there was a letting-go kind of love in the church, it would stay well and alive.' They had begun to apply that same kind of love to David.

"Mam!" David shouted at her for a second time. this time it brought her to attention. David walked toward her.

"You were day dreaming," he said and climbed up on the fence next to her. They watched the last of the setting sun slip down behind the broad field of wheat. The sky cast with a vivid pink and turquoise made the new green of the spring wheat rich in color.

"I love this time of year!" he commented.

"Mmm." They so often had watched the sunsets together from this spot. They stayed until the first faint star appeared.

"Make your wish," she said.

Nourished by the beauty, David thought of the hard work the summer would bring and the joy of the fall harvest; how he would dip his bare tan arms deep into the heaped cool grain embracing it as if it were his daily bread. He made his wish - 'Soon' - and let it float into the wisdom of God's universe.

"David, I've decided to have a dinner party for Thomas and Cridwyn, you and Evie and Megan. Can you come?"

"When?"

"How about Saturday."

"I'll check with Evie. I'm sure it will be fine. That's nice, Mam."

On Saturday they were all gathered together enjoying Betsy's wonderful food. Between the main meal and dessert John made their announcement. He and Betsy were turning over the management of the farm to David. He would stay on to help through the summer, but after the church's celebration on Labor Day week-end, he and Betsy were heading out. They were going on a trip to several places they had always wanted to see. David would have to get his own help with the harvest, they said. Being out of the scene would give David more freedom.

David was overwhelmed. He walked about the room smiling and hugging everyone and promised all the women that he would plow their gardens the very next day. Megan said she knew nothing about gardening.

"Oh, you have to have a garden," exclaimed Evie. "I'll help you." With such a promise, a sudden warmth sped through Megan that created a strong feeling of belonging in her. She was one of them now, doing what they would be doing and she would no longer feel alone.

The next morning, true to his word, David plowed up a patch of soil in her back yard, telling her to just let it be. The next day he came again and smoothed the soil ready for planting.

"Evie will be by with seeds this afternoon," he said and drove off.

Evie arrived right after lunch with tools, gloves, string and seeds and they proceeded to mark off rows, hoe troughs and plant the seed. Megan told Evie how much she was enjoying this.

"I feel just like a little kid playing in the dirt."

"It's a lot like going to church," said Evie.

"This is like going to church? You're going to have to explain that one, Evie."

"You have to get down on your knees, say a little prayer, have faith that God will bring the good weather to make the seeds grow. It's an act of faith, a plan for the future." She stood, looking at what they had accomplished. "Now, you just wait and see what comes."

At that moment, Jim came into view around the corner of the church and headed toward them.

"I have good news!" he shouted before he reached them.

They walked to meet him, not sure of what he had said.

"I have good news," he repeated. "My brother has received honorable discharge and is on his way home from Vietnam."

CHAPTER TWENTY FOUR – SUMMER

Urged on by the women's persuasive powers, the Anniversary Committee asked to speak to Megan about Charles. They questioned her extensively and told her they'd get back to her with their decision. Two days later they informed her they had wanted a unanimous decision but that two people were fearful. Megan asked who they were and made individual calls to each, taking Cridwyn and Betsy with her. It took some gentle persuasion and reasoning to get them to concede but then reluctantly, they agreed he could be invited.

When Megan called Charles to extend the invitation he immediately accepted. He would come on Friday in order to get acquainted with the instrument. Megan suggested he stay with her in the manse as that would be handy for him. She knew it would be difficult for him to find lodging elsewhere and Richard and her parents would all be in the house which should calm any eyebrow raising. Megan let Charles know how excited she was that he was coming.

"Dear Meg, you always were my most ardent admirer. Tell your people thank you for inviting me." She didn't tell him how hard it was. She wanted him to feel welcome.

Megan hung up and said a quick "Thank you, Lord" out loud that all had worked out. Then, working off the stress she walked around the house picking things up and putting things straight, the whole time talking out loud. She had begun doing that one day when the big house seemed too vacant.

"All my life I've been able to think for myself, God. You know that. Remember when you came to me in college and told me this young man was a good man, and I decided to be his friend? That was one of the best things you and I ever did. I learned so much from him. And when you came and told us we each had bigger things to do and we both went on to do them? You gave us the courage, God. You did it for us. Just look at what Charles did with his life. He's wonderful! And just look at all you've put me through in this place. I think we all deserve a celebration. I just know that this church is going to love Charles and celebrate and grow in a bigger way than they ever knew they could."

The door bell brought her back and she opened the door to find Bryn and Aycee.

"My goodness, come in," she said. "What brings you two to my door?"

They sat down beside each other. Aycee looked at Bryn with a shy smile so she spoke.

"We'd like you to marry us," she said, beaming, and Aycee nodded his head.

"Well, congratulations! I will be delighted. When?"

"June," said Aycee. "That there's the weddin' month."

"That soon? Then we'd better make some plans right now." They agreed to come for preparation sessions and she also suggested Aycee join church. They set the date on the church calendar, asked Megan to ask Cridwyn to play the organ for them and said that Bronwyn and Squire would be standing up for them."

"Where are you planning to live?" Megan wondered.

"Well, Jim had offered us to live in his new house except now that his brother's a comin' back he'll need it fer him ta live in. So then, Edwin said we could live in Tadcu's house. It's furnished so Bronwyn can keep most of our stuff."

"My! That's very generous of Edwin."

"With both of us working now we could afford to pay rent for the house but he said if we would just take care of the place he'll keep the rent low," Bryn explained.

"I'm sure you'll be very happy there." With everything settled, they left and Megan went back to her phone calls.

The legal document that made Cambria a dry town, did not prevent men from quenching their thirst in the near-by tavern of the catholic community. Farming was a lonely business and no one considered it a sin for a farmer to have a drink and a little talk with his buddies when wanted.

Squire was treating Aycee to a mug of beer. "Jeremiah was a Bullfrog," blared out from the juke box and the lights were dim in the smoke-filled room when John burst in on the scene.

"Dychi cymro," they greeted him waving their mugs.

John nodded and slung his jacket over the chair.

"Somethin' botherin' you?" asked Aycee.

"Nope! I'm free as a bird. Just turned everything over to David."

"Well, congratulations," they both voiced surprise.

"Yup. Figured it was time I saw a little more of the world and let him have his fill of the farmin'." He waved his arm at the bartender.

"That's great news, John. When are you quittin'?"

"Oh, I'll help the boy out during the summer but right after the Gymanfa Betsy and I will be headin' west. Wanta see those mountains."

"That's great." The bartender placed a pitcher of beer on the table and John began to fill mugs.

"Aycee and I were just talkin' about Buck. We think that man needs help."

"What's he done now?" He took a big mouthful and swallowed it.

"His wife left him. It got so bad she told Ruth Hughes Lloyd that she didn't feel safe no more. So she flew down to Florida to be with her sister. Buck's home alone, avoiding everybody," Squire explained.

"I said I think Pastor Brown better go see him," insisted Aycee.

"He won't open the door to her. She's been out there already," said Squire.

"The ol' goat. He done brought it all on his self."

"He's a lonely man." John felt sorry for him.

"He quit the church. I don't feel sorry for him." Squire shoved his empty mug across the table and John poured it full.

Aycee squinted his eyes and changed the subject. "How's them two love birds a doin'?'

"David and Evie? Just great. A man couldn't have a better daughter-in-law than that. These are happy days, I tell ya'"

"Guess you haven't heard about Aycee then, have ya John?" Squire winked at Aycee who grinned real big.

"What about Aycee?"

"He's engaged."

"In what? Makin' bird houses?" John let out a chuckle.

"Engaged. You know, engaged to be married."

"Married?" John set his mug down and stared at Aycee.

"Yep." Aycee nodded his head forward and back and wiped his mouth with his sleeve.

"Who to?"

"Bryn."

"Bryn?" He looked at Aycee for verification.

"Yep. Gettin' married in June and gonna live in Tadcu's house."

"Well I'll be a pop-eyed mule. Aycee! Here's to ya'" He raised his mug and they clanked theirs against his and drank up, laughing and joking on until closing time.

"Carpeting the whole sanctuary?" asked Paul again.

"That's what Cridwyn told me Thomas heard at the elevator." It was Megan who had called Paul.

"I want to clear this up with Haydn. Is he over at church, do you know?"

"I think so. His truck's in the parking lot." They hung up and Paul drove over to get Haydn to go see Saddler.

Saddler told them that the plans from the beginning were to paint the sanctuary, refinish all the pews and woodwork, build the broader platform in the front and carpet the entire area. So, yes, that's what they were doing.

"We also ordered a wooden cross for the chancel," he added. "It's beautiful."

"Haven't you boys gone a little overboard?" began Haydn.

"Never-mind that," interrupted Paul. "My concern here is more about the carpeting. I understood that it would cover only part of the sanctuary."

"What does it matter?" asked Saddler.

"We've already told the installers that it would only cover the front platform. Too much carpeting will deaden the sound of the organ unless they are warned ahead of time. Tell me, Saddler, how much is your committee planning on spending?"

Chapter Twenty Four

"The total estimate is around $8,000 I think."

"Is that too much?" asked Haydn.

"I had budgeted only half of that." Paul looked beaten.

"I've got an idea. Would your committee be willing to limit the carpeting to the aisles and platform only? Not go under the pews? That way, it not only would be cheaper, it would still hold the resonance of the organ where it should be."

"I see no trouble with that," said Saddler.

"Excellent plan, Haydn. I'll let the organ company know right away. That's a good compromise." So the carpeting problem was settled easily.

Jim's brother arrived home two days before the Memorial Day Parade. As Parade Marshall, David lined up the small parade. The color guard would lead carrying the flags and the armed guard behind them. Then himself on Duke followed by the high school marching band. Behind the band, Megan rode with Squire, as Mayor, in an open convertible followed by Jim's brother, who would be the honored speaker for the day, in another convertible. Veterans in uniform formed ranks and marched on foot. Onlookers fell in behind and all went to the cemetery and gathered around the memorials.

Jim introduced his brother Ben who had the somber attention of everyone there.

"Having now fought in a war, I have the greatest of respect for the men whose names are on these monuments," said Ben. He paused, and everyone waited for his next words. "When this war is over – there will be another monument built, and it will hold the names of some of your friends and mine. War is hell, folks but whether we're of English, Welsh, German or French background, we're all Americans. We'll fight for our rights together because this is America but war is destructive. In the future, I hope this country will find better ways than war to solve its problems. It should be our life-long duty to settle disputes through intellect, not brutality. I have nothing more than that to say to you except I'm just thankful that the Lord above saw to it to bring me home alive. We all should get down on our knees and thank God every day that we have such a peaceful life as this right here." He stepped back into the crowd and the National Guard gave the three gun salute. Everyone watched Ben stand at attention saluting the flag and everyone saw his jaw tighten and tears run down his cheeks. It was a solemn audience that Megan stepped up to, to pray and pronounce the benediction.

June first came in the middle of the week following the long Memorial Day week-end and was the day the organ pieces arrived. A semi-truck parked in front of the church, creating more curiosity than Megan's moving van. A gathering of curious onlookers assembled on the street to watch as the pipes were unloaded and carried in through the north vestibule. There, the high ceiling of the bell tower allowed them to raise up the larger pipes and redirect them into the sanctuary where they were laid across pews, along the aisles, and on the newly built platform. Aycee scurried around, counting. There were one thousand, six hundred and fifty-eight pipes, varying in size from one inch to sixteen feet long.

From that day on, until all the pipes were mounted, Aycee kept count to see that no one took any away. The two men, highly trained and talented, often played as they assembled and tuned, and the church was host to many a visitor who just stopped by to watch and listen.

Haydn, cognizant of the time schedule, knew it would take a few weeks for the painting to get done, so when the last pipes were removed from the pews and set in place he was ready to move painters in. He directed the painters to assemble their scaffolding to begin work on the ceiling.

The week before Bryn and Aycee were to be married they moved as much as they could into their new home. At one point, Aycee dropped a box and several of his belongings scattered across the floor. A small bag landed at the feet of Bryn.

"What's this?" she asked picking it up. As she did, dozens of small coins went tumbling across the floor. "Oh, my goodness!" exclaimed Bryn. "Are these real coins?"

"Oh, they was my mama's. I couldn't ever buy nothin' with 'em so I jus' kept 'em as souvenirs."

"Aycee, these are old five dollar gold pieces. They might have some value. We should take them to a coin dealer."

"Where would a body find one o' them?"

"Maybe, Chicago."

And so it was that they decided to go to Chicago for their honeymoon. The dawn of their wedding day rose like gray chiffon. It heated up under a steamy summer sun. The basement dining room stayed cool, though, and filled with friends. An altar area had two large bouquets of daisies and two candelabra. Bryn wore a white mid-length dress with short sleeves and a small head-dress with a short veil. She carried a small nosegay. Bronwyn's dress was a pale ivory made in the same pattern as Bryn's. Instead of a bouquet, she wore a small corsage of yellow roses to free her hands to hold Bryn's nosegay while they received their rings. Aycee and Jim wore ivory colored suits with white carnation boutonnieres.

It was a thoughtful and tender service for the two of them and afterwards Aycee kissed Bryn tenderly, blushing through his neatly trimmed beard. They visited with friends over cake and punch and soon Squire drove them away to catch the train to Chicago.

While there, they found a coin dealer who offered $8,000 for the rare gold coins which they decided to sell immediately. They came home with a nice sum of money.

True to their faithfulness they decided to share their good fortune with the church, so made a generous tithe of $800. It paid for the new wooden cross

Saddler had ordered carved for the chancel and would be named the Seawald cross. Aycee joined church the Sunday after they returned.

The summer was already a third of the way gone. Fourth of July arrived with no particular announcement of its unique character. Assignments were taken care of efficiently. By 9:30 the parade line was formed at the south edge of the village. David pranced back and forth on Duke in full parade regalia and fancy trappings. He wore a full brimmed white Stetson cowboy hat, white pants, a sparkling embroidered shirt trimmed with western fringe and hand-designed cowboy boots that he saved for just such occasions. The clip clop of Duke's hooves on the black asphalt road, warned participants to get ready. Other riders flanked him on either side at the head of the parade. The high school band, warming up their instruments; the American Legion color-guard, anchoring flags into their holsters; and the local fire wagon, with bells clanging, were all maneuvering into place. Behind them were several decorated bikes, small floats designed and built on tractor-pulled wagons, a 4-H float, a decorated truck with clown musicians, and several decorated hitches of carts, sulkies, and buggies. Bringing up the rear was the 4-H Pony Riding club.

At 10:00AM sharp they began their march through the village and out to the cemetery, where they disbanded. People meandered to the Lion's Club building where tables were packed with food. Lines formed and soon tables were filled with happy people eating, laughing and visiting. Two stands, run by the youth and young adult church classes offered lemonade and home-made ice cream, made on the spot. They were busy all afternoon.

Aycee had a stand where he and some of the youth sold bird houses. Megan circulated, making it her business to become acquainted with all non-church-going people. While the younger children scrambled for coins in a saw dust pit, the young men organized a Tug-0'-War game across the creek. Since most of the twenty-year-olds were in Vietnam, Squire had recruited the high school football team. Haydn was short a man and spotting David called him over to help.

They stretched a one-hundred-foot rope over the small creek and the team members took off their shirts displaying brawny arms and muscular backs, but kept on their shoes and jeans. They had ten minutes to pull the opposite team into the creek to win. Failure to do so was a tie. Megan joined the crowd of onlookers.

As the judges blew the whistle to begin, the shouting and pulling began. Quickly a crowd gathered. Squire's team went after it confidently. They were bigger and stronger than the opposing team, who only had middle aged men, but they hadn't bargained on Big Fred. He had moved into the area only a few weeks earlier. He had a large build. Few knew the power he held in his body.

At first, Squire's team seemed to be making strides by pulling the front three men of Haydn's team down the bank and close to the water's edge; but then, Big Fred caught on and when Haydn shouted at him to pull back, Big Fred slipped his hands to the tail end of the rope, gave it a clothesline wrap around his elbow and over his shoulder, turned away from the creek and dug in, pulling forward slowly and steadily. With David's added strength, they moved the three front men back onto dry ground where they regained their footing. As Squire's front man slid near the edge he shouted, "Dig In." Immediately, they leaned backward at a 45 degree angle and held with straight, sinewy arms. But Haydn's team had already hoisted the rope over their shoulders turning backs to the water and to Haydn's "Step - Pull - Step - Pull" commands, Big Fred hoisted and grunted the team forward until, one by one, Squire's big guys slid down the slippery bank into the shallow water. Both cheers and moans went up as Squire's team stood knee deep in the muddy water looking up with unbelieving faces at Big Fred who was being hugged and slapped on the back by the other team members.

"I don't believe it," said Squire. "Who is that guy?" Thomas was asking the same thing, "Who is that young fellow? Where did he come from?"

Jim's twins had the answer. "His family just moved in. They live a mile east of our house." They ran over to get a closer look.

"It won't take him long to get acquainted."

"I heerd he's a wrestler in some college," added Aycee. "That's his folks a standin' right over there." He pointed out a proud looking couple and Megan headed of in their direction.

"She don't miss a trick," commented Aycee to Bryn.

A ball game between fathers and sons took up most of the afternoon finishing just in time for getting the last snack of food before sunset. Fathers were grumbling because they had lost to a bunch of kids. They had assumed that because their older sons were in Vietnam that they would win easily.

A huge bonfire was built and they toasted marshmallows until it was dark enough for fireworks. Pete, the mail carrier, was the Fire Marshall and always set up the display. Mayor Squire stood by and Aycee did the leg work. Cars of people from neighboring communities assembled along the road at the edge of town to watch the annual display of the Welsh community.

Megan's thoughts drifted away. This American celebration of independence was typical of thousands of others being held across the nation by people who had come from many countries to claim America as theirs. While through their faith and music, the Welsh had held fast to their own traditions; in their labor and society, they embraced the American way. Proud of their heritage and unique and rugged life, they were as big a part of this country, its success and its wars as any other culture that had come to one coast or another and woven their ways together to become Americans. The Welsh were one of the largest and most influential. It was, for them, truly a home of the brave and the free. But what about those fighting for America in Vietnam? How did they feel? She recalled Jim's brother saying "War is so useless." There were questions about this war, faces tensed at the mention of it. Yet they carried the worry inside, seldom mentioning it aloud. On a day such as this, Megan knew their hearts were heavy, although they kept up the traditions of celebration for their young.

As the last explosion lit the sky with splendor and faded into darkness, Thomas's single voice rose from the crowd singing, "Oh, say can you see," and as others joined in singing "The Star Spangled Banner," a faint light in the sky grew brighter until the American Flag, flying high above the ball field, became visible. All faces turned toward it, some with proud chills of patriotism lifted their chins to sing; David and Megan, who had seen the flag burned on their college campuses sang out of duty but questioned in their minds what it stood for. This Fourth of July, 1972, was just four years short of America's 200th birthday. Megan wondered what that celebration would be like. She recognized the sheltered trend of the life of the community and wondered if she could ever balance their thinking and broaden their horizons to include the world around them. Charles would be a beginning. In ten minutes, everyone had driven out and the village was again, quiet beneath the stars.

By mid July, the two organ builders had finished their work. They invited Cridwyn in to try the organ and worked with her for a couple of hours. They promised to return for the concert and 125th Anniversary.

Megan, meanwhile had been filling in for anyone who couldn't get their jobs done; such as running errands to the printers for the Gymanfa and Organ Recital Programs, and following up on obtaining greeters and ushers.

In between she wrote her sermons, visited the sick, followed up on all the details and generally kept things happening. To settle her mind and get away from it all, she worked in her garden, harvesting tomatoes, cucumbers and corn. Oh, how good it all tasted and a peppering of pride fell over her at her own accomplishment. She had a sense, now, of why people stayed on the land, and why it was so important that it be handed down from one generation to the next.

Time was of the essence. There was one week left and she was determined everything would be in place and perfect for the big celebration. In the short, full year of being with them, she had learned that forcing people into one person's way was not the way to accomplish anything. In planting the seeds gently, letting the good soil, sun and rain nourish them, they would grow into what they were meant to be. We each find our own way under the sun, she thought to herself, but we all need community to survive.

With the final tack in the carpeting, they began to move the refinished furniture back into the sanctuary. People saw the need and came by to help. Aycee lowered the main ceiling light, cleaned it and put in new bulbs; a couple of men brought tall ladders and a plank and cleaned the stained glass windows; Cridwyn practiced daily as those who worked became accustomed to its new sound and a growing pride oozed from their faces and lifted their hearts. Finally, everything was in its place, ready for glory day.

Megan was tired but proud. Charles arrived tomorrow and Richard and her parents the day after. She was excited. She put in a call to Richard to check on final plans.

"Richard! It's Megan."

"I was about to call you. How is it coming?"

"Everything is ready. Richard, it looks beautiful. You will love it."

"I can hardly wait. Have you heard from Charles?"

"Yes, he'll arrive at the Dayton airport tomorrow noon so he'll have time to practice on the organ. When are you leaving?"

"Early tomorrow morning. I'll drive straight through to your folks'. I'll get your Distlfink on the way through Pennsylvania."

"Good. I'm glad you remembered. I've kept all day Saturday free so come as early as you can."

"I figure we can be there by noon. Are you sure you have room enough for all of us?"

"I do. Charles will have the small room with the day bed. You will have the extra bedroom which I now have nicely furnished, my folks will have my room and I will sleep on the couch in the living room so I can make breakfast."

"Sounds perfect. I can't wait to see you. Get some rest."

"I will. I'll see you about noon on Saturday, then."

"Megan."

"Yes?'

"I love you."

CHAPTER TWENTY FIVE - GYMANFA GANU

Megan watched for Charles as the passengers unloaded. When she saw him step through the doorway, her heart skipped a beat and she called out his name. They hurried toward each other, meeting in a clash of bodies. Holding tightly and swaying side to side they laughed and cried together, overjoyed at seeing one another again. Still holding each other's arms, they stretched back to study each other.

"How long has it been?" he asked.

"Four years."

"Seems like twenty."

"You look so great!"

"So do you." He picked up his small bag which he'd dropped onto the floor.

"This way," she said, and led him to her car, still holding his hand. When they got through the traffic and onto the highway, she said, "Tell me all the highlights of your last four years."

"That's my Meg," he said, and started right in from the day they had graduated from Ohio University. "Julliard for my Masters in a year and a half, Doctorate at Westminster, studied abroad, concerts in Europe. That's it in a nutshell."

"You're too modest, Charles. It must have been a fabulous experience to play all those great European cathedrals."

"You're right. It was a great thrill for me."

"And then for the invitations to come from the states as well. How did that feel?"

"That really surprised me."

"So, this job in Atlanta. Is it a steady job?"

"There's a young man training under me who fills in for me when I'm touring. But tell me about you."

"That's easy. Princeton and here."

"Were you the only woman in seminary?"

"There were two others, and they both got placed before I did. I think I only got this place because of Dr. Jarvis. He knew they were looking and since I had waited all summer he threw it my way."

"So, now that you've done what you wanted to do, how is it?"

"I haven't done all I wanted. It has been hard. I'm their first non-Welsh pastor, first woman pastor and, if I may say so, probably their youngest."

"Three strikes against you to start."

"It's been a tough learning experience, Charles."

"It must have gone well from the sound of this celebration."

"It's not over yet. Let's just say that there's something here that gets under your skin."

Saturday morning, Charles spent with Cridwyn at the organ. At 11:30 Richard drove in with her parents. They unpacked and by noon they were all seated around her dining room table, eating the meal she had prepared and laughing and visiting. Charles shared his praises for the new instrument, Richard assessed her first year at ministering as "marvelous" and her parents showered her with loving looks and smiles. Megan felt so full she could hardly contain it.

In the afternoon Charles practiced and the rest helped with setting up extra chairs in the prayer meeting room, putting out extra Gymanfa Hymnals, and setting up attic fans in the doorways to cool the sanctuary. It had been raining and the air was muggy.

Thomas mounted the Welsh green flag with the red dragon next to the American and Christian flags to the right of the pulpit. When a visitor saw it he commented, "Don't tell me you still use that old banner."

"So what's new?" asked Thomas.

"The new motto of Wales is Ich-Dien, the same as on the Prince of Wales' coat of arms."

"I thought that was Eich-Dyn," Thomas rebutted.

"Ich-Dien," said the man, "I serve."

"Eich-Dien. It means 'Your man' and it comes from the time of King Edward when he held up his new born son and said he would be their ruler."

"Not any more, man. Ich-Dien is the motto they use in Wales. You're behind the times."

"I have to say I like the new motto better, "inserted Megan.

"Then bring us a new one next year and we'll put it up," said Thomas a little put out.

The rain stopped just as people began to arrive, splashing a rainbow briefly overhead. The sun glistened on the wet leaves and the air freshened.

Megan, her parents and Richard sat together for the concert.

Charles performed splendidly. He began with a soft prelude settling people into a receptive mood and showed off the mellow tones of the instrument. He then, moved into Bach's "Sinfonia" from "God's Time is Best" and "Sinfonia" from "Cantata 29" interspersed with a "Tone Poem" and Monteverdi's "Lascitemi Morire," He ended the first part of the recital with Bach's "Sleepers Awake" from Cantata 140.

At the intermission, Megan's parents stepped outside for air and Megan and Richard discussed how well Charles had chosen his pieces to display the unique qualities of the new organ, show off his skills, and keep the audience interested. Megan was so happy to be sharing Charles' talent that she kept talking about how much she had learned about music and organs from him as well as some of their experiences in Africa and the Peace Corps those two years. She didn't realize how lovingly Richard was listening and watching her. Others noticed though. When Megan caught Betsy watching them, she blushed like a child caught in the act of stealing cookies.

"I think we are being watched," she whispered to Richard.

"So I noticed. Does it bother you?"

Before she could answer, her parents returned to the pew, Charles stepped back into the sanctuary and the congregation broke out in genuine applause. He had won their respect and admiration. He was a striking figure in his black tuxedo. Catching her eyes he bowed and stepped to the console, now turned so the congregation could watch his hands on the keyboards.

Beginning with "Trumpet Tune and Air" by Purcell, he moved through several lighter numbers to which the audience responded readily. They were hearing sounds they had never heard before as they watched his slender dark hands move back and forth from keys to the stops and his feet slide easily over the pedals. His whole body moved with the music, demanding the extremes of its capacity. Another prelude, a canon, a march, and a classic styled number that not only showed off the organ but himself, as well. He was never modest when he was seated at the organ, for as he explained, it was a greater power moving through him. He ended with two numbers in the extreme. The first, "Song of Ruth," a lovely romantic number, which he dedicated to Megan. Richard leaned over and whispered, "I didn't know he loved you, too."

"I think he was sending a different message," she replied and let it be a part of the intrigue about her.

Charles finished with a powerful Finale "Symphony 2" by Charles Marie Widor, which brought them to their feet with applause. He graciously received their enthusiasm and played one delightful encore. Afterwards, they crowded around him. Cridwyn and Thomas stood by to answer people's questions about the wonderful new instrument.

When it was all over, Megan served coffee and cakes at the manse so Thomas and Cridwyn, David and Evie, and John and Betsy could visit with her guests. Megan presented David and Evie the Distlefink for their new barn and David laughed heartily, remembering their talk about barns.

Evie came into the kitchen with an extra big smile on her face. "Do you have something to tell me?"

"What makes you think that?"

"You've been acting like you're in love."

"Who, me?" Megan teased.

"Megan."

"Could be."

Evie squealed in delight and hugged her.

"But don't get any big ideas yet."

Charles helped clear the dishes and Megan had a moment with him alone.

"He's in love with you, Megan, as I still am." He looked deeply into her eyes and with his own sad eyes told her, "But I think your best bet is your professor." They faced each other, knowing from their past all the reasons why.

Megan reached up to kiss him. "You were my first love," she said. "Thank you for coming to play for me."

"I was, you know – playing for you."

"I know."

They went upstairs together and after Charles settled in, Megan tapped lightly on Richard's door. He opened it and they stood in the darkened room.

"Richard, I think I'm falling in love with you."He took her into is arms, kissing her hair and holding her. "Not just 'I love you' love, but 'in love' love. Do you understand?"

"I will do anything you ask," he whispered.

"I want to be with you more, but — I'm not ready to leave Cambria. This is going to be such a hard decision."

"We'll find a way. For now, let's just take a day at a time until we're sure." He kissed her softly.

"Thank you, Richard, for understanding, and for being so patient." She kissed him good night and went to her room. *Richard, oh, Richard. Who would have thought?*

Visitors and members packed the sanctuary and overflowed into the balcony. Before the worship began there were several announcements. Then David called Megan to step out from behind the pulpit.

"We want you to have a small token of our appreciation for the year of devotion and hard work you have given to this church. As I recall, in your first sermon here, you asked how one could sing a new song in a strange land. I think it is safe to say that you found a way. But if you ever need the pitch to start singing a new song, here is a small organ pipe from the old organ. We couldn't snitch a new one because Aycee had them all counted." A chuckle went up from the congregation. "Thank you, Megan, for restoring our faith to us. We love you."

They stood applauding and Megan was nearly overcome with emotion. She hugged David and simply said, "Thank you all. I will treasure this always."

Richard then led a litany of dedication of the organ and Kevin sang "ymilwr bach" in his clear soprano voice. They dedicated the Seawald Cross and Bryn and Aycee were acknowledged. Then they dedicated the newly redecorated sanctuary to the glory of God and proceeded with the worship service. Richard led the closing prayer and benediction, and a rousing postlude played by Cridwyn drew applause.

A buffet with an abundance of food was kept replenished throughout the afternoon. People came and went as they liked. A harpist played background music. People were there from all over the country and there were several visitors from Wales, all with ties to the community. Most had sent gifts toward the purchase of the new organ.

Megan was amazed at the number of cars accumulating. They filled the parking lot and lined both sides of the street all the way through the village. By six o'clock, seats were being saved in the sanctuary. The damp earth and hot sun sprouted the typical muggy heat. Fans ran on high and people made good use of the paper fans in the hymnal racks. Ushers distributed extra hymnals, set up additional chairs which filled every vacancy, and hustled up and down the aisles trying to squeeze one or two more singers into the four-voiced sections.

The Cambria Choir was to sing "Ebenezer" (Ton-Y-Botel) for a prelude. Thomas had rehearsed the group stringently. They assembled on the center front platform and the drone of voices settled. Cridwyn played the new carillon chimes to mark the hour and the former pastor, Reverend Davis, spoke the Invocation in Welsh.

"Cenwch I'r Arglwydd ganiead newydd: cenwch ir Arglwydd, yr holl daear. Oh, sing unto the Lord a new song; sing unto the Lord, all the earth."

Thomas made a slight nod at Cridwyn and the 18 voices broke forth:

Send Thy Spirit, we beseech Thee
Gracious Lord, send while we pray;
Send the Comforter to teach us,
Guide us, help us in Thy way.
Sinful, wretched, we have wandered
Far from Thee in darkest night;
Precious time and talents squandered
Lead, Oh lead us into light."

An appropriate choice by Thomas, and it set the mood for singing hymns of praise and moved the congregation to the place of worshipful song. Mary Davis, a well-liked woman director from Wales, stepped to the front.

Megan found it difficult to read the Welsh hymnal as the music was by itself at the top of the page and the words were in both English and Welsh at the bottom. The accompaniment of both organ and piano was simply the four part singing harmonies that were played by both. The Welsh knew the music by part and heart. They began with "Rachie," which Megan recognized from the words as "Onward Christian Soldiers." However, as they began singing she realized it wasn't the familiar tune at all. She stumbled at first trying to keep up until she realized the harmonies were being sung all around her.

Richard shared his knowledge with her throughout the evening. "Part singing began with the Cymry, as the Welsh called themselves. One of the men who taught it brought the technique to America. The skill developed through the years and found its expression in the Gymanfa Ganu."

"It sounds like a well rehearsed choir," said Megan.

"I know. It's an expression of the soul like none other."

The director raised her arms and as if in one movement her arms and their voices met in a sound mellow and warm, lifting and lowering, flowing like a river carrying its burden to the sea. A finger to her lips brought softness, a fist and they burst with power. It was both pensive and powerful. Megan saw and heard and understood more about them in those two hours than she had seen the entire year and was deeply moved.

At intermission, David made his plea for funds. "Can you believe we've been singing these old hymns for 125 years?" Applause broke forth. "We've made some startling and distinct improvements in the sanctuary since you were here last year. I want you to meet the two women largely responsible: Reverend Megan Brown, and my wife, Evie, who gave the original challenge gift." They stood for applause.

The second hour of singing melted Megan into the minor harmonies of "Penpark" and "Sandon," but "Cwm Rhondda" seemed to lift the roof with the hwyl, their very souls in song.

> When I tread the verge of Jordan
> Bid my anxious fears subside
> Bear me through the swelling current
> Land me safe on Canaan's side;
> Songs of praises, songs of praises
> I will ever sing to Thee
> I will ever sing to Thee.

The director took all their voices in her hands and held them high above her head bringing a sound of power swelling in such splendor that it exploded in the air. They spread their chests, brought in the air and sang so that their voices struck the vaulted ceiling and poured back over them. Repeat after repeat of the chorus kept them going until their oxygen-starved faces and tired voices exhausted them. Megan felt the tears running down her own cheeks. They had given all of themselves to the devotion of God. They were as vulnerable at that moment as they would ever be.

Megan quickly wiped her eyes and slipped down the aisle to the front.

"I want to express for everyone here tonight, our deepest gratitude and appreciation to Mary Davis for the outstanding leadership we've just experienced." Immediate applause broke forth and everyone stood.

"Let us pray. Gracious God, one cannot sit amongst the Cymry and hear their singing without knowing you. You have heard the voices here rise to your gates in opulent praise. Accept them, for they are spirited gifts of praise in song, and they come from our hearts and souls.

We cherish you, God, for your presence in our midst tonight and in our daily journeys. Be with those who travel homeward this night that they may arrive safely and renewed.

Now may the Lord bless you and keep you. May God's voice sing through you all the days of your lives and may you live in God's grace forever. Amen." Joining hands across the room they sang "God be With You."

Immediately after, the decibel level rose as everyone began talking. Megan turned to thank Mary Davis and stepped over to Cridwyn.

"Beautifully done," she said.

"Did you enjoy it?"

"Powerful," was all Megan could say without choking up.

She thanked the pianist and Richard was there to escort Megan through the crowd to the front porch where they met David and Evie. Evie and Megan hugged and looked into each other's faces with great joy and greater knowing.

"Well?" David asked beaming at Megan.

"Tremendous. I have never heard any sound so God-filled. I wish I could hear it all over again."

"Next year," he said looking straight into her eyes.

"Yes," she nodded. "Next year."

"Good to see you again, Richard. Glad you could come."

"I wouldn't have missed it for anything." Richard answered politely and shook David's hand, but he had read the unspoken promise between David and Megan.

It took another hour for the crowd to "chew the meat," as Tadcu would have said, and finally they dispersed and the parking lot was empty. Aycee turned off the lights and closed the doors to the night, and all was still. But as Megan lay down in bed and closed her eyes, she heard the echoes in her head, as if the angels of heaven were singing it all over again. It swelled her heart with a profound gratitude that she had answered her Call to Cambria.

POSTLUDE

The church community on which I've based my story is in Venedocia, Ohio. The story and characters are fictional. Although the blood of the remaining Welsh families has been thinned by marriages and a transient society, a remarkable and durable pride has enabled the community to survive. They still hold their traditional Gymanfa Ganu each Labor Day Sunday. If you visit, you will be warmly welcomed and richly rewarded by the Welsh hwyl or spirit in their singing that will remain with you, as it has with me.

Postlude